Writing for the Media

FRANÇOIS NEL

SOUTHERN
BOOK PUBLISHERS

Copyright © 1994 by the author

All rights reserved. No part of this publication may be
reproduced or transmitted in any form or by any means without
prior written permission from the publisher.

ISBN 1 86812 506 8

First edition, first impression 1994

Published by
Southern Book Publishers (Pty) Ltd
PO Box 3103, Halfway House, 1685

Cover design by Kevin Gas
Set in 10 on 13 point Stone Serif
by Peter Green & Associates, Cape Town
Printed and bound by Colorgraphic, Durban

CONTENTS

Foreword   xiii

Acknowledgements   xiv

PART 1   THE BUSINESS OF WRITING NEWS

Essay "When it's good, it's really bad" (Denis Beckett)   3

Chapter 1   What is news?   6

1.1   Defining news   6
    1.1.1   News must be new   6
    1.1.2   News must have conversational value   7
    1.1.3   News must have commercial value   7

1.2   Traditional news tests   8
    1.2.1   Time   8
    1.2.2   Audience   8
    1.2.3   Consequence   8
    1.2.4   Proximity   9
    1.2.5   Peculiarity   9
    1.2.6   Prominence   9
    1.2.7   Conflict   9
    1.2.8   Package   9

1.3   Changing perspectives   10
    1.3.1   Changing views on information   10
    1.3.2   Changing standards   11
    1.3.3   Changing sources   12
    1.3.4   Changing interests   13

1.4   The subjective quality of news   14
    1.4.1   Our goal: fairness   14
    1.4.2   Do not just toy with words   16

1.5   A definition of news   17

1.6   Basic news writing terms   17

Assignments   20

Bibliography and recommended reading   21

Chapter 2   Inside newspapers   22

    2.1   Inside the newsroom: how a major metropolitan daily newspaper is organized   22

    2.2   What the primary editorial positions entail   23
          2.2.1   The editor   23
          2.2.2   Editorial-page editor   23
          2.2.3   Chief sub-editor   23
          2.2.4   News editor   24
          2.2.5   Photographers   24
          2.2.6   Cartoonists   24
          2.2.7   Graphic designers   24

    2.3   Other departments   26
          2.3.1   Advertising   26
          2.3.2   Circulation   26
          2.3.3   Business   26
          2.3.4   Production   27

    2.4   How copy flows from one editor to another   27

    2.5   Moving and printing the news   28

    2.6   Libraries   28

    Assignments   29

    Bibliography and recommended reading   29

Chapter 3   Writing in newspaper style   30

    3.1   Why using clear and concise English is important   31
          3.1.1   The product of bad habits   33
          3.1.2   Language is a political concern   34
          3.1.3   Not a call for traditionalism   35

    3.2   Some peculiarities of journalistic writing   36
          3.2.1   The reporter does not editorialize   36
          3.2.2   Eliminate unnecessary words   37

3.3   Some basic style rules   38
     3.3.1   Common style problems   38

Assignments   45

Bibliography and recommended reading   46

Chapter 4   The basics: getting started and organizing the story   47

4.1   Writing a lead   48

4.2   How to organize a story   52
     4.2.1   Types of conventional leads   53
     4.2.2   Closing with a kick   55

4.3   Wrapping it up   55

4.4   Different applications of the news writing style   56
     4.4.1   The news story   56
     4.4.2   The feature story   56
     4.4.3   The analysis story   56
     4.4.4   The investigative story   57
     4.4.5   Editorials   58
     4.4.6   Feature columns   58
     4.4.7   Reviews and criticism   59
     4.4.8   Sports writing   60

Assignments   60

Bibliography and recommended reading   61

Chapter 5   Sources of news   63

5.1   Organizing news coverage   64
     5.1.1   Beat reporter   64
     5.1.2   General-assignment reporter   64
     5.1.3   Special-assignment reporter   65
     5.1.4   Beats and sources   65

5.2 Generating story ideas   65

5.3 Developing personal sources   68
    5.3.1 Start your own telephone directory   68
    5.3.2 Visit the scene   68
    5.3.3 Do not forget secretaries   68
    5.3.4 Protect your sources   69
    5.3.5 Check the telephone directory   69
    5.3.6 Evaluate sources   69

Assignments   71

Bibliography and recommended reading   71

Chapter 6 Interviewing and note taking   72

6.1 Preparing for the interview   73
    6.1.1 Research   73
    6.1.2 Plan your time   75
    6.1.3 Formulate some questions   78
    6.1.4 Phrasing a question   78

6.2 Conducting the interview and planning your approach   79
    6.2.1 Possible approaches   80
    6.2.2 Keeping control   81
    6.2.3 Before you leave, take a look in the mirror   81
    6.2.4 Some tips   81

6.3 Taking notes   82
    6.3.1 Developing notehand   83
    6.3.2 Notebooks   84
    6.3.3 Tape recorders   84

Assignment   85

Bibliography and recommended reading   85

Chapter 7 Writing with flair   86

7.1 Writing with style   87
    7.1.1 Clarity   87
    7.1.2 Precision   89
    7.1.3 Pace   89

       7.1.4   Weaving with transitions   90
       7.1.5   Sensory appeal   91
       7.1.6   Alternative story structures   92

7.2   The Wall Street Journal method   93
       7.2.1   Applying the formula in steps   94

7.3   Other approaches   96
       7.3.1   Scenic leads   96
       7.3.2   Anecdotal leads   96

7.4   Features and fiction   97
       7.4.1   Types of feature stories   97
       7.4.2   Learning from the short story   99
       7.4.3   Using extended dialogue   107

Assignments   108

Bibliography and recommended reading   109

Chapter 8   Reaching the media   111

8.1   How to reach the media   112
       8.1.1   What does management want and what does the media want?   112
       8.1.2   Important news   113
       8.1.3   Know your company   113
       8.1.4   Know who will speak for your company   114
       8.1.5   Help your company spokesperson get to know the media   114

8.2   Targeting the right audience   115
       8.2.1   Creating a media profile   117
       8.2.2   Know the media   117

8.3   The right presentation – for readers and listeners   118

8.4   Reaching readers   118

8.5   Reaching listeners and viewers   120
       8.5.1   Format   121
       8.5.2   Style   123

       8.5.3   Media kits   126
       8.5.4   Working with the press   127

Assignments   132

Bibliography and recommended reading   134

PART 2   MAKING IT LOOK RIGHT, TOO

Essay "Designing for change" (Patti McDonald)   137

Chapter 9   Editing   141

    9.1   Complete, clear, correct – and exciting – stories   142
        9.1.1   Getting started   142
        9.1.2   Considering the content   143
        9.1.3   Matters of style   143
        9.1.4   Line-by-line editing   144

    9.2   Headlines   148
        9.2.1   Choosing a style   148
        9.2.2   Headline designs   149
        9.2.3   Principles of headline writing   151

    9.3   Captions   154
        9.3.1   Caption copy   154
        9.3.2   The format   155

Assignments   157

Bibliography and recommended reading   158

Chapter 10   Design   159

    10.1   Towards a design policy   160
        10.1.1   Basic guidelines   160

    10.2   Design starts with people   163
        10.2.1   Drawing up an editorial policy   163
        10.2.2   Publication profiles   165

10.3   Grid   167

10.4   Talking typography   170
    10.4.1   The anatomy of type   170
    10.4.2   Fonts   171
    10.4.3   Measuring type and layout   172
    10.4.4   Tips on typographic communication   172

10.5   Photography   176
    10.5.1   Getting the right shot   176
    10.5.2   Type of picture   178
    10.5.3   Types of picture story   180
    10.5.4   A few pointers about working with photographers   181
    10.5.5   You as a photographer   182
    10.5.6   Picture editing   183
    10.5.7   Cropping and sizing pictures   184
    10.5.8   Sending photographs to the printer   190

10.6   Layout   190
    10.6.1   The parts   190
    10.6.2   Putting it all together   190

10.7   Conclusion   193

Assignments   194

Bibliography and recommended reading   194

PART 3   DOING THE RIGHT THING

Essay   "Understanding ethics" (Dr Guy Berger)   197

Chapter 11   Doing the right thing   201

    11.1   Three ethical approaches   205
        11.1.1   Absolutism   205
        11.1.2   Antinomianism   205
        11.1.3   Situationism   206

    11.2   Freebies   208

11.3 Codes of conduct   212
       11.3.1   The South African Union of Journalists   212
       11.3.2   The Public Relations Institute of Southern Africa   213

Assignments   217

Bibliography and recommended reading   218

PART 4   MEDIA MILESTONES

Chapter 12   Timeline: significant events in the history of the press in South Africa   221

Bibliography and recommended reading   228

Index   229

FOREWORD

I am not stuck in the past. But I recall when I was an undergraduate student in Chicago, the most sought-after seats on campus (outside of the basketball stadium) were those in Professor Zenos Hawkinson's history classes – any of them.

Why did business, engineering, art and literature students all scramble to hear the white-haired professor?

Simply this: He told good stories and he told them well. That is what this book is about.

It is a book for journalists, whom I define the way Northwestern University media relations instructor Sandra Pesman does: "Journalists [are] all people who go out to do a story – regardless of whom they're writing for. They thoroughly investigate the subject, take to the street and interview as many people as possible, study the information they have gathered about it. Then, they begin to put it together in an orderly fashion, placing the most interesting facts first. Finally, they transform the facts into a clear, simple and interesting story. Anyone who does that for a living qualifies as a reporter in my book." (Pesman, Sandra, *Writing for the media*, Lincolnwood, IL, NTC Business Books, 1983, pp. 25–6)

This book draws on the expertise of journalists – from the mainstream and industrial media – who have studied and worked in Southern Africa, England and the United States. Many of the examples are from US-based publications. This is because for almost a decade I have worked there as a public relations writer, editor and newspaper reporter. Of course, the media game is increasingly being played on an international field and the rules are similar everywhere.

Learning to become a professional journalist is a tough task, but it is certainly not a boring one. And I hope you are ready for the challenge, because I am. And I have got more than a few stories to tell.

ACKNOWLEDGEMENTS

"The only qualities essential for real success in journalism are rat-like cunning, a plausible manner and a little literary ability. The capacity to steal other people's ideas and phrases – that one about rat-like cunning was invented by my colleague Murray Sayre – is also invaluable."
  Nicholas Tomalin, *Sunday Times* of London (Bates, Stephen, *If no news, send rumors: anecdotes of American journalism*, New York, St Martin's, 1989, p. 13)

To my contributors – Denis Beckett, Prof. Guy Berger, Patti McDonald, Diane Suchetka and Eddie Ward – and the other writers, editors and teachers whose advice and work have inspired and guided me, thank you.

PART 1

THE BUSINESS OF WRITING NEWS

WHEN IT'S GOOD, IT'S REALLY BAD

By Denis Beckett

We in the press are supposed to tell people what's happening in the world. That's the theory, anyhow. Of course we're entirely used to people taking swipes at us for not getting it right. Usually they say either that we're too full of Grim Reality and too thin on Light Escapism or they say the opposite, that we waste space on pictures of Claudia Schiffer when we are only telling half of a quarter of what we know about mayhem in Katlehong.

Those are the standard complaints. Once in a while a different one comes up and this week I heard a thought-provoking argument, from my friend Ueli. Namely, that we should not even begin to claim we are reporting "what's happening". We should admit that we are actually in the business of reporting what's happening **wrong**.

For instance, every day some 90 000 airline flights pass without incident. If we were literally telling people what's happening, we'd have on average 1,7 million stories saying "Successful Trip Completed" for every one story saying "Crash", and news consumers would have an image of airline flight as something remarkably safe and efficient. (Indeed you are statistically safer on an airliner than at your dinner table, where you are unlikely to be in the presence of personnel trained to save you from, for instance, choking on a food particle.) But in fact, of course, when you see a story about an airline, you're almost always seeing a story about a crash.

Or take the annual Easter Road Death Ritual. Year after year, the same crop of recurring headlines. Road Toll Up, Road Toll Rises, Road toll Fears . . . occasionally even Road Toll Drops, but always the toll, never the safe arrivals, never even a mention that in "what's happening" terms the safe arrivals are strictly speaking more newsworthy than the deaths. They go up at a faster rate, as road usage increases.

You could take the argument a long way. What *in fact* is happening is that maybe a million people go unmugged, unmurdered and unreported in the Transvaal each day for every one whose misfortunes hit the headlines. At least as many things are, literally, happening in

Switzerland as in Somalia. When did you last see Switzerland in the news?

What's really happening, with overwhelming dominance, is amazing normality – not the grimness and not the escapism either. If gunfire is not the world's chief reality, neither is Claudia Schiffer, and if the press truly told people "what's happening" both the guns and the Claudias would take a distant back seat.

Now you can see that Ueli is not about to get offered a job as a press consultant. If an editor tries to offer his readers Tannie Martha in the kitchen while his competitor is giving them Claudia in a miniskirt, he will rapidly become an ex-editor. Same if he gives them pictures of the mealie crop in Phuthadijaba while his rival splashes Casspirs in Katlehong.

That's the trouble with all the "give us good news" demands the people are constantly making of the press. People might think they want good news and say they want good news, but what they actually read is bad news. Bad news is crisp; good news is dull. Bad news is vivid; good news usually means complicated committee resolutions and proceedings. It's not that editors are ghouls; it's that people are more gripped by a snake striking than by a doe grazing.

More than that, bad news is on the whole easy to reach and easy to write. Good news is neither. Pitch up, for example, at a trouble-spot of the "racial tension" variety and one of the first people to greet you will be a photogenic AWB with a gun and a swastika and a big mouth, which he is using to utter quotably disgusting racial insults, whereas the dorp's average white resident ducks as far as he can out of the way of the press (who he thinks are going to shaft him) and if you can finally get a comment out of him at all it is something troubled and moderate, totally unblood-curdling and hard to see surviving the bottleneck struggle for limited news space.

The news media have by no means arrived at the end of history. If we look back now at the newspapers of a century ago, with their front pages devoted to advertisements and their middle pages consisting of huge slabs of leisurely grey small print, we can barely believe that anybody ever read that stuff. A century from now, of course, people will be looking back at today's ways and thinking exactly the same.

The trouble is, we don't know what it is that they, then, will know better than we know now. But I have a funny feeling that something along the lines of the "what's actually happening" theory might not be a million miles from the mark.

News media, to be true, aren't doing terribly well. Over the last 30 years or thereabouts, while populations and literacy rates have escalated dramatically, the circulation of the news media as a whole has barely increased at all.

Something is amiss, and nobody really knows what it is. There's a key waiting to be found, and it's likely that wherever the key is, it involves a way out of the current diet that presents depression as the main course and artificial relief as the sorbet.

Denis Beckett is a veteran journalist and political commentator. He was editor of the *Sunday Star* newspaper's "Insight" pages where this piece first appeared on 25 July 1993.

CHAPTER 1
WHAT IS NEWS?

To find out what is going on, we turn to the media. We pick up the daily newspaper or monthly house journal. We switch on the television or radio. We peruse magazines. These media all *report news*, but *news reports* are quite different.

Many reports focus on events, but not all events are news. People feature in many stories, but not all people are newsworthy. It is not always easy to see how editors decide which stories, among the scores of options, to use. Often we do not agree with their choice. Sensational, we say. Depressing. Boring. Biased. American Senator Adlai Stevenson, who helped found the United Nations, held this theory: "Newspaper editors are men who separate the wheat from the chaff, and then print the chaff" (Bates, Stephen, *Anecdotes of American journalism*, New York, St Martin's, 1989, p. 57).

Whatever the case, the first step in working for the media or with the media is understanding the process of making news.

> In this chapter you will learn:
> 1. Traditional tests of news.
> 2. Some viewpoints on news.
> 3. The subjective quality of news.
> 4. Basic news writing terms.

1.1 DEFINING NEWS

Admitting that a journalist cannot measure the essence of news the same way a scientist can measure the essence of water is key to our discussion of the nature of news. We will still try to formulate a definition, but only once we have examined the criteria journalists use to decide which facts make up news stories and which news stories are better than others.

1.1.1 News must be new

The basic element of news is clear from the root word: new. News comes from the Greek *neos*, the Latin *Novus* (and from later versions of the same), the German *neu* and the Middle English *newe*. A story may be many things –

well researched, finely crafted, cleverly composed – but if the information is not new to the readers it is not news. News is novel. News is different.

A snake biting a man is not news. But, as an article in the *Sunday Times* (20 September 1992, p. 3) illustrates, when farm worker Eddie Mkhize, 54, bit and battered to death a three-and-a-half-metre python which tried to bite him, the story made page three of the giant national weekly ("I have to thank God and my strong teeth for saving my life", Mr Mkhize was reported as saying afterwards).

1.1.2 News must have conversational value

Another aspect of news is that it is talked about. The *Miami Herald*'s Pulitzer Prize-winning crime reporter Edna Buchanan calls it the "My God! Martha" factor. She imagines a couple sitting at the breakfast table and, as the man scans the morning paper, he turns to his wife and says, "My God! Martha, did you read this?" (Buchanan, Edna, *The corpse had a familiar face*, New York, Random House, 1987).

Editors recognize the conversational value of news, even if they do not always appreciate it. An editor who does acknowledge this value of news in making editorial judgements is Reid Ashe, president and publisher of the daily *Wichita Eagle* in Wichita, Kansas. "Most readers don't think about it," Ashe says, "But if they did, they'd conclude that news has little intrinsic value. Its value is in the ways it stimulates and facilitates interaction with other people" (Ashe, Reid, "What readers really want", *Nieman Reports*, Spring 1992, p. 7). Much of what we consider news – the birth of triplets, the winner of the rugby test, the latest fashions in Europe – has little or no direct affect on our lives, but it is informative and helps us to socialize, to lean over the breakfast table and speak to our Martha . . .

1.1.3 News must have commercial value

News can be bought and sold. It is, quite simply, a product. Many starry-eyed reporters, and even some editors, are uncomfortable with the idea that newspapers are first and foremost a business. Readers buy newspapers because, like bread and socks, they want them. And editors and their newspapers give readers what they want.

People buy newspapers for different reasons – for the advertisements, for the news, or for the TV guide. Newspapers are a commodity for customers.

In Pedro Diederich's discussion of newspapers in "The fourth estate: a cornerstone of democracy", in De Beer, A.S. (ed) *Mass media for the nineties*, Pretoria, Van Schaik, 1993, p. 7, Diederichs recounts the history of newspapers: "An enterprising Roman named Chrestus began collecting information (from news about bumper crops to the burning of witches at the stake) and selling this on the contemporary local markets. In this sense he became one of the first journalists (from the Latin: *diurnarius*, diary writer)."

Diederichs also notes that in the Middle Ages news was spread by messengers who would recite the stories to those willing to pay a coin, an Italian *gazetta*.

Several South African newspapers, past and present, highlight the commercial nature of the industry in their titles: *The Cape Town Gazette and African Advertiser, South African Commercial Advertiser, Gold Fields Advertiser, Business Day* and *Graaff-Reinet Advertiser*.

1.2 TRADITIONAL NEWS TESTS

In addition to the three considerations we have just discussed concerning defining news, journalists have traditionally considered the following factors when deciding what is news:

1.2.1 Time

News, like milk, is perishable. News reports on what happened today, or since the previous issue. Readers need news as soon as possible, although this does not mean only recent events are newsworthy. Events that occurred many years ago – how the African National Congress planned to spring Nelson Mandela from his Robben Island prison, for example – become news when they are revealed today.

1.2.2 Audience

The readership profile guides editors in deciding which items are newsworthy. When the Afrikaans-dominated Conservative Party's late leader, Dr Andries Treurnicht, stalked out of a Dutch Reformed Church fuming about the (more) liberal minister's sermon, the event got scant attention in the English-language press, but made headlines in many Afrikaans newspapers.

1.2.3 Consequence

When the reader will be affected, how the reader will be affected and to what degree the reader will be affected often determines the news value of an item. Increases in the price of caviar may receive a mention in the newspapers, but a rise in the price of bread and milk, which will affect most people, will probably make the front page.

1.2.4 Proximity

Most events become more newsworthy the closer the action occurs to the audience. Usually, the same event is bigger news if it happened in your town than if it occurs 1 000 or even 10 kilometres away.

1.2.5 Peculiarity

The unusual or unexpected often captures the imagination and provides moments of diversion. In the words of *New York Sun* editor Charles Dana: "I have always felt that whatever Divine Providence permits to occur I am not too proud to report" (Bates, *Anecdotes of American journalism*, p. 76).

1.2.6 Prominence

Names do not always make news. Although some readers may not have a genuine interest in politicians, they do recognize their names. Students meet in class and fall in love all the time, but when President F.W. de Klerk's son Willem took up with his Cape Technikon classmate, Erica Adams, the liaison remained in the newspapers until the couple split up.

1.2.7 Conflict

From the front page – with reports of wars, politicians taking each other on, and differences in ideologies – to the back page – with tales from the rugby field and the boxing ring – conflict makes news.

1.2.8 Package

These were the headlines in the 14 July 1993 edition of the *Cape Times*:

- "Fundtrust liquidators sue ex-chief Marais"
- "Alleged killer linked to rightists"
- "Death toll in massacres rises to 14"
- "Arrests bid on Tollgate: Bosses face charges of fraud"
- "Woman, 82, in ticket shock"
- "New US call to invest in SA"
- "Berg traps top canoeist"
- "Dial-a-yuppie"

For its eight front-page stories, the editors selected five hard-news items and two lighter stories (including one about an 82-year-old woman who was summonsed to court for allegedly travelling at 110km/h in her 1970 Mini). Five of the stories originated in Cape Town, one each in Johannesburg, Washington and Perth.

Editors usually strive for a variety in tone and topic, and package stories accordingly.

We have just discussed the major elements journalists traditionally have used to decide the relative importance of stories competing for space in a newspaper or time on the air. But recently criteria of news standards, news sources and topics have shifted, and continue to do so.

1.3 CHANGING PERSPECTIVES

1.3.1 Changing views on information

"The problem with newspapers is that they've grown too good at the wrong things and ignored the things readers and society value most" (Ashe, *Nieman Reports*, p. 7). Newspapers have refined the art of compiling and delivering information – and convinced themselves that's their main function – at a time when information has become cheap and abundant.

For many people, news has become something you get by flipping a switch: you wake up with the radio alarm and fall asleep to the sound of CNN. In between, you have your car radio, television news and "Agenda". At work, there are memos, meetings and the proverbial grapevine. When the house journal and newspaper come along offering more information in greater depth – at a price in time and money – lots of people just do not buy. I already have more than I need, they reason. Why should I have to pay more?

Newspapers are ignoring – at their peril – the reader's hierarchy of values, says Ashe (p. 8). Things that are plentiful, like air and water, are cheap, even though they are vitally important. But if something is scarce, like caviar or diamonds, it is highly valued despite its limited usefulness.

General news is cheap because it is freely available all around us. What is scarce (and, therefore, potentially valuable) in South Africa, where people have for decades been kept apart by force, is the respect for different people and views that comes from meaningful social interaction. The United Nations, the Institute for a Democratic Alternative to South Africa and the Institute for a Multi-Party Democracy, amongst others, recognized this. When they held a conference several months before the country's first free election, the Institute for a Multi-Party Democracy asked the media to help promote voter education and political tolerance.

In response, South African Union of Journalists' Yvonne Grimbeek was reported as saying that the primary responsibility of journalists was to report events fairly and accurately and that imposing extra duties on the media could inhibit the free flow of information (*Argus*, 2 August 1993, p. 5).

To say that the role of the journalist is just to deliver information is too limiting. It ties us to the low-value aspects of what we do. Anybody can recite the headline news that most people consider sufficient. And everybody, including the telephone company and the post office, can deliver an advertising message. Newspapers and house journals need to stake a claim on something more valuable and less abundant, as well as more difficult for competitors to copy. The mission of newspapers should not just be to deliver information but rather to bring people together. For journalists this means newspapers need to help people to relate to their neighbours, help foster a sense of community, help bring the political process, i.e. national politics and corporate politics, within the reach of the individual and the control of the electorate. It means orienting the reading within a community of humans, and not just a system of institutions (see par. 1.3.3 for an example of how this has been done).

We should not neglect the news. News can help to bring us together. It gives us something to talk about as well as reasons to reach out to each other and work together to make things better. For those who believe this, the concept can guide the way in which every story is selected and placed.

This does not mean stories have to be short or "dumbed down". But it certainly means they need to go beyond what was on TV1 last night or the conversation in the canteen.

We have to understand that raw information is cheap, understanding is valuable, and something you can act on is precious. Too often, stories that are pure information, that the reader cannot do anything about and that will not change his or her life in any identifiable way, win the competition for space and display in our papers. Certainly, these stories have their place, but the other kind of story, the ones that grab the reader and let the reader react, deserve more of our scarce resources.

1.3.2 Changing standards

Some newspapers are already accepting the challenge of providing news that grabs the reader and allows the reader to react. On 31 January 1993, for example, Johannesburg's redesigned *Sunday Star* devoted almost two thirds of the news space on its front page to a series of teasers under this headline: "The Paper that helps you lead a happier, brighter life". Many of those stories cannot be judged accurately by traditional standards. Few dealt with anything bizarre or featured prominent people. Time is only a minor factor in some. In most, proximity is hardly considered.

"Throw away your scales – with a revolutionary mind-and-body diet", "Are you better off than your parents?", "Our sex fantasies" – these stories are considered **soft news**, and they are examples of a mainstream newspaper's move towards so-called "news you can use"; these stories not only highlight an issue, like the tight job market, but give the readers some hints on how to react.

1.3.3 Changing sources

In selecting sources, newspapers have traditionally followed this criteria: The higher the official, the better the quote. But by simply printing statements from official news sources, the press has allowed itself to be manipulated by community leaders in politics and commerce, especially at election time. As a result, citizens often feel alienated from the political process. The Poynter Institute for Media Studies in St Petersburg, Florida, is trying to change that.

When the 1992 US presidential election rolled around, the Institute teamed up with the *Charlotte Observer* and WSOC-TV in North Carolina to take up the challenge issued by David Broder of the *Washington Post*: "We have to try to distance ourselves from the people that we write about – the politicians and their political consultants – and move ourselves closer to the people that we write for – the voters and the potential voters" (Miller, Edward, "Institute, media partners reinvent election coverage", *Poynter Report*, Winter 1991, p. 2). The experiment began with an extensive opinion survey almost a year before the election. That survey was the first of many attempts to identify the "voter's agenda", and to base political coverage on the results, says the Institute's Edward Miller (Miller, Edward, *Charlotte Observer*, "WSOC-TV begin innovations in election coverage", *Poynter Report*, Spring 1992, p. 4).

Let us see how the *Observer* announced the initial poll results to its readers:

Listen, candidates, your neighbours are worried. Worried about losing their jobs, their health insurance, and even the moral values that glue their communities together. Worried that taxes – and the cost of a decent life – will go up so much they won't be able to afford a home or send their children to college.

And, as more are touched by the scourge of drug-related crime, they worry about simply going outside their home – or about someone breaking in.

As a new election year unfolds, a *Charlotte Observer*/WSOC-TV poll of 1 003 Carolinians found people are deeply troubled about the future. And nine out of 10 in the 14-county Charlotte region doubt their elected leaders are in touch with the powerful forces tearing at their personal lives. They want their worries heard. They want them to become the priorities of politicians.

"The *Observer's* reporting took on a different tone," Miller said. "The political reporters and columnists didn't declare what the issues were. The voters made the case in their own words. One South Carolina woman described what economists call a recession: 'People don't know around here from one day to the next whether they have a job.'. . . And on they went, citizen after citizen, raising the issues they wanted addressed by the candidates."

The point of the project was this: to show that an aggressive media need not be the victim of the spin doctors and campaign manipulators; the media can take charge of the process by voicing the concerns of readers, viewers and listeners, and then holding candidates accountable.

One reader told Rich Oppel, the *Observer's* editor: "It's the people's government and country, and we've got to do something about it. Thanks for helping us." (Miller, Edward, *Poynter Report*, Spring 1992, p. 5.)

1.3.4 Changing interests

We have discussed how the news value of events is measured by traditional standards, and how new kinds of stories are competing for space with the traditional official news. We have seen the challenge the media faces in covering news events, like an election. Let us see what newspaper readers – or consumers of news – consider important or interesting.

Of course, the best way to find out is to ask the readers, and this is just what the *Weekly Mail* did early in 1993. The result was a redesign which combined the *Weekly Mail* with its international supplement *The Guardian Weekly*. In response to a readers' survey, *The Weekly Mail & Guardian* increased business and sports coverage, added a new features section and redesigned entertainment listings with "intelligent choices of the best entertainment available, rather than simply lists of events" (*The Weekly Mail & Guardian*, 23–29 July 1993, p. 3).

Listening to their readers made good business sense, too. While most political weeklies were battling to survive, this news brief appeared several months later ("Advertising Record", *The Weekly Mail & Guardian*, 5–11 November 1993, p. 3):

> During the month of October, despite a recessionary climate in which most media lost advertising, this newspaper broke all records for advertising revenue in its eight-year history by selling more than R500 000 worth of space.

Both advertising and newspaper sales have boomed since *The Weekly Mail* and *Guardian Weekly* merged into one product earlier this year.

1.4 THE SUBJECTIVE QUALITY OF NEWS

When South African Broadcasting Corporation newsman Calvin Thusago was hauled from his car and stabbed to death in April 1993, journalists, politicians and community leaders were unanimous in their plea: media workers must be protected. Some of the reasons offered, however, were surprisingly naive.

One media union representative argued that journalists should be protected because they are non-partisan and act merely as channels of information, relaying facts to the public. That journalists relay facts is true enough, but that this process occurs objectively, is not.

We have seen that throughout the process of making news, editors and reporters have choices to make: Which topic is newsworthy? Who is the best source? How should the information be arranged in the story? Where and when in the paper or broadcast will the story be placed? How, where and at what cost should the media be distributed? And, finally, how will the audience be allowed to respond?

It is indisputable that the answers to these questions are influenced by time, money and (of primary importance to this discussion) the reporters' perspectives. Like everyone else, reporters are moulded by their societies, education and exposure – even by their state of mind. News choices are ultimately made by subjective editors who base their decisions, by and large, on subjective interpretations of facts and hearsay provided to them by journalists. Accordingly, the notion of an objective media is ridiculous.

This last statement may upset media workers. For, as political correspondent John Battersby says, "Objectivity is the holiest of holy cows. . . . It is taken for granted as the cornerstone of a free Press and an essential prerequisite for the functioning of the Press in a democratic society" (Battersby, John, "Objectivity – the holiest of cows", *Equid Novi*, 2(1), 1981, p. 17). But, as Battersby and others have asked, is the idea of a clinical-like objectivity realistic? The answer? No!

1.4.1 Our goal: fairness

This does not imply that journalists should simply brush aside any effort to keep their personal perspectives in check. On the contrary, media workers should acknowledge their own biases and, if their goal is to serve a wide audience, actively work to be fair. Fairness in selecting stories should prompt sports editors, for example, to feature woman athletes as prominently and frequently as their male counterparts.

Fairness in reporting makes it conceivable that a reporter with left-wing sympathies can, for example, write a fair story about the assassination of South African Communist Party leader Chris Hani. The journalist could give a detailed account of how the murder was committed and then, after interviewing a number of people, describe the affects the killing had on people from across the political spectrum – including those who were celebrating Hani's demise.

Fairness in displaying stories means a union newsletter would display a story of a corporation's management training programme as prominently as a report on wage negotiations.

Fairness in responding to their readers make it necessary for newspapers to print letters and display corrections to stories as boldly as the original, faulty report.

The objectivity/fairness debate is a heated one, because both sides agree that the media is powerful and, by extension, so are those people who select what is news and decide what to do with it.

Story selection is important because a newspaper or house journal with a well-known and respected institution, can influence what a community thinks and does. Says Bernard C. Cohen in his *The press and foreign policy* (1936, p. 13):

> The press is significantly more than a purveyor of information and opinion. It may not be successful much of the time in telling what to think, but it is stunningly successful in telling its readers what to think about. And it followed from this that the world looks different to different people depending not only on their personal interests, but also on the map that is drawn for them by the writers and editors, and publishers of the papers they read. The editor may believe he is only printing things that people want to read, but he is thereby putting a claim on their attention, powerfully determining what they will be thinking about, and talking about, until the next wave laps their shore.

But it is unrealistic to assume that any news, even fairly processed news, can equal the reality it presumes to report.

"News – even the best-written – never comes close to equalling or approximating reality," says John Merrill, professor and director of the Louisiana State University's School of Journalism (Merrill, John, "News media, news, objectivity – ontological questions in journalism", *Equid Novi*,

5(2), 1984, p. 82). "In Alfred Korybski's words: 'The map is not the territory'. Abstracted bits and pieces of an event presented in symbols do not equal the event."

Therefore, as reporters must often struggle with the questions of fairness in a story, editors who assign stories and layout pages must ask themselves the broader question: Does this edition give a fair account of the newsworthy stories in my target community?

1.4.2 Do not just toy with words

Clarifying the distinction between objectivity and fairness is not merely a matter of semantics. Fairness affects not only the manner in which the news is presented, but also how news is consumed. Let me clarify: Only when journalists stop insisting they are objective, will the public stop expecting them to be – and judge them harshly when they are not.

Take the South African Broadcasting Corporation (SABC). Beleaguered by charges of bias, the national broadcaster fought back with a campaign which included these full-page newspaper ads (*The Guardian Weekly*, 21–27 May 1993, p. 9): A grid of portraits stereotypically depicting six segments of their audience, from a conservative white Afrikaner extremist to a radical Pan Africanist Congress supporter sporting a "one settler, one bullet" button on his T-shirt. Speech bubbles from each character showed their objection to the SABC's coverage. Below the images ran the bold headline "Precisely". The copy explained, "If you're after objective coverage of what's happening in South Africa you can't beat TV1. We spend more time than any other medium in this country to make sure all parties are heard. All the views, all the issues, from all the faces of South Africa."

However, many of the SABC's critics were not convinced and when, months later, a new board was appointed to the group, the company's biased news coverage featured high on the list of issues to be addressed. Nevertheless, no amount of reprogramming, no matter how well-intentioned, will make news programmes objective. An hour-long show which takes, for example, four politicians from rival groups, touches up their faces with make-up, sits them in a make-believe lounge and questions them about a complex issue such as women's rights cannot lay claim to having objectively discussed the issue. The best that can be said is that for 60 minutes the show provided a fair platform for a variety of specific voices to discuss a few aspects of the issue.

Only when journalists become aware of the limits of work and, in turn, educate their audience, will demands for the impossible – the objective news report – cease.

1.5 A DEFINITION OF NEWS

Considering the factors above, a popular definition of news is: *News is whatever newspapers print and radio and television stations broadcast.* This is true enough, but still incomplete. The definition ignores a crucial party – the audience. Journalists' best decisions are ultimately judged by the audience, and if a news reader glances at a story and says, "This isn't news," then it is not news – at least not for that person.

News, therefore, whatever else it may be, is in the eyes of the beholder: reporters, editors, and readers.

Nuus: 'n definisie

Nuus is moeilik om te definieer, maar die volgende is seker: Nuus moet nuut wees. Nuus moet gemeensaamheid aanwakker. Nuus moet kommersiële waarde hê.

Nuusitems word tradisioneel aan die volgende faktore gemeet: tydigheid, gehoor, gevolge, aardigheid, nabyheid, verhewenheid, konflik en die algehele nuuspakket.

Hoewel nuus nie objektief is nie, kan 'n akkurate berig wat duidelik geskryf is 'n regverdige weergawe van 'n storie wees. Regverdigheid affekteer nie net hoe 'n berig geskryf word nie, maar ook watter berig geskryf word en hoe die berig gebruik word.

1.6 BASIC NEWS WRITING TERMS

Some words you should know about the organizing, writing, and use of news stories:

Add (Byvoegsel)	Additional material to be included in the story; a way of numbering pages (second page is FIRST ADD, third page is SECOND ADD).
A-matter (Vooraf-kopié)	Material prepared in advance; background information, with the lead called in from the scene of the news event.
Angle (Nuuspunt)	Special quality of interest or marketability that makes an idea usable.
Bed (Van die steen af)	A newspaper put to bed is ready to be put on the presses for printing.

THE BUSINESS OF WRITING NEWS

Book
(Trek)
A page of copy is called a book; see also "take".

Box
(Kassie/raam)
The border around a story to set it aside or call attention to it.

Break
(Breek)
The place where a story is continued on another column or page.

Breaking
(Breek)
A breaking story is one which has just happened or is still happening.

Bright/Brite
(Stoepie)
A short item, maybe only a paragraph, that elicits a chuckle or is upbeat in some way.

Budget
(Nuuslys)
A list of stories, with priorities indicated, for the day.

Bulletin
(Korte/brok)
A short item, usually a paragraph, of great importance, usually arriving too late to be developed into a story.

Bullets
(Kolle)
Round dots (often in place of numbers) used to highlight one-paragraph topics or items on a list.

Column
(Kolom/Rubriek)
Standard line width of printed type in a newspaper with a standard depth; an opinion, analysis, or entertaining piece of writing, usually of predetermined length with byline.

Copy
(Kopié)
An article or material prepared for publication or broadcast.

Correspondent
(Korrespondent)
A non-staff person who writes a story, often a regular contributor representing a distant area.

Dupe
(Duplikaat)
An extra copy of a news story.

Edition
(Uitgawe)
Total unchanged press run; when new material is added to a new run within the day and it is so designated, this is another edition. Large papers have as many as a half dozen editions in one day.

Editorial
(Hoofartikel)
An unsigned article or essay, often very brief, appearing on an editorial or opinion page, usually expressing the views of the management of the paper.

Enterprise
(Inisiatief)
An effort to find news or picture idea on one's own.

Feature
(Artikel)
To make a story look more prominent in the paper, to lead off with it; name for a human interest, non-timely article (in contrast to hard or breaking news).

File
(Instuur/roep)
Sending (by wire) or calling in a story.

Fluff (Wolligheid)	Vague and often unimportant copy; poor writing, non-factual writing; also, light, non-serious topic.
General assignment (Algemene nuusdekking)	Availability to cover any topic.
Hard news (Harde nuus)	Straight, factual news, usually of a compelling nature.
In depth (In diepte)	Emphasis on the background of a story.
Jump (Oorloop)	Part of a story that is continued on another page or column.
Kill (Pen/skrap)	Eliminate designated words, stories, or parts of stories.
Lead/lede (Intro/inleiding)	The beginning of a news story.
Lift-out (Uittreksel/ prikkel/lokker)	Sentence or paragraph from a story repeated with headline for display purposes.
More (Meer)	Notation at the bottom of a page indicating more is coming.
Move (Aanstuur/ versprei)	A story is sent by wire or edited copy is sent into production.
Mug shot (Nabyskoot)	A head-and-shoulders photograph.
News hole (Gat)	Space available for news stories in an issue after advertising space is allocated.
Newsprint (Koerantpapier)	Paper used for newspapers (cheaper, poorer grade paper).
Peg (Nuuspunt)	An idea or event on which a story is based.
Play (Gebruik)	The way a news story is handled in the paper, such as where it appears and how much space is allocated to it.
Rewriter (Insetter/ herskrywer)	A person who edits and rewrites stories; a person who takes calls from reporters on breaking stories and writes them in the office.
Second day (Oorstaanstorie)	A story on the same topic that appears a day later.
Sections (Afdelings)	Parts of a newspaper dedicated to one topic, for example, the sports section.

THE BUSINESS OF WRITING NEWS

Sidebar (Byvoegsel)	An additional short news story that is split off from the main story but which is printed alongside it, often in a box.
Slant (Aanslag)	Direction or emphasis to appeal to a particular audience.
Spot news (Harde nuus)	Breaking news; also firsthand, on the spot.
Stringer (Medewerker)	Correspondent; often a part-time, out-of-state contributor who calls in stories. Sports desks, for example, use local stringers in peak seasons.
Story (Storie)	News article or feature.
Subs desk (Subkantoor)	Where material is edited, headlines added, and so on.
Sub-editor (Subredakteur)	The person who edits, rewrites copy, and puts on headlines.
Take (Trek)	A page of copy.
Top-off (Nuwe intro/inleiding)	Put a new lead on a story.
Trim (Sny)	Cut back length of a story; a portion that is trimmed.
Update (Aanpas)	Add more recent facts to a story.

(Afrikaans translation provided by Willem Eksteen and Stephanie Hefer, *Die Burger*)

Assignments

1. Read a newspaper and make a list of the 10 best stories. Identify what makes each story newsworthy. Refer to your list and choose six stories you would have put on the front page. Compare your decisions with the original and those of your classmates. Explain how you made your choices.

2. Compare national and local editions of Sunday newspapers printed on the same date. Choose five stories which appear in both and discuss how the stories were treated in each paper. Consider traditional news factors as well as changing perspectives on news.

Bibliography and recommended reading

Ashe, Reid, "What readers really want", *Nieman Reports*, Spring 1992, pp. 7–10.

Bates, Stephen, *If no news, send rumors: anecdotes of American journalism*, New York, St Martin's, *1989.*

Buchanan, Edna, *The corpse had a familiar face: covering Miami, America's toughest crime beat*, New York, Random House, 1987.

Battersby, John, "Objectivity – the holiest of cows", *Equid Novi*, 2(1), 1981, pp. 17–23.

Diederichs, Pedro. "The fourth estate: a cornerstone of democracy", in De Beer, A.S. (ed.), *Mass media for the nineties*, Pretoria, Van Schaik, 1993.

"Eddie puts the bite on a giant python", *The Sunday Times*, 20 September 1992, p. 3.

Merrill, John, "News media, news, objectivity – ontological questions in journalism", *Equid Novi*, 5(2), 1984, pp. 79–82.

Miller, Edward D, "Institute, media partners reinvent election coverage", *Poynter Report*, Winter 1991, pp. 2–3.

Miller, Edward D, "*Charlotte Observer*/WSOC-TV begin innovations in election coverage", *Poynter Report*, Spring 1992, pp. 4–5.

"This is what to look out for next week", *Weekly Mail*, 23–29 July 1992, p. 3.

Tuchman, Gaye, *Making news: a study in the construction of reality*, New York, Free Press, 1978.

CHAPTER 2
INSIDE NEWSPAPERS

When I started work at a bureau of North Carolina's Pulitzer Prize-winning daily, the *Charlotte Observer*, Dan Huntley was the oldest reporter in the newsroom. When I last heard, he still was. Armfuls of accolades for his work and nudges from the paper's management were not enough to move Huntley up the corporate ladder. He even tried a stint as a news editor once, but asked to return to his beat. "I don't want to be so far removed from the action," Huntley once explained. The thrill of hunting down a tip, interviewing sources and telling a story well was the only job Huntley wanted to do. Positions like sub-editor, news editor, assistant-editor or even editor – which, though they sound similar, require diverse skills – held no appeal for him.

Understanding the requirements of each position and the role each person in the newsroom plays in creating each edition of the newspaper is crucial for any aspiring media worker.

> In this chapter you will learn:
> 1. How a major metropolitan daily newspaper, and its editorial department in particular, is organized.
> 2. What the primary editorial positions entail.
> 3. How copy flows from one editor to another.

2.1 INSIDE THE NEWSROOM: HOW A MAJOR METROPOLITAN DAILY NEWSPAPER IS ORGANIZED

The management structure of a modern newspaper is as complex as in any other contemporary business. The newspaper institution has its hierarchy of staff, just like any other major corporation. Most South African newspapers are part of conglomerates; they are a subsidiary or business among a group of businesses under one ownership. Nasionale Pers, for example, owns a number of businesses: several newspapers, including Cape Town's *Die Burger*, Pretoria's *Beeld* and Johannesburg's *City Press*, as well as book publishing companies, like Tafelberg.

Even if it is part of a conglomerate or chain, a newspaper functions independently, using its ties with a central administration and sister newspapers to bring in additional stories. Argus Newspapers, for example, has a special wire service that allows the sharing of stories among its nine sister newspapers which include the *Daily News* (Durban), *The Star* (Johannesburg) and *Diamond Fields Advertiser* (Kimberley). The group also has national and international reporters who serve its network.

There are exceptions, but in all newspapers someone has to gather and write the news, someone has to check the copy for clarity, someone has to evaluate the stories and pick the best ones and someone has to compile the pages accordingly. There are, therefore, enough similarities to make some observations about key personnel and their functions.

2.2 WHAT THE PRIMARY EDITORIAL POSITIONS ENTAIL

2.2.1 The editor

Also known as the editor in-chief at some newspapers, the editor is responsible for overall policy and management of the newspaper. He does not deal with day-to-day operations in the news department and, unless you begin work as a reporter at a weekly or small daily newspaper (or create some real trouble), you will probably have little contact with the editor. The editor's influence is exerted through those who report directly to him, namely the deputy editors and assistant editors.

2.2.2 Editorial-page editor

This person is responsible for producing the editorial page: writing the daily editorial column – which is seen as the official position of the newspaper – as well as editing the letters-to-the-editor section and political columns.

2.2.3 Chief sub-editor

This editor (often just called the chief sub) controls the copy desk, where the final editing of stories is done, pages are designed and headlines are written. Working for the chief sub-editor are sub-editors (called subs), specialists who polish the stories. They check verifiable facts, including the spelling of names and addresses, and write headlines.

Some newspapers, like the *Weekend Argus*, have a single-page editor who helps the chief sub design and lay out all the newspaper's news pages. Across town at *Die Burger*, for example, the chief sub sends stories to individual page subs who have control over designing certain pages, as well as polishing the stories and writing the headlines.

Whatever the brief, the copy desk plays an important role in producing the newspaper. It is charged with enforcing deadlines so the newspaper is produced on time. Although deadlines affect everyone in the newsroom, you will have little contact with the sub-editors unless they have questions about something you have written. Even then, the questions may be channelled through the news editor.

2.2.4 News editor

The news editor supervises the reporters who gather local news. He or she directs the news desk, which is the hub of the newsroom (local news is the primary news product of most newspapers).

The editors of special sections like entertainment, art, property, sports and business all liaise with the news editor, who also often supervises the chief photographer or, at some large newspapers, works with the photography editor.

2.2.5 Photographers

The new designation – photojournalists – seems a more precise description for the work of camera-toting newsroom staff. Photographs play a vital part in attracting readers and enhancing the written story or copy. *Newsweek* (24 May 1993, pp. 60–61) ran a promotional advertisement highlighting the role of photojournalists under the headline "Every week our readers *see* the news" [their emphasis]. The double-page spread shows work by three of the magazine's award-winning photographers and says, "Their pictures involve our readers in the immediacy of the moment, bringing drama and emotion to each news story." Often pictures are used independently with a simple caption (called "stand alones"). Photographers, reporting to a Chief Photographer, are usually under the authority of the news editor.

2.2.6 Cartoonists

Cartoonists have long had a place on newspaper's editorial pages. "The task of the cartoonist is to be insulting to everyone, criticize mercilessly – but equally," wrote cartoonist Dov Felder in the *Rhodes University Journalism Review* (June 1991, p. 24). Editorial cartoonists usually report to the editorial page editor.

2.2.7 Graphic designers

Another type of journalist is gaining a place on the news pages: the graphic artist. Editor Dave Hazelhurst says the successful redesign of the *Sunday Star* is based on these three cornerstones: "News you can handle. . . . News that touches your life. . . . News you can see" (*Rhodes Review*, December

INSIDE NEWSPAPERS

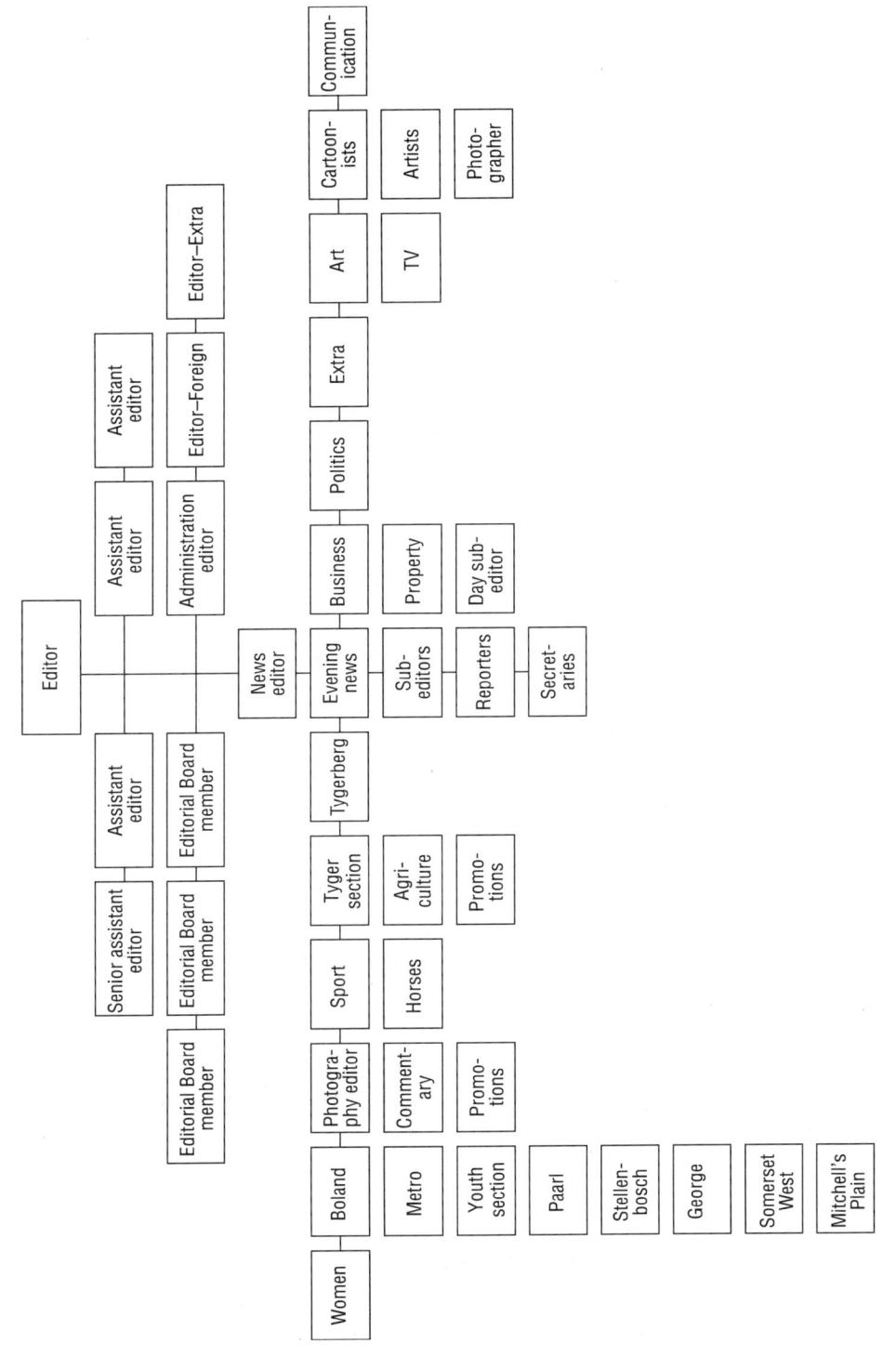

FIGURE 2.1 Typical organisation of the newsroom of a daily newspaper

1992, p. 27). Graphics are used extensively, not just to illustrate stories, but also to tell them. Hazelhurst has used graphics to show how French rugby players out-smarted South Africans with complex manoeuvres and also to show how Ciskei soldiers and African National Congress supporters clashed at Bisho.

The journalism school at the University of Missouri (which claims to be the oldest journalism school in the world) has created a programme for graphic journalists who are trained to report a story, the way writers do, and return to their computers and create their story in images. Industrial editors, like Deon Meyer of Sanlam, have also seen the value of graphics and use graphics extensively in their publications. Graphic artists, like reporters, are usually directly responsible to the news editor.

2.3 OTHER DEPARTMENTS

Like any business, newspapers are profit-making institutions. However, they differ from traditional business in one significant way: the clearer separation between departments. The news department gathers and reports news, even though some of the news may conflict with management. The business and advertising departments are relatively independent of the news-gathering operation, ideally at least.

2.3.1 Advertising
Most of a newspaper's revenue is generated by the advertising department. Some newspapers, like the *Argus*, devote as much as two-thirds of their pages to advertising. Usually the department is divided according to the two major forms of advertising: display and classified sections. Classifieds (often called smalls) account for the largest chunk of advertising.

2.3.2 Circulation
The job of getting the newspapers in the readers' hands belongs to the circulation department. Revenue from copy sales is the second leading source of income.

2.3.3 Business
From a reporter's point of view, this department's most important function is handling the payroll, benefits and insurance. The business department also handles billing, accounts and related functions.

2.3.4 Production

This is where the creative work of the reporters, photographers and editor is translated onto the page. Production departments are usually divided into sections which handle composing, where type is set and pages are assembled, plate-making, and printing.

2.4 HOW COPY FLOWS FROM ONE EDITOR TO ANOTHER

It is inevitable. The telephone rings and on the other end is an irate reader. Your side of the conversation is likely to go something like this:

"Yes, sir, I understand your disappointment with the headline, but I did not write it.

"Mmmm. Yes, but I did not choose to place the story about your new hotel next to the one about the national housing crisis.

"Yes, sir, I noticed that your name was spelled incorrectly in the caption, but . . . yes, Mr. Jones, I did not write it.

"Yes, yes, Mr Jones, I know my by-line is on the story – but I am only the reporter . . ."

Understanding how a story evolves and moves through the newsroom before finally landing up in the reader's hand is essential.

| Reporter | → | News editor | → | Chief sub-editor | → | Sub-editor | → | Chief sub-editor | → | Production |

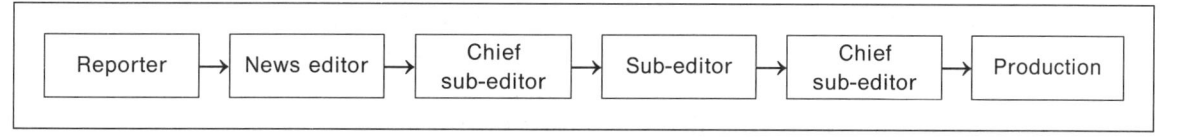

FIGURE 2.2   The copy flow pattern in a typical newsroom

Let us look at the stages of evolution of a story in a newsroom.

- **Stage 1: Reporter**
  Collects facts, writes story, checks accuracy, passes to news editor (a discussion of news sources can be found in chapter 5).

- **Stage 2: News editor**
  Edits story, returns to reporter for changes or more details (if necessary), forwards story to chief sub-editor.

- **Stage 3: Chief sub-editor**
  Prepares a page dummy, or layout plan, which determines where stories are placed in the newspaper, their exact length as well as the headline size, before forwarding the piece to the sub-editor.

- **Stage 4: Sub-editor**
  Checks for accuracy and clarity, polishes the writing and trims the piece to fit the exact column size, writes the headline, and then returns the piece to the chief sub or a designated revise sub for the final check. At this stage, the sub-editor also writes the caption for any pictures or graphics that may accompany the story.

- **Stage 5: Chief sub-editor**
  Verifies that the story is trimmed as specified and the correct headline has been written, then transmits the story to the composing room for typesetting.

2.5 MOVING AND PRINTING THE NEWS

Since the 1970s most newspapers have steadily moved out their old typewriters and hot metal type printing methods and moved to computer technology. The sophistication of the systems varies greatly. The now-defunct *Rand Daily Mail* and the *Cape Times* introduced the Atex Video Display Terminal (VDT) system in 1979 to become South Africa's first computerized newspapers. Nasionale Pers' *Die Burger* switched to the same system in 1980. When sanctions forced American-owned Atex, a division of Kodak, to divest from South Africa, newspaper groups were forced to look elsewhere and have now developed their own systems.

2.6 LIBRARIES

Some newspapers, like *Die Burger*, have also computerized their libraries (sometimes called "morgues"), allowing researchers near-instant access to stories written since 1 March 1986. However, earlier items have to be retrieved manually from files which patient librarians have created by clipping daily stories and pasting them into books. Some newspapers also store their editions on microfiche, miniature photographic negatives of each page which are then viewed through an enlarger. Newspaper libraries commonly are open to the public during restricted hours and provide copies of articles and photographs at a fee.

Assignments
1. Answer *true* or *false*:
    a. The editor supervises the news reporters.
    b. The reporter submits his story to the sub-editor.
    c. News editors assign the headline sizes.
    d. The chief sub-editor coordinates the design of the news pages.
    e. News stories are designed around the advertisements on each page.
2. Divide your class into two or more groups. Arrange visits to your local daily newspaper as well as a weekly newspaper or magazine. Study how the staff in each is organised and scheduled. Draw up charts which show the organisational hierarchy and the flow of copy. Present the findings to the rest of the class.

Bibliography and recommended reading
Diederichs, Pedro, Newspapers: "The fourth estate – a cornerstone of democracy", in A.S. de Beer (ed), *Mass media for the nineties*, Johannesburg, Van Schaik, 1993, pp. 71–98.

Felder, Dov, "Pen sketches: Dov Felder", *Rhodes University Journalism Review*, June 1991, p. 24.

Hazelhurst, David, "Why and How", *Rhodes University Journalism Review*, December 1992, p. 29.

CHAPTER 3
WRITING IN NEWSPAPER STYLE

The writer George Orwell once noted that most people who bothered about the matter at all admitted that the English language was in a bad way (Orwell, Sonia and Angus, Ian (eds), *The collected essays, journalism and letters of George Orwell*, Vol. IV, London, Secker & Warburg, 1968, p. 127). What would he have made of this article from a Cape Town newspaper?

- **Example 1**

  Former editor of the *Cape Times* Mr. Tony Heard will continue his defamation action in the Supreme Court despite losing a skirmish this week.

  Mr. Heard lost an exception application.

  A report in the *Argus* on Friday incorrectly stated that the defamation action, brought by Mr. Heard against his employers, Times Media Limited, and the editor of the *Financial Mail*, Mr. Nigel Bruce, had been dismissed with costs.

  In fact, the exception application brought by Mr. Heard to a plea of fair comment by Mr. Bruce and TML was dismissed by Mr. Justice Gerald Friedman. . . . In his judgement Mr. Justice Friedman said the comment in question was "clearly based on the facts set out in the article" and it was unnecessary for any further facts to be alleged in the plea.

  He said there was sufficient "substratum of fact" in the article to form the subject matter of the plea of fair comment.

  He dismissed the exception with costs.

  (*Weekend Argus*, 20/21 February 1993, p. 3)

After shaking his head, Orwell would probably have offered the editorial staff at that paper the same advice he gave to readers of *Horizon* in 1946. The themes from that essay, "Politics and the English Language" form the basis of the first part of this section.

> In this chapter you will learn:
> 1. Why using clear and concise English is not only good practice, but also a political concern.
> 2. Some peculiarities of journalistic writing.
> 3. Some basic style rules.

3.1 WHY USING CLEAR AND CONCISE ENGLISH IS IMPORTANT

The struggle against poor English is a tough one. And, Orwell noted, many feel the effort is in vain:

> Our civilisation is decadent and our language – so the argument runs – must inevitably share in the general collapse. It follows that any struggle against the abuse of language is sentimental archaism, like preferring candles to electric light or hansom cabs to aeroplanes. Underneath this lies the half-conscious belief that language is a natural growth and not an instrument which we shape for our own purposes.
>
> Now, it is clear that the decline of a language must ultimately have political and economic causes: it is not simply due to the bad influence of this or that individual. But an effect can become a cause, reinforcing the original cause and producing the same effect in an intensified form, and so on indefinitely. A man may take a drink because he feels himself a failure and fail all the more completely because he drinks. It is rather the same thing that is happening to the English language. It becomes ugly and inaccurate because our thoughts are foolish, but the slovenliness of our language makes it easier for us to have slovenly thoughts.

However, Orwell was optimistic:

> The point is that the process is reversible. Modern English is full of bad habits which spread by imitation and which can be avoided if one is willing to take the necessary trouble. If we get rid of these habits one can think more clearly, and to think clearly is a necessary first step towards political regeneration: so that fight against bad English is not frivolous and is not the exclusive concern of professional writers.
>
> (Orwell & Angus, *Collected essays*, pp. 127–8).

It is difficult to believe that Orwell was writing nearly a half-century ago. His concern is as valid today, as the passage above and two others we will also discuss show. (The examples are numbered so I can refer back to them.)

- **Example 2**
  It's make or break for SA future now. (*Argus*, 5 March 1993, p. 1)

- **Example 3**
  The government's insouciance as the gravy rises to the horses' bits is not just outrageous. It is putting this country in jeopardy. (*Cape Times*, 4 March 1993, p. 6)

These newspaper excerpts have not been picked because they are especially bad – I could have quoted far worse – but because they illustrate what Orwell called the "mental vices from which we now suffer": stale images and lack of precision (Orwell & Angus, *Collected essays*, p. 128). Here is a break-down of the main causes:

• *Dying metaphors*

A newly created metaphor helps by invoking a visual image and a technically dead metaphor (like "iron resolution") has the effect of reverting to an ordinary word, and can generally be used without being vague. In between these two categories is a huge dump of worn-out metaphors which save people the trouble of inventing phrases for themselves: ring the changes on, ride roughshod over, toe the line, stand shoulder to shoulder, fishing in troubled waters, etc.

Some of these are used though their exact meaning is unclear and frequently incomparable metaphors are mixed – a sure sign the writer is not really interested in what he is saying. Others are distorted without the writer being aware of it. For example, "toe" the line becomes "tow" the line. Another example is the hammer and the anvil now used to imply that the anvil gets the worst of it, whereas in life the hammer always gets the worst of it. The anvil always breaks the hammer, and not the other way around. If writers stopped to think about it, they would not pervert the original phrase.

• *Operators or false limbs*

These save the trouble of choosing appropriate verbs and nouns, and at the same time pad the sentence with syllables to make it appear symmetrical. For example: render inoperative, prove unacceptable, play a leading part, make itself felt, take effect, give rise to.

Why eliminate simple verbs? Instead of simple words like break, stop, spoil, mend, kill, a verb becomes a phrase made up of a noun or adjective tacked on to some general purpose verb such as prove, serve, play or render. The passive voice is also used: by examination of, instead of by examining.

• *Pretentious diction*

Words like phenomenon, element, effective, virtual, facilitate, utilise and liquidate are used to dress up simple statements and give the air of impartiality to biased judgements. The current media favourite is "radical elements".

Adjectives like historic, epic, triumphant, veritable and unforgettable are used to dignify sordid and forgettable processes in politics. Phrases like *status quo* and *deus ex machina* are used to give an air of culture and elegance. Except for some useful abbreviations (i.e., etc.) there is little need for many of the foreign phrases in current English.

• *Meaningless words*

In certain kinds of criticism, especially in art and literary criticism, it is normal to come across long passages which seem meaningless, like: "her work is filled with a vivid blackness". Many political words are similarly abused. The word "Fascism" has now no meaning except in so far as it signifies something not desirable. Democracy, socialism, freedom, patriotic, realistic and justice each have several meanings. In the case of democracy, not only is there no agreed definition, but the attempt to define it is resisted from all sides. It is almost universally agreed that to call a country democratic is to praise it. Subsequently, we have the South African Communist Party on the one side and the Afrikaner Weerstands Beweging on the other side and everyone in between calling for democracy in South Africa.

Words like these are often consciously used in a dishonest way. A speaker who uses them has his own private definition, but allows the audience to interpret them in a different way.

3.1.1 The product of bad habits

Now that these swindles and perversions have been catalogued, here is an example of the kind of writing they lead to. Take this well-known verse from Ecclesiastes: "I returned, and saw under the sun, that the race is not to the swift, not the battle to the strong, neither yet bread to the wise or yet riches to men of understanding, nor yet favour to men of skill; but time and chance happeneth to them all."

Here is Orwell's rewrite of the same passage, in modern English (Orwell & Angus, *Collected essays*, p. 133):

> Objective consideration of contemporary phenomena compels the conclusion that success or failure in competitive activities exhibits no tendency to be commensurate with innate capacity, but that a considerable element of the unpredictable must invariably be taken into account.

This is a parody, but not a gross one. Example 3 contains the same kind of English. Now analyse Orwell's translation and the biblical text more closely.

The original contains 49 words with only 60 syllables and all of these words are from everyday life. The modern English version contain 38 words of 90 syllables. The first contains six vivid images, and only one phrase –

"time and chance" – that could be called vague. The second contains not a single fresh, arresting phrase and in spite of its 90 syllables is a shortened version of the main point in the first.

Modern writing at its worst does not pick out words for the sake of their meaning and explore images to make the meaning clearer. It consists of glueing together long strings of words which someone else has ordered. This way of writing is attractive because it is easier, for example, if you are in the habit of saying "In my opinion it is not an unjustifiable assumption that . . ." rather than, "I think". Stale metaphors, similes and idioms save mental effort – at the cost of leaving your images vague, for the reader and for you.

Look again at the three examples. What is particularly disturbing about the first passage is that it intended to clarify a previous article which was even more vague. What is an exception application? Of a survey of about 300 students and 20 Technikon faculties, only those with law degrees gave the correct answer.

Journalists should know vague statements do not automatically clarify themselves when placed between quotation marks, as the last sentence illustrates: "He said there was sufficient 'substratum of fact' in the article to form the subject matter of the plea of fair comment."

The generic banner headline in the *Weekend Argus* (Example 2) is probably rolling around in some sub-editor's head and hauled out when the second cup of coffee fails to inspire.

What is the writer of Example 3 trying to say by mixing the battered metaphor "riding the gravy train" with the "horse's bit"? Words and meaning seem to have parted company. And is it necessary to throw in a pretentious word like "insouciance"? How many newspaper readers know what the word means without reaching for a dictionary? Would it not have been better to use a word like "indifference" or "unconcerned"?

3.1.2 Language is a political concern

In our time, political speech and writing are largely the defence of the indefensible. Things like the American-led assault on Iraq and the shooting of panga-carrying protesters near Johannesburg can indeed be defended, but only in language too brutal for most people to face, and which does not square with professed political aims. So when defenceless Iraqi civilians are bombarded from the air by American-led forces their deaths are referred to as "collateral damage". When boys die in a war they do not believe in their deaths are referred to as "casualties". When protesters are shot in the back, the act is referred to as the "eradication of radical elements".

Such phraseology is needed if one wants to name things without calling up mental pictures. As Orwell said: "The great enemy of clear language is insincerity" (Orwell & Angus, *Collected essays*, p. 137). In these times there is no such thing as keeping out of politics. All issues are political issues.

When a business writer in a daily newspaper uses language that only degreed business people understand he is saying that those who do not understand do not matter.

If a political writer uses acronyms and jargon that keeps ordinary people guessing about who is doing what, the writer is saying, in effect, that the matters of government are not the concern of ordinary people.

Like children in a playground who use in-phrases to create a clique and only allow "cool" kids in on the passwords, writers – political, economic, legal, sport – are saying to those who do not understand "you are not cool enough – and we do not care".

3.1.3 Not a call for traditionalism

The defence of language does not have to do with archaism, with salvaging obsolete words and figures of speech, nor with the setting up of a standard English from which we may not deviate. On the contrary, it is especially concerned with scrapping every word that has outworn its usefulness. It has nothing to do with correct grammar and syntax, which are not important so long as the meaning is clear, or with the avoidance of Americanisms, or having so-called "good prose style". On the other hand, it is also not concerned with fake simplicity or the attempt to make written English colloquial.

What it does imply is using the fewest and shortest words that will convey one's meaning. What is needed is to *let the meaning choose the words* and not the other way around. In prose, the worst thing one can do with words is to surrender to them. When you think of a concrete object, you think wordlessly, and then, if you want to describe the thing you have been visualizing, you probably hunt around until you find the word that fits. When you think of something abstract you are more inclined to use words from the start, and unless you make a conscious effort to prevent it, the existing dialect will come rushing in and do the job for you – at the expense of blurring or even changing your meaning (Orwell & Angus, *Collected essays*, p. 138).

One can often be in doubt about the effect of a word or a phrase, and therefore rules are needed that can be relied upon when instinct fails. Orwell suggests these guidelines:

- Never use a metaphor, simile or other figure of speech which you are used to seeing in print.
- Never use a long word when a short one will do; it saves energy – both your reader's and your own. As journalist and author Mark Twain said:

THE BUSINESS OF WRITING NEWS

"I never write 'metropolis' for seven cents, because I can get the same price for 'city'. I never write 'policeman', because I can get the same money for 'cop' (Bates, *Anecdotes of American journalism*, p. 63).
- Never use the passive where you can use the active.
- Never use a foreign phrase, a scientific word or a jargon word if you can think of an everyday English equivalent.
- Break any of these rules sooner than say anything outright barbarous.

These rules sound elementary, and they are, but they demand a deep change of attitude in anyone accustomed to writing in the style now popular. You could, of course, keep all the rules and still write bad English, but you could not write the kind of stuff quoted earlier (Orwell & Angus, *Collected essays*, p. 140).

3.2 SOME PECULIARITIES OF JOURNALISTIC WRITING

The language many newspapers are written in today has its roots in the 1920s, 1930s and 1940s, when newspapers began to standardize the presentation of information to a public that still got most of its news from the press. In those days, newspaper leads worked much as today's television and radio summaries. As American columnist Charles McDowell, who is a leading critic of newspapers' "artificial" prose, points out: "We jab, hit, lambast. . . . We have peculiar adjective clauses: 'The re-married, 25-year-old mother of three' " (Teel & Taylor, p. 165).

The traditional newspaper language is much the language of headlines. The news story is a form of abbreviation and contraction of sentences (Teel & Taylor, p. 166). Here are some of the peculiarities of newspaper writing, including techniques journalists use to make their writing shorter and tighter:

3.2.1 The reporter does not editorialize
A news reporter's job is to report on the action, not take part in it. Consequently, he does not use I, me, my, we, us or our in a news story except when quoting someone. (Certain types of by-line stories are exceptions to this rule).

Instead of: The lawyer lost his temper.
Write: The lawyer threw down his pen.

Instead of: She is well qualified for the job.
Write: She is a graduate of the University of Cape Town and has 10 years of experience.

3.2.2 Eliminate unnecessary words

- *Connectives*

The word "that" is one of the frequent syntactical interruptions which is avoided.

Instead of: Aldsworth said that he was not a crook.
Write: Aldsworth said he was not a crook.

- *Clauses*

Instead of: The man *who* was driving the car . . .
Write: The man driving the car . . .
or: The driver . . .

- *Unnecessary articles*

Instead of: The union members attended the meeting.
Write: Union members attended the meeting.

Instead of: He returned a part of the money.
Write: He returned part of the money.

(Note: only unnecessary articles should be avoided. For example, the article in "He returned part of the money" cannot be cut. This also applies to "a" and "an".)

- *Lengthy word forms*

Instead of: The union will hold a meeting.
Write: The union will meet.

Instead of: The judge arrived at a decision.
Write: The judge decided.

- *Adjectives, adverbs, prepositions*

Instead of: The men were completely irrational.
Write: The men were irrational.

Instead of: He stepped off of the platform.
Write: He stepped off the platform.

- *Phrases*

Instead of: The tests took a period of ten days.
Write: The tests took ten days.

- *Redundancies*

Instead of: Past experience taught her how to react.
Write: Experience taught her how to react.

3.3 SOME BASIC STYLE RULES

When is a woman not a Miss, a Ms or a Mrs? In South African journalistic circles at least nine answers are correct:
- If she is a celebrity (Ms Madonna?).
- If her name appears in the sports pages (However, Zola Pieterse is also called Mrs Pieterse, Ms Zola Budd-Pieterse and even just Zola).
- If she is convicted of a crime (crossbow killer Louisa Chatburn).
- If she is a police or defense-force officer (Major Jill Jackson).
- If she is a member of the clergy.
- If she is a professional doctor or professor.
- If she is an advocate or a judge.
- If she is a member of parliament.
- If she is quoted in *Business Day* or the *Weekly Mail* which do not use honourifics.

It is all a matter of style. And, as in fashion, style rules in newspapers vary greatly – as does editors' support of style. Louis Boccardi of The Associated Press noted that journalists approach the issue with various degrees of passion: "Some don't think it's important. Some agree that basically there should be uniformity for reading ease if nothing else. Still others are prepared to duel over a wayward lower case." Boccardi's observation is in the foreword to *The Associated Press stylebook* which, with the *United Press International stylebook*, is the major source of American newspaper style.

In South Africa no such standard stylebook exists. Most publications have their own manual; therefore, our discussion will focus on the common ground.

Style refers not only to uniformity, but also to clarity. Both aspects are important, and both rely on a solid understanding of the rules of English grammar.

3.3.1 Common style problems

The style rules that follow are far from conclusive. Instead, they clarify some of the most common errors, and learning them will help cut down the time you spend referring to a stylebook.

3.3.1.1 Abbreviations

Abbreviations save much space for newspapers in a year, but editors should only allow them when the reader will recognize them instantly. Saving space at the expense of understanding is an intolerable offence.

3.3.1.2 Acronyms

Do not follow a group's full name with an abbreviation or acronym in parentheses. If an acronym would not be clear on second reference without this arrangement, avoid it.

Generally, abbreviations of one or two letters take fullstops and abbreviations of three or more letters do not. Therefore, write:

U.S. and U.N. and RSA, FBI and etc.

An exception is made when abbreviations without fullstops spell an unrelated word. Write c.o.d. and not cod, which is a kind of fish. Some other exceptions include TV (no fullstops).

3.3.1.3 Dates

Months are abbreviated only when followed by the day in constructions such as Sept. 16. The following five months are never abbreviated: March, April, May, June and July.

Days of the week are only ever abbreviated in tables, such as stock market listings.

3.3.1.4 Addresses

The words "street", "avenue" and "boulevard" can be abbreviated, but only when preceded by a street name and number:

She lives at 18 Queen St.
He drove down Queen Street.

When referring to the plural, write:
They ran up Longmarket and Adderley streets.

3.3.1.5 Measurement

Write out millimetre, centimetre, metre, kilometre, gram, kilogram, tonne (metric ton) and litre when used without a number, for example:

He ran a kilometre.

Abbreviate measurements (mm, cm, km, g, kg, t, l) when used with numbers and fractions:

She picked up the 20 kg weight.
Add 1.5 g of sugar.

Abbreviate speed:
   The car went 75 km/h.

The Americans still use inches, miles, ounces, and pounds. If you need to use those measurements, write:
   The car went 75mph.
   He is 5 feet 7 inches tall; the 5-foot-6-inch woman; the 6-foot-2 man, the 6-foot lady.
   The rug is 9 feet by 12 feet; the 9-by-12 rug.
   The baby weighed 9 pounds, 7 ounces.
   She had a 9-pound, 7-ounce baby.

3.3.1.6 Capitalization

The basic rule of capitalization applies: Proper nouns – specific persons, places and things – are capitalized; common nouns are not. The rule is simple, but knowing when to capitalize words in other usages may not be as obvious. If in doubt, consult your dictionary.

- *Direct quotations*

The first word in a direct quotation should be capitalized only if it starts a complete sentence; if it is separated from the source with a comma; or if it appears in direct quotation marks. Therefore, you may write:
   De Klerk said, "It will end soon."
   De Klerk said "it will end soon".
   De Klerk said it will end soon.

Do not write:
   De Klerk said "It will end soon".
   De Klerk said, "it will end soon."
   De Klerk said, it will end soon.

- *Trademarks*

This advertisement appeared in the *Columbia Journalism Review* (March/April 1993, p. 9):
   You can't Xerox a Xerox on a Xerox.
      But we don't mind at all if you copy a copy on a Xerox copier.
      In fact, we prefer it. Because the Xerox trademark should only identify products made by us . . .
      As a trademark, the term Xerox should always be used as an adjective, followed by a noun. And it is never used as a verb. Of course, helping us protect our trademark also helps you. Because you'll continue to get what you're actually asking for.
      And not an inferior copy.

Such warning of trademark infringement is courteous enough, but companies are generally very concerned about the correct use of trademarks or brand names. In general, use a generic equivalent unless the trademark is vital to the story.

• *Plurals of pronouns*

You would write National Party and Conservative Party when they are used in the singular form. The plural, however, would be National and Conservative parties. The same rule applies when writing about streets: Buitenkant and Adderley streets.

• *Religious terms*

Capitalize proper nouns referring to deities: God, Allah, Buddha.
   Lowercase pronouns are used to refer to deities: he, she, thee, thou.

3.3.1.7 Numerals

Spell out numbers from one through nine, and use digits for all numbers from 10, except in the following cases:
- Spell out numbers at the beginning of sentences.
- Spell out ordinal street names: Third Street
- Instead of thirty-fourth write 34th, with the exception of centuries: fourth century.
- Use figures for whole and fractional numbers: 8.2; 9½.
- Spell out fractions, except after whole numbers.
- After dates, do not use st, nd, rd or th, instead write: 10 June 1993 or June 10, 1993

3.3.1.8 Punctuation

• *Apostrophes*

Apostrophes are used for the plural of letters, but not of numbers:
   B's, 1970s

Use apostrophes when abbreviating calendar years:
   '70s, '80s and '90s

• *Colons*

A colon introduces a formal series:
   The following officials were fired: Barend du Preez, Winnie Manfred, . . .

A colon separates chapter and verse in referring to the Bible:
   John 3:16

Use a colon before minutes when writing the time of day:
8:30 a.m.

• *Commas*

Commas at the end of a passage are always placed inside quotation marks.
"We have to succeed," Mr. Johan Pieterse said.

Use a comma to indicate cents only when the figure is more than one rand and when the rand sign is used. Otherwise, write the word "cents".
R1,01   37 cents   eight cents

Use commas to set off the identification of a person, unless the identification is preceded by "of":
Michael Wofford, 222 Clarkson St.
Michael Wofford of 222 Clarkson St.

Do not use a comma between a man's name and Jr, Sr and II:
Fred Jones Jr
Jerry Aldsworth Sr
George V

• *Dashes*

Use dashes to set off important parenthetical information:
Supporters crowded around the prison entrance, but Rohan – whose name they chanted – did not appear.

Use a dash to separate a dateline from the first word in the lead:
CAPE TOWN – Two bullets ended the . . .

Use dashes in Q. and A. quotations, omitting quotation marks:
Q. – Where were you?
A. – None of your business.

• *Fullstops*

A quotation mark is placed outside a full stop at the end of a sentence when only a fragment or partial quote is used. When the quote is complete, the fullstop goes inside:
Mr. Simon Ismail said people are "going wild".
Mr. Simon Ismail said, "People are going wild."

A fullstop can also be placed inside or outside a closing parenthesis, depending on the usage. If the parenthetical phrase is a complete sentence, the period goes inside the parenthesis. If it is not a complete sentence, it goes outside:

Mrs. Nkoli took all the dogs to the kennel (except the doberman).
Mrs. Nkoli took all the dogs to the kennel. (The cost was R147,50.)

Use three fullstops (ellipsis) to show quoted material has been left out. When a sentence ends and another sentence follows use four periods.
"Going shopping . . . exhausts me."
"Going shopping exhausts me. . . . But what can I do?"

Omit fullstops in headlines, subheadings, captions and letters used in a formula.

- *Quotation marks*

If your publication does not use italic body type, use quotations to set off titles of books, plays, movies, poems, paintings, articles or television programmes:
"Beautiful Screaming of Pigs"
"Boesman and Lena"
"Mona Lisa"

Set off coined words or slang terms with quotation marks on first reference. Do not use quotation marks if the word is used again.

Use quotation marks to set off nicknames when the proper full name is used. However, do not use quotation marks when a nickname is used instead of a given name:
James "Loverboy" Smith
Pik Botha

If the punctuation marks belong to the quotation, the quotation marks follow the punctuation:
"Where are we going?" he asked.
"Sing," she commanded.

Otherwise, the quotation marks precede the punctuation marks:
Can you play "New York, New York"?

Use single quotation marks for a quotation within a quotation.
Use single and not double quotation marks in headlines:
'YOU'RE FIRED!'

- *Semicolons*

Semicolons should be used to separate lists of names and addresses or similar series containing commas:
Among the delegates were Jane Mandela, 27 Green St.; Bruce Johnson, 207 Kloof Ave.; . . .

43

In headlines semicolons are used instead of fullstops:
Eight convicts escape; prison guard arrested.

3.3.1.9 Hyphens

Hyphenate compound adjectives:
50-year-old woman
old-fashioned singer
well-known drink
so-called hero

Use a hyphen with prefixes to proper names:
un-Christian
pre-National Party

Use a hyphen in writing figures and fractions:
sixty-nine
three-quarters

A hyphen between two figures indicates the inclusion of all intervening figures:
7-21 July

Use a hyphen to substitute *to* when giving scores: 21-8

3.3.1.10 Spelling

Most South African publications refer to the *Collins dictionary*, choosing the English rather than the US spelling where there is a choice. Oxford Press' *Guide to South African spelling* is also a useful tool and includes names of cities, towns and rivers.

3.3.1.11 Titles

Women may choose either Ms., Miss or Mrs., depending on their own particular status. Most newspapers allow them this choice.

A wife has no claim on her husband's professional title. Therefore, write Mrs. John Smith, not Mrs. Dr. John Smith.

Men are all called Mr.

In the medical profession, general practitioners are called Dr. and specialists Mr.

Occupational titles – those more descriptive of a person's job than a formal status – are lowercase:
comedian Michael Banks
singer Lucky Dube

Clergy are generally referred to as Rev., on first mention, and thereafter as Mr. but the person might be a Right Revd., a Very Revd., or a Most Revd., depending on rank. Some churches do not use titles, besides common courtesy titles.

Police and defense-force officers are referred to by their rank.

Titles are capitalized before the name, but are written in lowercase afterwards:

President Robert Mugabe

Ms. Jane Reed, minister of defense

In reports of criminal proceedings, persons convicted of crimes lose their courtesy titles.

Courtesy titles are not used on the sports pages.

Youngsters who are in school or younger do not usually get courtesy titles; after the first reference, only the first name is used.

Following international style, some magazines and newspapers, like *The Weekly Mail & Guardian* and *Business Day*, do not use honourifics.

Assignments
1. Correct the following sentences, where necessary:
    a. She moved to R.S.A.
    b. The deadline was extended from Jan. 15, to Apr. 12.
    c. He was described as a Greek God.
    d. "let's have a coke," the barman said.
    e. They said they would be there at seven p.m., but did not arrive until 8.
    f. He rode down Fourth St.
    g. "Mister Livingston, I presume"?
    h. She is an out of town guest.
    i. I love 60's music even more than 80's music.
    j. Who wrote *A Tale Of Two Cities*?

2. Correct the style errors in the following story:
   So, you say it's tough to read certain articles? And boring, too? Well, get out your calculators and we'll measure just exactly *how tough* and *how boring*.

   Research into the readability and human interest-levels of prose go back to the 1920s. Early work identified various factors – like sentence length, word length and prepositional phrases – that affect the readability of prose. Dozens of formulas were developed, though only a few are still used. Probably the best-known are those proposed by Dr Rudolph Flesch* in the 1940s.

---

* Among the more significant of Flesch's books are *Say what you mean*, *The art of plain talk*, *The art of readable writing* and *How to be brief: an index to simple writing*.

To use Flesch's formula you need 100-word samples of text; get one from a weekly international news magazine, your local newspaper and a textbook. Divide the number of words by the number of sentences to get the average sentence length (asl). Next count the syllables (that's syl-la-ble) and divide by the number of words to get the average word length (awl). Then insert these values into Flesch's formula:

Reading case = 206.835 − (84.6 × awl) − (1.015 × asl)

Your score should fall between 0 and 100; the higher the score, the easier the material is to read. A score in the 70–80 range is "fairly easy"; a standard four pupil could understand it. Scores below 50 are considered difficult reading. Scores below 30 are generally found in scientific and technical journals.

NOTE: when counting words, consider contractions and hyphenated words as one word; when counting sentences, count clauses separated by colons and semi-colons as separate sentences.

But we know it takes more than short sentences and short words to keep us interested. Flesch figured that out too and came up with a "Human Interest" formula. It's based on the number of personal words per 100 words and number of personal sentences per 100 sentences. Personal words are pronouns and any other words that are either masculine or feminine. Personal sentences are direct quotations, exclamations, questions – questions that address the reader directly. The formula:

Human Interest = pw/100 words × 3,635 + ps/100 sentences × 0.314

A score below 10 is dull; 20 to 40 is interesting; above 40 is very interesting.

So when you wonder if your own writing is on track, get out the calculator!

Bibliography and recommended reading

Goldstein, Norman (ed), *The Associated Press Stylebook and Libel Manual*, New York, Addison-Wesley, 1992.

"Heard action to continue after application", *Weekend Argus*, 20/21 February 1993, p. 3.

Harris, Julian *et al.*, *The complete reporter: fundamentals of news gathering, writing and editing*, New York, Macmillan, 1981.

"It's make or break for SA future now", *Argus*, 5 March 1993, p. 1.

Orwell, Sonia and Angus, Ian (eds), *The collected essays, journalism and letters of George Orwell*, Vol. IV, London, Secker & Warburg, 1968.

Sparks, Allister, "Only control on corruption in politics is accountability", *Cape Times*, 4 March 1993, p. 6.

Teel, Leonard & Taylor, Ron, *Into the newsroom: an introduction to journalism*, 2nd ed, Chester, Connecticut, Globe Pequot, 1988.

CHAPTER 4
THE BASICS: GETTING STARTED AND ORGANIZING THE STORY

On my first night sub-editing for a Cape Town newspaper, I worked on a story about what officials at the nearby Koeberg nuclear power plant predicted would happen to the facility once its nuclear reactors had expired.

It was a fairly long piece, as I recall, around a thousand words. However, when I finished reading at least one crucial question remained unanswered: When were the reactors expected to expire? I was not impressed. And, of course, neither would the readers have been if I had not called the reporter and inserted the missing fact.

Reporting all the relevant facts of a story is the reporter's first duty (and the one our Koeberg reporter obviously forgot). The next is to write them as directly, simply and clearly as possible. Unlike other forms of writing, news writing ordinarily does not allow journalists to build suspense until the last line (like an Agatha Christie mystery), because readers may stop reading at any time. The most common news-writing formula is called the inverted pyramid, in which information is arranged in descending order of importance.

Journalists do not all agree to what extent the first paragraph should be packed with facts. Some say all the basic details should be there; others argue that they can be worked into the first few sentences. Both parties agree that the most important and interesting facts should be available to the reader right at the start. And to all crafting the first lines of a story – called a lead – has become a high art form.

One of the most famous leads (which is probably apocryphal) concerned the death of Richard Loeb (Carey, James W, "The dark continent of American journalism" in Manoff, Robert Karl & Schudson, Michael (eds) *Reading the news*, New York, Pantheon, 1986, p. 147).

In 1924 Loeb and a fellow graduate student at the University of Chicago were convicted of murdering a 14-year-old boy and sentenced to prison. Some years later, Loeb apparently made advances to a fellow inmate who turned on Loeb and killed him. For his obituary, according to legend, a *Chicago Daily News* reporter wrote this lead: "Richard Loeb, the well-known student of English, yesterday ended a sentence with a proposition."

THE BUSINESS OF WRITING NEWS

> In this chapter you will learn:
> 1. How to write a hard-news lead, with flair.
> 2. How to organize a story using the inverted pyramid method.
> 3. How to weave your story together using transitions.
> 4. The different applications of the news writing style: hard news, features, editorials, columns, sports, and reviews.

4.1 WRITING A LEAD

It is easy to grasp news writing if you imagine how a friend would tell you about a shooting she had just witnessed. Would your friend say this? "I was walking down the street this afternoon. I had just come from the supermarket, where I had bought some eggs, milk and some really nice French bread, when suddenly a car drove by, somebody got out and pointed a gun . . ." It is unlikely. Anxious to share the news, your friend would probably get right to the point: "This boy was just shot in the back by a bunch of guys who were driving down the street."

When somebody is waving a loaded gun around, even a non-journalist knows the lead (pronounced lede). In your friend's report are responses to four of the six questions news reports are traditionally expected to answer:

Who?   a boy
What?   got shot in the back
Where?   in the street outside
When?   "just now"
Why?   not clear
How?   this is implied by the action, but the weapon may have been a pistol, revolver, rifle, or even a crossbow.

A journalist must go through essentially the same process to analyse information and determine the lead. Whereas your friend served you, the reporter must serve the readers, and ask: What is important to them?

When the shooting is over, the reporter has to attempt to piece together the event. Among the questions a reporter would routinely ask are the following:

Was the shooting fatal?
Who is the victim?
Did anyone witness the event?
Who was the gunman?

Has the person or people been arrested?
How did it happen?
Why did it happen?
Who reported the shooting?
When was it reported?
How long did it take the ambulance to respond?
How many such shootings have occurred in this neighbourhood this year?
How does that compare to figures in previous years?
How does that compare to figures in other areas?
What is being done to find the people responsible?

With this information, our reporter can start to write the story. She starts looking over her notes and picks out these facts:

Who? John Smith, 18, a matric pupil at Oak Hill High School, who lives at 1651 Memorial Drive with his aunt, Mattie Brice Featherstone, and uncle, Eddie Brice. John had moved in with them five years ago when he left Johannesburg.

What? Shot in the back with a handgun by a young man who had been expelled from school a few weeks earlier. A neighbour, Eunice Rohan, called the ambulance which took John to City Medical Centre; just before deadline, a spokesperson for the hospital said the boy's condition was critical.

Where? The shooting occurred outside the garage of a house at 1648 Memorial Drive in the College Downs neighbourhood.

When? About 5 p.m. Thursday.

Why? A fellow student, Chris McCullough, who had been with John for most of the afternoon said the shooting came after John and another student argued and then had a fist-fight during the bus ride from school.

How? The boy John had fought later returned in a dark grey Nissan sedan accompanied by three other boys. The gunman got out when he spotted John and his friends sitting on a porch. When the group spotted the boy with the gun, they scattered. Four shots rang out; one hit John in the back.

Our reporter also found out that this had been the second shooting in this neighbourhood so far this year, which was the same figure as the previous year. No arrests have been made.

Our reporter sits down to write. Easy, she thinks, and begins to type:
JOHN Smith, 18, was shot in the back by a hateful former Oak Hill High School student.

Not bad, thinks our reporter. She has summed up the main news in only 19 words and she is supposed to hold every lead to under 35 words, if possible. She decides that maybe she can add a time element as well – the when – and rewrites:

> JOHN Smith, 18, was shot in the back yesterday afternoon by a hateful former Oak Hill High School student.

Just then, the news editor walks by and glances at our reporter's story. "Who is John Smith?" he asks, frowning. "That is such a common name, don't you think the victim could be confused with someone else? And how do you know the gunman was hateful? Keep your own opinions out of the story!"

Our reporter realizes she has made several basic mistakes in news writing: she started a story with a name of a person whom few people would recognize and she let an opinion which had not been attributed slip into the story.

Before her next attempt, our reporter decides to review the elements that make a lead good. They are:
- A good lead needs a newsworthy action or result.
- A good lead appeals to a wide readership.
- A good lead gives readers some human interest.
- A good lead gives the reader the most important facts.

As she starts writing, her editor calls to her: "And did you check the spelling of the names?"

What could be wrong with John Smith, our reporter thinks, but she decides to call the boy's uncle to confirm the spelling anyway. She finds out the actual spelling is: J-o-n S-m-y-t-h-e. Relieved that the error did not make it into print, she looks at her lead again. It is OK, she decides, but it is pretty dull. In her head one image keeps coming back: the kids, surprised and terrified, running for cover as a gunman fires at them. "If it has grabbed my imagination," she thinks. "Chances are it will also grab the reader's imagination. Let me see if I can use it." With that, she turns back to the keyboard:

> AN Oak Hill High School matric was shot in the back Thursday afternoon when a gunman fired four times into a group of terrified youths running for cover.

"Not bad," says her editor. "You have included some of the most important information in the lead and created some drama by describing the scene. Now support and develop the lead." Our reporter takes up the story:

JON Smythe, 18, of 1651 Memorial Drive, was in a critical condition late Thursday at City Medical Centre, a doctor said.

Witnesses say those bullets, fired around 5 p.m., were the last round in an argument that began on a school bus two hours earlier.

The gunman and three other young men fled the scene in a dark grey Nissan sedan, witnesses said. No arrests had been reported Thursday night.

"OK," thinks our reporter. "If people stop reading now they will know the key facts of the story." This story's main emphasis is the "how" and "why", neither of which our reporter can answer first-hand. So she organizes her story by taking the reader to the scene and describing how she got her information:

LIKE dozens of other folk who live in the modest brick houses at College Downs, Eunice Rohan was outside talking to a neighbour, enjoying the sunny spring weather after a day at work. Next door at 119 Clement St., Jon and some other students sat on the porch chatting.

"I heard sounds and I thought it was firecrackers," Rohan said. Then, pointing at Chris McCullough, she said, "Then he came running and said the boy had been shot."

Chris, also in matric at Oak Hill High, was with Jon for most of the afternoon. Chris said he and Jon got on bus no. 42 as usual, when school ended at 1:15 p.m. Another young man, who had been expelled from the school weeks before, also sneaked aboard, he said.

During the 30-minute bus ride, Jon and the young man began arguing, Chris said. At first they flung insults at each other. By the time the bus pulled into the College Downs suburb, someone had thrown a punch and a tussle ensued.

Minutes later the bus stopped at a designated stop near 1651 Memorial Drive, where Jon lives with his aunt, Mattie Brice Featherstone, and uncle, Eddie Brice.

The boys got off the bus, along with other students who live nearby. Jon and the other young man yelled at each other a few more times, before Jon turned towards home.

Brice said his nephew came home nursing a bruised hand and said he had been in a fight.

"He said he whipped the boy," Brice said. "The boy had told him that it was not over and that he would be back."

Brice went inside and Jon walked diagonally across the street to the home of George and Geraldine Nichols.

Jon, Chris, the Nichols' daughter and four other youngsters were sitting on the front porch when the Nissan pulled up at the end of the 20-foot long driveway.

The young man who had fought Jon earlier jumped out and pulled out a gun, Chris said.

"Everyone ran," he said. "We were scared." Four shots rang out.

Jon fell in the carport, a few yards from the rear corner of the house.

Jon, born in Johannesburg, had been living since 1989 with Featherstone, who is his mother's sister. His parents had sent him to College Downs, Brice said, because they thought it was a better environment.

"This was supposed to be his last year," said Brice, taking a deep drag from his Winston cigarette. "I hope he makes it."

(The names in this story, which first appeared in the *Charlotte Observer*, have been changed. Used with permission.)

4.2 HOW TO ORGANIZE A STORY

To recap then, here is a breakdown of how the hard news story is put together using the inverted pyramid method illustrated below.

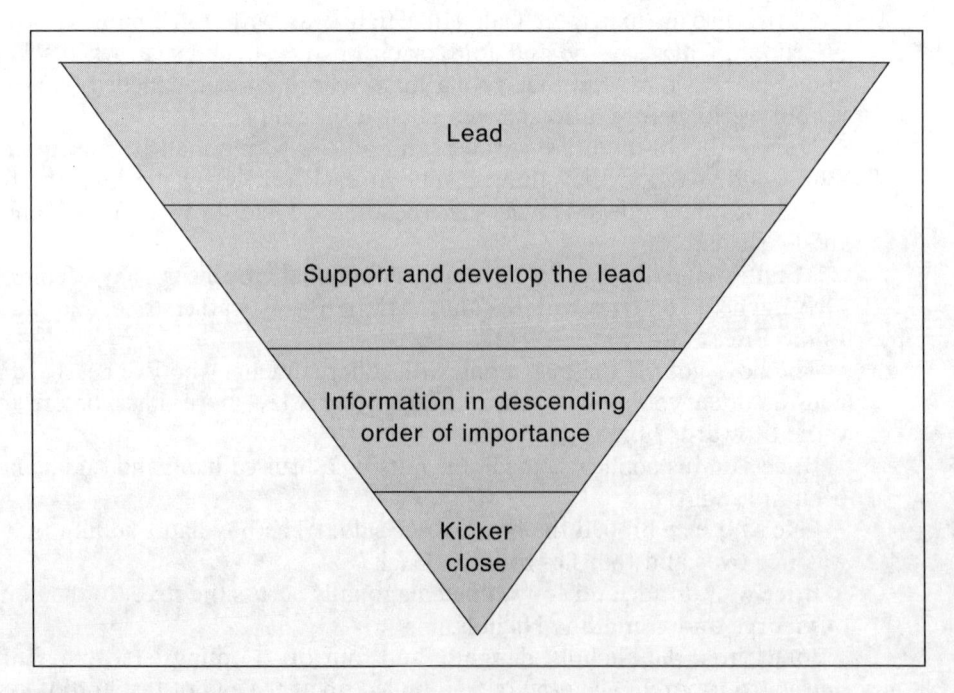

FIGURE 4.1 The inverted pyramid method

Now let us examine a few of the parts in more depth:

4.2.1 Types of conventional leads

Suspended interest lead. Question lead. Dialectic model. Many efforts have been made to label different types of leads. This discussion is not intended to add to that confusion. However, conventional hard-news stories usually rely on a lead which summarizes the action, often in the first paragraph. And that is not a bad idea. Since the inverted pyramid requires that you deal with facts in descending order of importance, the best way to establish what is most important is to summarize at the outset.

The major types of hard-news leads include:
- Immediate identification leads.
- Delayed identification leads.
- Summary leads.
- Multiple elements leads.

4.2.1.1 Immediate identification leads

LONDON – Former *Sunday Times* columnist Jani Allen and AWB leader Eugene Terre'Blanche had sex in her Pretoria flat and were "sexually active" in a car outside the Krugersdorp civic centre, the Royal Courts of Justice were told here yesterday.

This lead, which appeared in the *Cape Times* (21 July 1992, p. 1), started with the names of the people involved in the story because of their prominence. It would be safe to assume that men and women have for many years had sex in Pretoria flats and some have even cuddled in cars in Krugersdorp. That Allen and Terre'Blanche were alleged to engage in these pursuits was the news.

Note: Even those two well-known personalities were introduced as "former *Sunday Times* columnist" and "AWB leader". This practice is true for most personalities, even stories about prominent world leaders, e.g. US President Bill Clinton.

4.2.1.2 Delayed identification leads

Our rookie reporter used a delayed identification lead. She first described the victim in the shooting as an Oak Hill High School matric pupil and later, in the second paragraph, gave his name and age. There are two instances when this type of lead is most suitable:

- When the person's action, position or responsibility is more prominent than who they are. Take this lead by Walter Schwarz [sic] for *The Guardian Weekly* (28 May–3 June 1993, p. 5):

The Archbishop of Birmingham is being sued by the parents of two children who were sexually abused by a priest in his parish.

- When the lead is too crowded:
PIETERSBURG – Seven National Party ministers today lead 4 000 of their followers down the city's main street to mark the start of their election campaign in this region.

In the second example, it would be impractical to crowd the names of all seven ministers into the lead.

4.2.1.3 Summary leads

Reporting from parliament, *Sunday Star* political correspondent David Breier summed up the day's action this way (31 January 1993, p. 10):

IT was a bloody Friday for the apparatchniks of apartheid as President F.W. de Klerk announced a ruthless spring-cleaning of highly-paid left-overs of failed political experiments.

In this opening speech at what could be the last full session of the tricameral Parliament, De Klerk announced widespread purges.

Breier went on to list, in point form, the President's planned dismissals of several hundred officials.

The basic question a journalist should ask is, "Is the whole of the action more significant than the parts?" If the answer is yes, a summary lead is appropriate.

4.2.1.4 Multiple-element leads

The ANC leadership is struggling to keep the lid on the South African peace process, amid extraordinary scenes marking the funeral of Chris Hani, as President F.W. de Klerk warned parliament of the threat of civil war.

The lead above topped a story in *The Guardian Weekly* (23–29 April 1993, p. 6) under the following by-line: "By David Beresford in Soweto and Phillip van Niekerk and Chris McGreal in Boksburg."

In this story choosing one theme for the lead would be too restrictive. Both the action (the violence surrounding Chris Hani's funeral) and the reaction (from the ANC leadership and President F.W. de Klerk) are important enough to be in the lead. Note how the lead ranks the various elements of the story in order of perceived importance.

Use multi-element leads sparingly. Simpler leads are preferable.

4.2.2 Closing with a kick

Although an inverted pyramid story assumes the end of the story is the least important and can, if necessary, be cut, it need not be dull.

Our reporter decided to save a reflective quote from the victim's uncle for the end, thereby creating what is sometimes referred to as a "kicker close". The scene rounds off the story. And, in a sense, it rewards the reader for sticking with you all the way.

Editors are becoming more sensitive to writing style and will often work to cut from other parts of the story, if length is a consideration, in order to keep a good ending.

4.3 WRAPPING IT UP

There are several lessons you can learn from our reporter's experience:
- Keep the lead short, no more than 35 words.
- Attribute opinion (firing a gun is a fact, that it was motivated by hate is an opinion).
- Find answers to the who, what, where, when, why and how. But if they do not add to the story, some points might be omitted (our reporter left out the statistics about shootings in the neighbourhood, because there was nothing out of the ordinary to report).
- Always check the spelling of names.
- Do not name the someone alleged to be involved in a story until you have confirmed it with an official source – the gunman in our story had not been positively identified by officials, like the police.

Wenke

1. Hou die aanhef van hardenuusberigte kort, dit wil sê nie langer as 35 woorde nie.
2. Maak seker dat jy alle opinies aan die bron kan toeskryf. Hou dus jou eie opinie uit die storie uit.
3. Vind uit wat die antwoorde is op die vrae: "wie?", "wat?", "waar?", "wanneer?", "waarom?" en "hoe?". Onthou egter dat dit nie noodsaaklik is om al die inligting in die storie in te sluit nie.
4. Kontroleer altyd, maar altyd, die spelling van name.
5. Moenie 'n persoon se naam in 'n storie noem tensy jy absoluut seker is van sy betrokkenheid nie.

4.4 DIFFERENT APPLICATIONS OF THE NEWS WRITING STYLE

Now let us take a look at other ways in which these principles can be applied:

4.4.1 The news story

We have discussed how to write a news story, we have not actually discussed what it is. Georgia State University journalism lecturers Leonard Teel and Ron Taylor (1988, p. 169) have this to say about the news story: "To solidify its place at the heart of the newspaper scheme of things, editors have given its content macho names, such as hard news, to distinguish it from sissy soft news, or spot news, to give that we-were-there quality."

There can be little argument, however, that the news story is the foundation on which all other newswriting is based. And editors usually value this type of story above all others.

4.4.2 The feature story

Scribbling notes while ducking bullets or following police sirens is not everyone's idea of the ideal reporter's life. For those people, there is the feature story.

This does not mean news and features are mutually exclusive. For by magnifying society's eccentricities and styles, feature stories help put the news into context much the way the colour commentary at a sports broadcast supplements the play-by-play.

Also called human interest stories or people news, features usually allow the writer more space: not only more words, but also latitude to experiment with language. Although feature stories seldom follow the strict inverted pyramid format, the news angle (Why?) should be clear within the first three or four paragraphs.

Popular feature stories include profiles, service pieces and trend stories. Profiles are in-depth looks at people, organizations and places. Most feature editors like to provide readers with some informational service and regularly provide weekly entertainment listings and "How To" features. The most timely feature stories are those that reflect trends – interests, moods and activities that are moving across the city or country and affecting the lives of your readers.

4.4.3 The analysis story

The analysis story, also called a think piece, interpretive story and explainer, normally takes up some pressing issue and attempts to make people understand. Not uncommon are headlines such as: "Why I want this: Mining St Lucia is an emotive topic that has the Greens buzzing like flies. But what is the truth? What is best for the country?" *The Sunday Star*'s Denis Beckett analysed the controversial issue of mining the dunes at St Lucia in the "Insight" pages of the newspaper (31 January 1993, p. 27).

In his story he also illustrated an important aspect of such stories: it is best to do most of the interpreting yourself in the written version, since experts tend to speak expert-ese, a language foreign to most of your audience. For example:

> Earnings from the utilization of the natural resources at St Lucia, estimated at 0,15% of GDP, would facilitate the exponential decrease in the nation's unemployment.

Beckett decided it would best be explained to his readers in more basic terms, as if he were having a conversation:

> **Is the mining right, then?** For sure. It adds 0,15 per cent to the wealth of the nation, and that means 16 500 jobs.
> **Huh? Sounds glib.** Of course, it's brief. But at bottom it is unarguable. SA has a R270 billion GDP and 11 million jobs. Add X per cent to the GDP and you add X per cent, give or take, to the jobs.

Beckett's readers can probably all understand that much. "It is not your purpose in the interpretive story to establish that you have learned something," say Leonard Teel and Ron Taylor. "It is to help your readers learn something."

4.4.4 The investigative story

"Every government is run by liars and nothing they say should be believed." This premise, articulated by I.F. Stone (Bates, *Anecdotes of American journalism*, p. 91), is the basis from which the investigative journalist operates. But its application extends beyond politics to celebrities, commerce, community groups and even religion.

Investigative pieces, maybe more than other stories, should be approached with the suspicion of a poker player and the fairness of a judge (though even the latter may need to be investigated).

Sometimes it is enough just to lay out the facts: "To keep the student failure rate down and avoid criticism from parents and academic regulators, technikon officials often change the marks of poor students, informed lecturers say." It is always important to attribute the facts, to clearly show the source of the data and the allegations.

When a person or institution is portrayed negatively, it is vital to have it backed by irrefutable facts otherwise the target may claim libel and sue you. To present a balanced story, journalists often ask the target to respond to the allegations. A *South* reporter followed this procedure when investigating union officials' charges of racism and sexism at a Plessey Tellumat plant in Cape Town. The company rushed to court to stop the small weekly newspaper from printing the story. (That move, however, backfired and the courtroom incident – along with the allegations – subsequently received coverage in newspapers nationwide.)

Because of incidents like this, newspapers routinely ask their attorneys to scrutinize investigative pieces before going to print.

4.4.5 Editorials

On the editorial pages, writers are allowed to be exactly what critics often accuse them of being: biased, subjective, one-sided and opinionated. And this is how it should be.

The editorial pages, which are usually clearly set apart from the news pages, usually carry three types of copy: the unsigned editorial, which reflects the opinion of the editorial board; the editorial column, which has bylines and mug shots that identify the writers; and the letters to the editor, which gives readers a chance to be biased, opinionated, one-sided and subjective.

4.4.6 Feature columns

This is where experienced – and talented – writers get to think aloud about life. Jon Qwelane, Barry Ronge and David Biggs are among the best known South Africans currently writing feature columns. Such columnists usually deal with human problems, rather than cosmic problems. The tone is sometimes humorous, sometimes sentimental, sometimes gossipy – and almost always personal.

Feature columns are the stuff of which legends and acclaim are made. Todd Matshikiza, for one, deserved it. Matshikiza's regular columns for *Drum* magazine are some of the best examples of South Africa's "Jazz Age" writers of the 1950s and 1960s. This piece, "Jazzing the Blues", appeared in March 1955:

> Then said Louisa Emmanuel to Isaac Peterson, "Will you be my turtle dove, or not?" Isaac replied (in the English used in Show biznes), "No I ain't no turtle an' I ain't no durv. So I can't be yo' turtle-durv."
>
> Louisa said, "I'm looking for man to sing with me. He must coo as I purr. Coat as I fur. In other words, his voice must match mine."

Says Isaac, "Baby I'se got ze voice. Dunno if I'se got ze match. We'll figure it out. I reckon you'se got ze figure anyhow."

That's how this partnership started.

I was interested in that conversation as I listened through the stage curtain. Louisa was nervous. The lights were on. Bright. Very bright. Isaac wasn't nervous. Not very. If stage fright got him, Louisa's pretty confident smile would hide his fright. Louisa. One hundred and twenty pounds of vocal dynamite packed into four yards of lace and taffeta ... Or four yards of nylon net and sequins across the chest. Louisa. Pearly white teeth that grace the mouth that lets out the voice that thrills from Johburg [sic] to Rustenburg. Even listening to her speak. I wasn't listening. I was hearing, hearing, hearing ... and hoping she wouldn't stop.

And Isaac. Son of Peterson. Bound by ties of brotherhood to American clothes.

Commanded by a little birdie inside him to sing ... sing ... sing to save the sorrows of ten million black voices. You wouldn't know him if you met him at home in Vrededorp. Sits around the corner looking lazy like a lord. Slumps down in a chair like was waiting for some luck. Looks at you with black beady eyes like he's blaming you for it all. And thanks you for his gift of song as if you gave him all.

These two little kids, Louisa Emmanuel (aged twenty), and Isaac Peterson (twenty-three), surprised me once by saying, "We two see thing the same way. We met and we're tied hand and foot to the stage. And what showbiz puts together, let no man put us under. We want to stay on the top all the time."

They love a song called "Confess". In fact it's one of their most famous items. The people say, "We wish those two could fall in love each time they sing, 'Confess' ". But Louisa and Isaac take love right out of their musical profession. In fact Louisa is "still in mother's care," (as she says) and love will begin to come to her, a little later than now. Meanwhile, Louisa and Isaac are proudly your very own Lord and Lady of Song. They might find time to talk to you between factory hours. Or if you'd like to meet Louisa, her Mom lives with her, and Dad and a fiery dog "Danger", in Vrededorp.

(Reprinted with permission from *Drum*, March 1955)

4.4.7 Reviews and criticism

They are usually courted and often despised – at least by some. Critics basically write editorials about the arts. Some, like Clive Barnes of *The New York Times*, are ruthless. A typical (and legendary) example is his one-word review of the play "The Cupboard": "Bare." (Kessler, Felix, "Clive Barnes:

man on the aisle" in A. Kent MacDougall (ed), *The press*, Princeton, NJ, Dow-Jones, 1972, p. 99).

Reviewers are traditionally more merciful than critics as they merely sum up the subject, be it a new art exhibition or an episode of "Agenda". Often, though, the terms are used interchangeably.

Increasingly, newspapers are employing specialists in these areas, rather than tap someone in the newsroom who merely likes – or hates – films, television, food, visual or performing arts.

4.4.8 Sports writing

Once when a fellow first-year journalism student complained that reading the newspaper each morning generally depressed her, our lecturer gave this advice: Start with the sports. On the sports page, life is ordered. You get to see the score. The winners and losers are clearly defined. And, unlike the front page, there are always winners.

Sports writing is essentially news and feature writing about sports. Sports offers a reporter all the elements of which good stories are made – triumph, passion, heartbreak, courage, conflict, comedy, artistry, even love and hate. The latitude given sports journalists is implicit in the common reference to sports writers, instead of sports reporters. Unfortunately, this latitude often gives way to laziness and sports writers trying to be colourful, frequently spew out clichés instead. But it need not be so. Some of the finest, most imaginative writers have been among their ranks, including Ernest Hemingway and Tom Wolfe.

As sports become more complex, sports writers increasingly have to move beyond the stadium and locker-room into the boardroom, courtroom and even the jail. To understand professional soccer and athletics, sports writers have to know about contracts, sponsorships and anti-trust lawsuits. To understand some troubled athletes, sports writers need at least an academic understanding of cocaine, steroids, bribery and assault with a deadly weapon!

Assignments

1. From several newspapers collect the leads from five stories. Paste them on a sheet of newspaper and identify the 5 W's and the H.

2. Using newspapers available in the library, compare the leads on five stories in both a morning and afternoon newspaper in the same city or the same story which appears in different language newspapers. Note the differences in these leads.

THE BASICS

3. Notes for story leads are given below. List and identify (as "who", "what" and so on) the fact or facts you think deserve the most prominent play in each lead. Then write the lead.
   a. African Chemical Corp.
      Automotive Products Division
      To lay off 350 hourly workers
      At its plant in Bellville
      Plant Manager Robert Nkomo
      Said layoff to start Friday
      Does not anticipate more layoffs
      Blamed reduced orders from major car manufacturers
      Hopes to call back employees in a month
      Plant employs 2 100 workers
      (*Source*: Nkomo)
   b. Cape Education Department officials
      National Democratic Teachers Union representatives
      To meet at 10 a.m. tomorrow
      Civic Centre
      Opening meeting in contract negotiations
      Teachers seeking R35 000 minimum salary
      Current minimum is R28 000
      Threaten strike if they don't get it
      Department officials won't comment on demands
      Union represents 3 700 teachers
      Last year's strike lasted two weeks
      (*Source*: Ms. Stephanie du Plessis, union representative)

4. Select from a newspaper a hard-news story and a feature you think are particularly well written. By circling phrases and drawing lines, show how the writers used transitions to keep the stories flowing. Make a list of the transitional devices used.

5. Evaluate ten endings in stories and try to establish a list of five guidelines for writing successful kicker closes.

Bibliography and recommended reading

Bates, Stephen, *If no news, send rumours: anecdotes of American journalism*, New York, St Martin's, 1989.

Beckett, Denis, "Why I want this", *Sunday Star*, 31 January 1993, p. 27.

Beresford, David *et al.*, "Hani buried as de Klerk warns of civil war", London, *The Guardian Weekly*, April 23–29 1993, p. 6.

Breier, David, "Black Friday for apparatchniks", Johannesburg, *Sunday Star*, 31 January 1993, p. 10.

Carey, James W., "The dark continent of American journalism" in Manoff, Robert Karl & Schudson, Michael (eds), *Reading the news*, New York, Pantheon, 1986, p. 147.

Kessler, Felix, "Clive Barnes: man on the aisle" in A. Kent MacDougall (ed), *The press*, Princeton, NJ, Dow-Jones, 1972.

Teel, Leonard & Taylor, Ron, *Into the newsroom: an introduction to journalism*, 2nd ed, Chester, Connecticut, Globe Pequot, 1988.

Ward, Hiley H., *Professional newswriting*, New York, Harcourt Brace Jovanovich, 1985.

CHAPTER 5
SOURCES OF NEWS

The basic rule is: the more information you discover, the sounder will be your judgements and the more accurate your story

Teel & Taylor, *Into the newsroom: an introduction to journalism*, p. 67.

Imagine this: "Due to nothing new happening today, the South African Broadcasting Corporation has cancelled tonight's TV1 news programme. John Bishop will return tomorrow – if something interesting happens."

What about a special musical interlude at 5 p.m. on Radio 702? Or a newspaper with blank columns, broken only by lively advertisements? This is highly unlikely (except if press censorship returns, that is).

Such scenarios, says Gaye Tuchman, a professor of sociology at New York's Queens College (*Making news: a study in the construction of reality*, New York, Free Press, 1978, p. 17), are plausible only in a system where news judgements are made objectively; a system where, if no item was to meet the clearly defined criteria, there would be no news for that day.

Cancellations of news reports are unlikely because the news media claim to sell news. And they have to find news to fill the spaces between money-producing advertisements, the media's primary source of income. On a Saturday, for example, journalists have to find more items to fill the spaces between the greater number of advertisements in the thicker Sunday edition. On weekdays, however, thinner newspapers are produced and fewer advertisements and news items are required. For this reason, stories that may have been considered newsworthy on the weekend are now sometimes discarded.

Whatever else the media is – an information service, a voice for the people, a watchdog, an educator, a community builder, an entertainer – it is a business. And to keep going, they need news. Therefore, the most valuable players in the newsroom are those who consistently deliver the goods.

> In this chapter, you will learn:
> 1. How news media are organized to systematically gather news.
> 2. How to generate ideas.
> 3. How to develop and evaluate sources.

5.1 ORGANIZING NEWS COVERAGE

To fill a daily newspaper – which easily prints as many words as a novel – takes planning and organization. Generally, news staff writers are organized into three primary categories: beat reporters, general-assignment reporters, and special-assignment reporters.

5.1.1 Beat reporter

As a beat reporter, you usually know how to plan your day, at least at the beginning. A steady routine is the basis of beat reporting. Each day a court reporter, for example, checks the court role, attends trials of interest and makes routine stops with the court staff. One day your routine may yield little more than a businessman convicted of assaulting a rival, on other days you might witness a serial killer confessing to his crimes.

5.1.2 General-assignment reporter

In contrast to the beat reporter, a general-assignment reporter seldom knows what to expect when they walk into the office. The news editor often calls on the general assignment reporter, without a moment's notice, to write about whatever comes up. You learn to live by your wits and, like a Boy Scout, you are expected to always be prepared.

Lolo Pendergrast could teach the Boy Scouts a few things. When Hurricane Hugo, *en route* across the Atlantic to the American East Coast, suddenly changed direction and instead of heading to Florida churned several hundred miles north towards Charleston, South Carolina, the editors wanted someone at the scene, quickly. Lolo was ready. In her car was a sleeping bag, toiletries, food, water, torch (with spare batteries), hiking boots and extra clothes. Within minutes she was off, racing to get to Charleston before the hurricane struck. Her detailed account of the "Night of Fury" was riveting stuff and anchored the *Charlotte Observer*'s coverage of the disaster (1989, p. 1). The next day's stories were introduced this way:

> The hurricane that a generation of Carolinians had dreaded brought with it a night of unexpected terror.
>
> As Hurricane Hugo turned tropical storm and departed the Carolinas Friday, 10 people were dead. Hundreds of buildings were damaged at a cost in the billions. Nearly a million people were stripped of the basics of daily life – electricity, telephones, water and sewer service – along an arc from Charleston to Charlotte and beyond.
>
> But long after the property is repaired, Hugo's legacy will survive, seared into the minds of millions who spent a night in September 1989 huddled in the dark.

They will know helplessness. They will know a new kind of fear.
And they will know how good it feels to survive.

5.1.3 Special-assignment reporter
On special assignment, the task at hand is the most predictable. You know where you will be and what you will be doing. Some large papers create departments or pinpoint a few reporters to take on special assignments.

5.1.4 Beats and sources
The criteria newspapers generally use to organize their reporters are: location and topic. A reporter located at a bureau may have to cover everything from police affairs to country fairs. At the main newsroom, editors usually assign reporters to cover the following:
- Police stations, jails, fire departments and hospitals
- City Hall (headquarters for city legislative and executive officials)
- The courthouse
- National government and opposition groups
- Schools, colleges, technikons, universities as well as affiliated groups and unions
- Civic, fraternal and professional organizations
- Churches and associate organizations
- Youth organizations and welfare agencies. Also health associations, such as heart, cancer, mental health, alcohol and drug counselling
- Cinemas, radio and television stations
- Groups offering theatrical productions (symphony, drama, cabaret) and other forms of entertainment, like promoters of national and internationally famous music groups
- Funeral homes
- Tourism groups, convention centres, hotels, airlines and other firms engaged in accommodating meetings and visitors
- Local, national and international sports teams and organizations
- Businesses and markets
- Various local news sources, such as ships and shipping, mines and mining, agriculture, oil, environmental groups.

5.2 GENERATING STORY IDEAS

Philip Graham, the late editor of the *Washington Post*, described news as "the first rough draft of history" (*Newsweek*, 1963, p. 13). The job of gathering the information and writing that "rough draft" can be exciting, demanding and rewarding for the journalists. Of course, much depends on the journalist's attitude.

A key quality for a journalist is the ability to "get interested" in something that minutes before held absolutely no interest. Veteran reporters Leonard Teel and Ron Taylor (*Into the newsroom*, p. 56) think it is essential: "There is no substitute for this sort of blank-cheque enthusiasm: If you don't have it, life gets less exciting when you're suddenly assigned to interview the toothless man on a cross-country trip collecting autographs of celebrities. In fact, if you can't get interested in other people's ideas, you ought to reconsider your choice of career."

Although at first you will mostly be assigned to work on other people's ideas, reporters are usually encouraged to be enterprising and come forward with story ideas of their own. An idea becomes an assignment when there is commitment. If an editor approves an idea, the story will be assigned for a certain edition and entered on the budget, or content list, for that edition. That is when deadlines are set.

Generating story ideas is not easy. Certainly, a journalist taking the reigns of a company newsletter can keep herself busy for a few months following the popular subjects – dress codes, gender stereotyping, smoking. But filling the newsletter every week or month with interesting, relevant stories takes discipline.

Here are some suggestions to make the task easier:

- *Listen*

Journalists often find it hard to leave their work at the office and frequently spend hours regurgitating the day's activities after hours. This is not bad. But be careful not to become one of the reporters (and there are many) who are shunned at social gatherings because they routinely dominate discussions with talk of their own exploits. Focus on your next story – and that means listening, at least as much as you speak.

- *Circulate*

Get around. Once a month, at least, go to some kind of event you have not attended before.

- *Be friendly – to everyone*

Some new journalists, enthralled by landing a job in this competitive business, consider themselves better than others. The best reporters make friends with street vendors, clerks, bartenders, security guards and prison inmates.

- *Identify and meet leaders*
  Make the effort to identify and get to know key people on your beat. Take them to lunch, or plan to meet them at a social occasion or club.

- *Read*
  Read widely, including newsletters, brochures, magazines and out-of-town newspapers. Stories are copyrighted, not ideas. Localize and adapt good ideas to suit your publication.

- *Visit the library*
  Do not only browse through the racks, look at the notice boards and posters as well. Scan the new book lists and periodical section, especially journals like the *Rhodes University Journalism Review* and *Publisher's Weekly*.

- *Read records*
  Government agencies are full of records. Scan data to find out about employment, property sales, travel, new businesses, bankruptcies and other activities of businesses and individuals that may turn up good stories.

- *Subscribe*
  Get your name on as many mailing lists as possible. A story about a new invention or a business scam may be waiting in your post box.

- *Consider the opposites*
  Be sceptical. If somebody wins an award, the unsuccessful competitors may be disgruntled and have theories of rigged judging. When a company moves offices, there might be a story in discussing the future of the old building. When statistics are released detailing the poor performance of matric students, there is likely to be a story if you can track down a few who have managed to beat the odds.

- *Develop expertise*
  Journalists, especially those on general assignment, are expected to be experts on a wide range of issues. The best way to handle an assignment on a topic about which you know little – say, medicine, law or labour

relations – is to ask questions. Of course, the reporter with specific knowledge about the issue is likely to ask the most perceptive questions. So check out seminars, evening classes, books and journals which will help you learn more about the area you are covering.

5.3 DEVELOPING PERSONAL SOURCES

Face-to-face, on the telephone, by fax or by mail, most of the information used in stories comes from personal sources: people. To distinguish between types of personal sources, journalists differentiate between contacts, tipsters and informants.

A contact is an established, usually visible person who provides information. Some groups and corporations appoint a specific person, referred to as a "spokesperson" (the politically-correct pronoun). A tipster often prefers to remain anonymous and may have only partial, unsubstantiated information. A tipster may also direct you to the source. An informant gives information not available through regular channels. Informants may want to barter their information; an informant or informer may negotiate with the police, for example, for protection from prosecution.

One of the first challenges of a new reporter is to develop their own personal sources. Here are some suggestions on how to do this:

5.3.1 Start your own telephone directory
Use a directory, a notebook or file cards. Whatever system you devise, hold on to every name and number that comes your way. List them so they can easily be retrieved. For example, under "education", you might have the school board, government, unions, colleges, universities and technikons.

5.3.2 Visit the scene
Get out of the office. Visit the departments on your beat and identify at least one cooperative person in each. Attend functions, sports meets and seminars.

5.3.3 Do not forget secretaries
If the secretaries do not actually do the work for their executives, they often make sure it gets done. They have access to the people, if not most of the information you need. And when you need it most – right before deadline – a secretary can help you reach the boss, whether by slipping into a meeting to deliver a note or letting you know where she's playing golf.

5.3.4 Protect your sources

This is not just good advice, it is expected of good reporters. The South African Union of Journalists formalized this directive in Item no. vii of their code of conduct: "A journalist shall protect confidential sources of information."

Many people have lost their jobs because they have spoken to reporters. This happens in public and private concerns, and it happens regardless of the truth of the source's information. If information is given to you in confidence, you are honour-bound to keep to the deal. Your source's livelihood – and, in some cases, even his life – may depend on it.

Allister Sparks, for one, kept his word (*Cape Times*, 21 June 1993, p. 4). For 16 years he kept secret the source who told him anti-apartheid activist Steve Biko's death in detention was not due to a hunger strike – as then Minister of Justice, Jimmy Kruger, had announced. Only after Dr Jonathan Gluckman's death did Sparks reveal it was Gluckman who called Sparks, then editor of the now-defunct *Rand Daily Mail*, to show him the post-mortem report that said Biko had died of brain damage.

Careful to protect his source, Sparks attempted to substantiate what he knew by having a reporter confront the doctors who had attended to Biko. The paper then ran a story which began: "An investigation by the *Rand Daily Mail* – which included interviews with doctors who examined Steve Biko in detention – has revealed that the black consciousness leader showed no signs of a hunger strike in detention."

Kruger protested that the report was false and called for a hearing of the Press Council. Still Sparks would not reveal his source. The presiding retired judge eventually ruled against the paper and "severely reprimanded" it for its actions.

"History has vindicated us, of course," wrote Sparks in a newspaper column detailing the episode. "But the verdict still stands in the records of the Press Council, and the newspaper is dead because of the wounds like that which it suffered in its final years. Now Jon Gluckman is dead too. Only the truth survives."

5.3.5 Check the telephone directory

Apart from helping you track people down, telephone directories are helpful when verifying names and addresses.

5.3.6 Evaluate sources

Trisha Greene, an editor at the *Charlotte Observer*, had this advice for young reporters: "Don't trust anyone. If your mother tells you she loves you, check it out. Get a second source."

The motives of sources are not always clear. Some sources are obviously self-serving, as when a politician maligns a rival. Others may be concerned citizens, like the person who calls to report a factory which dumps its refuse in a river. Still others may be revengeful, like the disgruntled employee who, after being fired from his company, called a journalist with information about the corporation's fraudulent business practices.

A source's motives can be complex and many. A journalist needs to be sure that, whatever the case, the information is accurate.

Consider the following:

- *Always be sceptical*
  Use sources as starting points for stories, but make sure you double- or even triple-check the information. Discard information you cannot substantiate.

- *Be careful with confidential or "anonymous" sources*
  Some sources, in an attempt to manipulate the press or avoid responsibility for what they say, may ask you not to use their name. Henry Kissinger did that. As an American Secretary of State, Kissinger routinely briefed reporters but insisted he be identified only as "a senior US official" (Bates, *Anecdotes of American journalism*, pp. 178–80).

  Some reporters dropped clues in their stories. On CBS radio, he was referred to as the mysterious official "who often shows up in various parts of the world where Henry Kissinger is visiting," an official who "knows a lot about foreign policy." In the *Boston Globe*, he was described as "the senior US official was last seen entering a long black limousine with Nancy Kissinger."

  The "senior official source" spoke for the last time on Kissinger's final trip abroad and the Associated Press filed an obituary: "America's second most famous diplomat – the 'senior U.S. official' who always travels aboard Secretary of State Henry A. Kissinger's jet – disappeared Tuesday somewhere across the Atlantic."

  Anonymity also invites sources to distort information and take cheap shots at opponents. Do not lead them into temptation.

- *Many publications discourage sources that cannot be named*
  There are two concerns: credibility and integrity. Many readers are sceptical when they read such vague attributions as "a man said". They wonder if the source exists, and rightly so. During a social gathering, a newspaper editor acknowledged that when pressed to find a source for information or opinion he thought was valid he attributed the information to an unnamed person.

He is not alone. On September 28, 1980, the *Washington Post* published "Jimmy's World", the story of an eight-year-old heroin addict in Washington DC's black community (Bates, *Anecdotes of American journalism*, pp. 87–8). The story described how Jimmy's mother looked on as a man injected the boy with heroin: "The needle slides into the boy's soft skin like a straw pushed into the centre of a freshly baked cake." The story was riveting. Riveting enough to earn the reporter, Janet Cooke, a Pulitzer Prize. But when reporters and finally editors tried to confirm Cooke's story, she broke down and confessed: Jimmy did not exist.

The incident ended Cooke's career, embarrassed the *Washington Post* and gave more credence to sceptics who tell us not to believe what we read in the papers.

My rule: Avoid unnamed sources.

If you cannot find someone who will talk on the record, look further. Only in extreme cases – say when a life or the national security is endangered – should you quote someone anonymously. If someone is anxious, read back the quotes you are likely to use. Never use an unnamed source just because you are too timid or lazy to ask the person's name.

When it comes to sources – as in other things – do not create situations where it would be easy for you, or others, to be dishonest.

Assignments

1. Study an in-depth article in a newspaper and list who you think the sources might have been for the reporter. Make a composite list of the sources in class, then invite the reporter concerned to class to discuss the sources, as far as she is free to do so.

2. Go to the library and find 10 ideas for interesting articles (but not tied in with the day's headlines) based on resources in the library. Choose one idea and write out a story budget, which includes the audience, the length and angle of the story, as well as details about all the sources you would need to contact.

Bibliography and recommended reading

Bates, Stephen, *If no news, send rumours: anecdotes of American journalism*, New York, St Martin's, 1989.

"Night of fury", *Charlotte Observer*, 23 September 1989, p. 1.

"Philip L. Graham, 1915–1963", *Newsweek*, 12 August 1963, p. 13.

Sparks, Allister, "Dr Gluckman exposed truth on Biko's death", *Cape Times*, 21 June 1993, p. 4.

Teel, Leonard & Taylor, Ron, *Into the newsroom: an introduction to journalism*, 2nd ed, Chester, Connecticut, Globe Pequot, 1988.

Tuchman, Gaye, *Making news: a study in the construction of reality*, New York, Free Press, 1978.

CHAPTER 6
INTERVIEWING AND NOTE TAKING

A reporter who begins an interview without the proper preparation is like a pilot flying without a navigator. Both may make it, but flying blind is not the best way to get there.

The Missouri Group, *News reporting and writing*,
New York, St Martin's, 1980, p. 94.

Information is the merchandise of journalists (The Missouri Group, *News reporting and writing*, p. 94). Some data is collected from records, some from observation. But by far the most common source is person-to-person conversations.

However, interviews are tricky – as off-beat journalist P.J. O'Rourke noted after interviewing Bill Clinton while the former governor was campaigning for the US presidency (*Sunday Star Life/People*, 4 October 1992, p. 2).

"On the subject of interviews, I'd like to ask the reader a question," wrote O'Rourke.

Do you think Governor Bill Clinton was suddenly going to lean across the table and say: "P.J., if I'm elected, taxes will be on steroids, regulatory agencies will spread like sexually transmitted diseases, inflation's going to look like my midsummer opinion poll rating, the stock market will do a cordless bungee jump . . .?"

Successful politicians did not get to be successful politicians by being dumb enough to tell reporters the truth. Or tell reporters much of anything.

Then there's the matter of charm. It is the business of successful politicians to have some, and even the most loathsome have enough to last through an average interview.

I count myself a hard-bitten newsman – cynical, world-weary, you get the picture – but I have been charmed in my time by [New York] Mayor [Ed] Koch, Imelda Marcos and the Lebanese Shi'ite terrorist leader, Hussein Mussawi.

You start out asking tough questions and before you know it, you find yourself saying, "I loved your last car bomb. It had real style and, dare I say it, wit."

The third and worst problem with political interviews is essential dishonesty of the interviewers. Sometimes this is wilful, but mostly it is uncontrollable, like the action of the aorta. . . .

Exempli gratia, I am a blowed in-the-glass Republican. . . . I have never voted for a Democrat in my life. Bill Clinton could know the location of the Holy Grail, possess the secrets of the philosophers' stone and have the value of Pi worked out to the last decimal and I'd fudge it.

Interviewing is an imperfect process, that much is clear. Some of the variables can be controlled, but it is tough – sometimes impossible – to control the two that matter most: the interviewer and the source. So, good reporters work hard to hone their interviewing skills.

There is much to learn: You simultaneously ask questions, evaluate answers, take notes, nudge the source on, gauge reactions and check for details. This is not a task for the unprepared.

In this chapter, you will learn:
1. How to prepare for an interview.
2. How to plan your approach.
3. How to take notes.

6.1 PREPARING FOR THE INTERVIEW

The success of an interview depends as much on what you do before you ask the first question as it does on the questioning and writing. Research your subject. Plan your time. Formulate some questions. Then, go with your instinct.

Let us take a closer look at each step:

6.1.1 Research

How you research a subject depends on the assignment. Sent to do a special interview with a model-turned-actress whose first major feature film was about to be released, I called the film company to ask about an advance screening. I was told by the distribution manager that this was impossible to arrange before the interview, so I asked for any publicity material to be faxed to me (at least I would know the plot). Then I checked the newspaper's electronic library for stories about the woman – since this was a new career move, there were not many.

I went to chat to the newspaper's fashion editor who was able to fill me in on the woman's modelling career and point her out in some magazine cosmetic advertisements. I also found out that the model had attended the same university as I had, although she had left a few years before I enrolled. I telephoned a professor I thought may have taught her. Following a hunch I learned the woman's older sisters had also been to the university and the professor suspected that the young woman's role in a sexy film would raise some eyebrows in her conservative home town. I made a note reminding myself to ask the actress about this.

On the way home, I rented a video of a film in which she had played a small part about six years earlier. I noticed something odd: the fashion editor said the woman's career had taken off after appearing in a TV commercial in which, oozing characteristic Southern charm, she had drawled the line: "Nothing comes between me and my Calvins." Yet in the film, she spoke with a crisp British accent. Now I knew I had an angle:

> Andie MacDowell is Southern – she grew up in Gaffney, SC – and she's convinced her newest film is "definitely stuff that especially older Southerners will find uncomfortable".
>
> She's talking about "sex, lies and videotape" which won the Cannes Film Festival's top prize this summer and opens Friday in Charlotte. In it, MacDowell, a 31-year-old actress and model, plays an uptight woman trapped in a disastrous marriage.
>
> "Everyone will get something different from it, I think," said MacDowell. What the former Winthrop College student could get is a new-found reputation: that behind the auburn hair and coltish eyes that earn her $500,000 yearly as the "face" for L'Oreal cosmetics is an actress with substance.
>
> Certainly, after MacDowell's first feature-film role – the un-plain Jane to Christopher Lambert's Tarzan in "Greystoke: the Legend of Tarzan, Lord of the Apes" – she has something to prove. Director Hugh Hudson cast MacDowell halfway into the project, only to dub out her Southern drawl and dub in Glen Close's crisp British clip – without MacDowell's knowledge.
>
> "I was already doing publicity for them," MacDowell said. "And I called and said, 'When am I supposed to do the looping?' And they said, 'Well, we decided to use a British accent.' So that was that. I was pretty much powerless at that point.". . .

Try to get as much information as possible about the subject before you begin an interview. Not only will it allow you to ask more insightful questions, but sources are less likely to fudge answers if they know (or think you know) what is going on. And, of course, it will save you time.

6.1.2 Plan your time

Time magazine writer Margaret Carlson was assigned to interview actress Katherine Hepburn, who had recently published her autobiography, *Me: the story of my life*. Carlson arrived late. "How dare you keep me waiting? Are you stupid?" were Hepburn's first words (*Time*, 29 June 1992, p. 54).

"Not a good beginning," wrote Carlson. "Not good at all." The two women sparred for a few hours and Carlson's story portraying Hepburn as an "arrogant", "overbearing", "bully" ran under the headline, "A bad case of Hepburn".

In letters to the editor a few weeks later, readers aired their opinions of the piece (*Time*, 20 July 1992, p. 10). Some applauded the reporter: "The interview was a fine piece of journalism – really excellent. Give a raise to Carlson," wrote a reader from Helsinki, Finland. Many, like this reader from Denver, Colorado, did not: "I read Margaret Carlson's 'interview' with the legendary actress Katherine Hepburn, but found it a total waste of time learning how Hepburn apparently gave poor Carlson heartburn because the reporter was 10 minutes late. If Carlson had taken the time to learn something about the eccentricities of Hepburn beforehand she would not have been late."

On this occasion, Carlson got her interview despite poor time planning. But she might not have been so lucky (and she will probably not be visiting Hepburn again soon).

Time is precious – both your source's and yours. Often the person you most want to interview is precisely the person who has the least amount of time to spend with a reporter. A good policy, when approaching someone for an interview, is to say exactly how much time you would like. It is also good manners.

You are more likely to get an audience with a busy or reluctant source if they think you will not be wasting their time. If you set specific parameters, stick to them. Do not say you want to talk for 10 minutes and then stay for 20. The next time you want to talk to that person, they are unlikely to believe you if you say you will be brief. If your source invites you to stay longer, take up the offer only if there is important information you still need – your time is precious too.

One of the most common gripes heard around newsrooms is that there is never enough time to work on stories. Editors, keeping track of deadlines and budgets, are often seen as tyrants who never stop asking when the next story will be done. Most reporters are expected to write at least one story and sometimes three or four stories a day. Forced to produce under such pressure, reporters need to carefully plan what information they want from an interview and how best to get it.

There is no substitute for in-person interviews which allow a reporter to collect the colourful details which distinguish good writing. Being on the scene does not only allow you to observe the person but also to absorb the atmosphere, as these lead paragraphs by Gus Silber show:

In a glass cage in the foyer of the Piet Meyer Building, Auckland Park, Johannesburg, a stubble-faced man in stonewashed denims and a Mickey Mouse T-shirt taps out a tattoo on his knees and throws his hands up in the air.

"Hey," shouts Alex Jay, 31, father of two, owner of the spearmint-white Mercedes Benz convertible gleaming in pole position in the SABC parking lot, "I don't want any more! What's the point? Please! I'm in enough trouble with the taxman as it is."

Alex Jay is talking about money. He's learned his lesson. It can buy you a Mercedes Benz. It can buy you a holiday in Disneyland. It can buy you a fully-equipped digital recording studio. But it can't buy you Love, Peace and Happiness. So who's complaining?

(*Sunday Times Magazine*, 11 October 1992, p. 24)

When pressed for time reporters may have to make do with getting information by telephone. With the right questions, though, you can still get plenty of details in this way.

One Saturday morning I arrived in the newsroom where an anxious editor told me a teenager had died at a Halloween party the previous evening and they needed a story, quickly. The incident had happened at the boy's aunt's house in a town a half-hour drive away and the child's family lived in a city 45-minutes in the other direction. I had no choice but to get the bare-as-bones police report and hit the telephone for the rest. The next day this front-page story ran under the heading, "Teenager Strangles At Party":

YORK – Mock terror turned to real horror when a 15-year-old Charlotte boy playing a hanged man at a private party was strangled by the noose.

William Anthony "Tony" Odom, a ninth-grader at Garinger High School, was pronounced dead Friday night by York County coroner Jim Chapman amid spider webs and plastic bats decorating the dirt-floor basement of his aunt Diane Boyd's home.

Shortly before 9 p.m. Tony and several of his friends staged the annual event's grand finale: a haunted house in the unfinished basement of the single-story home on Mission Road.

Tony crouched inside a freestanding wooden cupboard, intending to fake a hangman scene, said his grandmother, Hattie Carpenter, who was at the party.

He was dressed as a pirate wearing black trousers, a red shirt and gold hoop earring. Around his neck was a three-foot nylon ski rope tied into a hangman's knot.

"It was a slip-knot type noose; the more pressure you apply the tighter it gets," said the coroner.

"One of the kids checked on him before the show began and he was fine, jumping around and waiting for things to begin," Chapman said. "She didn't hear anything from him and went back to check two to three minutes later and he had slumped over inside the closet.

"Evidently, it was tight enough to cause some problems with his breathing and he either passed out or panicked."

The noose was attached to a bar about $4\frac{1}{2}$ feet from the ground, York County deputy coroner Don Johnson said. Odom was 5 foot 9 inches, York County sheriff's reports show.

"He would have had to stoop down to show that he was hung," Chapman said. "He could have stood up and loosened the rope; his hands were not restrained."

Odom's 13-year-old cousin found him and ran upstairs to get her mother. Boyd tried to free the noose and had to return upstairs for a kitchen knife before she could cut the boy free.

Chapman said the circumference of the noose was $14\frac{1}{2}$ inches: Odom's neck was $15\frac{1}{2}$ inches. Tony's grandfather, Harvey Carpenter, said he and Boyd tried to revive the boy. The county 911 dispatcher received a call at 9:36 p.m., Chapman said. Rescue workers arrived at 9:45 p.m., but Chapman estimates the boy died between 9 and 9:15 p.m.

"What was really sad was that the kids thought we were going to be able to revive him, but it was too late. They were scared when we got there, but then they became hysterical," Chapman said.

"It's a real shame. Maxie and Diane (Boyd) go to so much trouble for their kids to have fun at home," said a family friend who asked not to be identified. "I really felt sorry for the boy's family, but it must have also been really hard for those little kids at the party. I don't think Halloween will ever be the same for them."

Johnson said tests showed the boy had not been drinking. . . .

All the information in this story came from telephone interviews, except for the boy's height and neck size which were on the police report. I called the coroner and deputy coroner, who had both investigated the accident and, after warning them that I was going to be very picky, I started: When did you get the call? What time did you arrive? Was the boy already dead? What time did he die? What type of house was it? How many storeys? Was the basement renovated? How was it decorated? Was the cupboard built-in? How big was it? How tall was the boy? What was he wearing? How long was the rope? How was it secured? What type of rope was it? What type of knot was it? Why couldn't the boy free himself? Was it possible that he had been drinking?

Next, I called the home where the accident happened, but no-one would speak to me. I rang up the boy's home where I spoke to both his grandparents. Just before deadline, I called the high school principal to double-check that the boy had been enrolled at his school.

The story closed with three paragraphs from an in-person interview with the boy's mother, conducted while she sat on a weight-lifting bench in her son's room. And finally, there were details about the funeral which I got after a call to the mortuary.

6.1.3 Formulate some questions

Among journalists a story does the rounds of a reporter assigned to write about legendary comedian Bob Hope's trip to entertain Allied troops stationed near the Iraqi border.

"Absolutely no time for an interview," Hope's manager said. "Please," the reporter pleaded, "just five minutes."

Eventually, the request was granted. The reporter got permission to walk with Hope from the airport terminal to the plane. What would he ask Hope?

After much thought, the reporter came up with one simple question: "Mr Hope, what's your latest joke?"

The other information – like what Hope's schedule would be, where he would be performing, when he would return, why he was going, and how the trip had come about – the reporter could get from other sources. But what joke Hope was going to use to try to relieve the troops' tension (albeit briefly) was unique.

Some editors advise young reporters to write down 10 questions before starting an interview. It is not bad advice since it allows the reporter to clarify what he or she is after. But interviews seldom go according to plan. You may find after the first question that the rest on your list become irrelevant because your source introduces more important elements. Let the interview take its natural course and, above everything, *listen*. If something is unclear, ask. Do not be afraid to push for clarification, especially on technical matters. Once, when interviewing a doctor, I had to stop him and say, "I am sorry but you are going way over my head. Let us try this: think of me as your teenage cousin, now explain to me what is chronic otismedia."

Do not be afraid to let someone know you are searching blindly. Many interesting details have come from simply asking, "Is there something else you think may help me?"

6.1.4 Phrasing the question

Take care in phrasing your questions. Open-ended questions are less direct and less threatening. A worker may not respond frankly if asked if he likes his supervisor; the question calls for a yes-no response. But an open-ended question like "What do you think of Mr Bigwig's managerial style?" is not so personal. Open-ended questions are more exploratory and flexible and it is a good idea to use a few when you start your interview.

There are times when the reporter needs to close in on the subject to get specific answers. Instead of asking an accused whether he thinks the charges against him are fair, you simply ask, "Did you forge the cheque?"

Knowing when to put the question depends on the flow of the interview and the chemistry between you and the source. You must make on-the-spot decisions.

6.2 CONDUCTING THE INTERVIEW AND PLANNING YOUR APPROACH

Television presenter Freek Robinson is known as a sharp interviewer. Some say he is cocky, even arrogant. Robinson says he is only doing his job:

There is apparently an attitude among certain South Africans that a person must have an absolute respect for authority, and that you have to ask questions from your knees ... I don't think that's right. Each one of us, as ordinary citizens, has our own claim on human rights. Obviously a person makes certain concessions if, for example, you are speaking to the president of the country, like giving him more time to answer his questions and interrupting him less. But that does not mean that you give him a blank cheque to say in a monologue exactly what he wants. Then it's no longer an interview, but a propaganda session. (*DeKat*, September 1993, p. 38)

That is, Robinson's approach is straightforward. Usually it works, although good journalists know that getting information depends on more than just asking questions.

Rapport – the relationship between the reporter and the source – is crucial to the success of an interview. The relationship is sometimes relaxed, sometimes tense. Some situations may require the gall of a salesman; others, the genuine sympathy of a priest. A journalist works between two factors: (1) the public has the right to know most information, yet (2) nobody is legally required to talk to you (Teel & Taylor, *Into the newsroom*, p. 119). Therefore, getting what you want requires versatility and plenty of imagination.

6.2.1 Possible approaches

- *Direct approach*
Introduce yourself and tell the person what you want, like Robinson.

- *The wide-eyed approach*
On a routine check of police reports, I ran across an account of a traffic accident caused by a drunk driver; the name looked familiar – that of the elderly local high school vice-principal. I called the school. No, said the secretary, the man was at the courthouse serving on a jury. I called a clerk at the court. No, said the official, the man had called in sick. I knew I had to call the principal. I also knew that a story about the incident, which had put a young woman in hospital, might jeopardize the man's job (a group of parents at the school, calling themselves MADD for Mother's Against Drunk Driving, had recently run a much-publicized "don't drink and drive" campaign in the town).

On the advice of a colleague, I tried this approach: "Hello, Mr X. I am François Nel at the *Observer*. While checking police reports this morning, I came across one with your name on it. Could it possibly have been you?" Then, quite demurely I added, "Tell me, sir, what happened?" The strategy worked and the man gave me his version of the events. (We eventually ran a small story on page three, as I recall. The man went into counselling and joined Alcoholics Anonymous – and kept his job.)

- *The sit-in*
If you really need to see a person and the protectors – secretaries, associates – insist the person is too busy and could not possibly see you today, tell them you will wait. Taking along a lunch and a book helps to show you are serious. Although persistence does not always pay off, it is likely to yield greater dividends than no persistence at all.

- *The assault*
If you glimpse a reluctant source within earshot, make your appeal as quickly and directly as possible: "You have been sentenced to death, Mr. Ratheart, do you think the judgement was fair?"

- *Be understanding*
Convicted mass-murderer Antonie Wessels gave a reporter an exclusive interview because he was the only person who ventured to find out what Wessels was feeling. People in trouble with the law, or otherwise, will

often respond to simple manners, for example, "There are always two sides to every story. I would like to hear yours."

6.2.2 Keeping control

Few interviewees will give you everything you want to know, clearly and concisely, and nothing more. Therefore, most conversations, if undirected, will touch on this and that and meander over there and beyond. This is just not productive, and it makes wading through your notes and piecing together a story a nightmare. In a note to a young reporter, veteran journalist and editor of *Sarie* magazine, Andre Rossouw, gave this advice:

> I get the impression that you allow people in your interviews to speak as they wish and wander off track, to lose the train of thought. Don't do that. You are the "chairman" of the meeting. If a person is busy with a subject and he/she wanders off, you must immediately interrupt them and take them back to the subject at hand.
>
> [This story] was a case where you obviously didn't play "sheep dog". Every so often the article wanders from the subject so that the reader always feels something is incomplete. . . . Every good story is told in blocks . . . complete each one from front to back before you continue. . . .

6.2.3 Before you leave, take a look in the mirror

Even the best prepared interview can fall apart because of something as petty as your appearance. You would probably frown if your bank manager greeted you in her office wearing shorts – and vice versa.

Most reporters choose to fit in with the environment. As the four University of Missouri journalism professors, known as The Missouri Group, point out: "It is your right to wear your hair however you wish and to wear whatever clothes you want, but it is the source's prerogative to refuse to talk to you" (Brooks, *et al., News reporting and writing*, p. 97).

6.2.4 Some tips

- *Be on time*
  There is no law that says people should speak to reporters, so respect your source's concession.

- *Make it clear why you are there*
  Sources usually relax when they know what you want from them (unless, of course, you are investigating something they want to hide).

- *Start with broad questions first*
  Open-ended questions are usually less threatening.

- *Stick to the topic*
  Do not indulge your source – or yourself – in long, unfocused conversations, unless you think they will pay off at a later stage. Remember: it is your job and you are being paid for your time.

- *Save your interruptions*
  Give the interviewee a chance to relax before you challenge a point.

- *Occasionally, murmur and chuckle – and keep quiet*
  A simple "mmmmmm" or a chuckle will let your source know you are listening and encourage them to keep on talking. A pause may do the same, but it can signal more: that the answer was inadequate, that you did not understand or that you are sceptical of what was said.

- *Be nice to people*
  This advice is one of business consultant Mark H. McCormick's "success secrets" from his video *What they still don't teach you at Harvard Business School* (1990). Journalists would do well to pay attention.

- *Keep calm*
  Keep your cool, grit your teeth, count to 10 or do whatever it takes to maintain a professional attitude.

- *Listen*
  Always listen closely to what your source is saying and probe when something is unclear. Do not stop listening once the formal interview has ended. That is when some sources loosen up. You are not violating any ethical code if you keep asking questions after you have put your notebook down or switched your recorder off.

- *Do not leave until you have got the basics*
  Never say goodbye before you have the correct spelling of the person's name, title, company, address and, if possible, age.

6.3 TAKING NOTES

You may have had a fantastic interview, but your efforts are in vain if you have not recorded it in a way you can use. Inexperienced reporters often lose excellent facts and quotes because they do not get the information down fast enough or, in their haste, scribble it so that later even they cannot decipher their handwriting.

Reporters' notepads are covered in strange, sometimes quirky symbols, abbreviations and shortcuts that help them quickly jot down what is said. Because few reporters are trained in secretarial or recording techniques they usually devise a system that lets them record speedily, accurately and completely – and to go back and retrieve the information with relative ease.

6.3.1 Developing notehand

Some of the helpful notehand symbols include the following:

atny	attorney
bk	book
cr	classroom
eg	example
f	father
gg	going
hpd	happened
i.e.	that is
invu	interview
j	judge
m	mother
nfa	not for attribution
OR	off the record
ple	people
px	police
rep	representative
Sa	South African
sitn	situation
sldr	soldier
std	standard
u	you
u r	you are
u/stng	understanding
wh	what
w/	with
w/o	without
Xn	Christian
y.p.	young people

Also use symbols:

@	at
> <	greater than or less than
#	numbers
∴	therefore

Using these shortcuts to taking notes is a little like learning a new language, you will only become fluent with practice.

6.3.2 Notebooks

Reporters will write on anything: envelopes, cocktail serviettes, cigarette boxes, backs of cheques and cheque-books. There are even tales of desperate journalists writing on their hands and up their arms.

Ideally, you should consider choosing a notepad that is convenient for you, but discreet. Many people are nervous when reporters start taking notes and if they do it on large, obtrusive pads that crinkle when the pages turn, it increases the source's discomfort.

A good idea is to get a spiral-bound notepad with a hard back which you can comfortably hold with one hand. It makes it easier for you if you have to stand during an interview. Consider numbering and dating your notepads so that you can file them for reference. Remember to write your name and telephone number on the cover; it will increase the chances of getting it back should you leave it somewhere.

6.3.3 Tape recorders

More reporters are swopping traditional notebooks for miniature tape recorders. This little gadget has many advantages:
- It provides total accurate recall, which is especially useful when quoting dialogue or extended parts of speech.
- When a reporter is not bent over a notepad, she has greater freedom to observe and react to the interviewee.
- The interview is captured verbatim and disputes with sources over being misquoted can be settled more easily.

But the tape recorder has its disadvantages too:
- Some sources feel uncomfortable being taped, while others mumble, rendering the recording unintelligible.
- Technology fails. True, your pen may run out of ink halfway through an interview but it cannot happen without you noticing it in good time, as is the case when the batteries go flat or the tape jams.
- Reporters are not forced to listen as carefully as when they are taking notes.

The strongest argument against using a tape recorder may be that it is too complete. Instead of returning to the office with selected facts and choice quotes, the reporter has to wade through the entire interview again to transcribe the information. This process steals a scarce commodity: time.

Having said that, I own a small tape recorder and usually have it close at hand. When doing important interviews, I usually ask the source if they mind if I switch on the tape and then I take notes as well. The notes help me focus on what is being said and serves as an index of the taped interview. It is also a back-up in case something goes wrong. Back at my computer, I review only the recorded sections I want to double-check and those I want to quote.

Assignment

Invite a newsworthy student or alumnus to class for a group interview. Have the lecturer tape-record the session, but use only your notes to write a 250-word story for the student newspaper or alumni journal. Include at least three direct quotes in your piece.

Compare the completed articles in small groups and read the best of each group to the whole class. Discuss:

1. The various approaches taken to the story (all based on the same information). How does this relate to our earlier discussion about the subjective nature of news?

2. Evaluate the quotes with the recorded conversation. Were they accurate?

3. Send the best stories to the intended publications.

Bibliography and recommended reading

McCormick, Mark H., *What they still don't teach you at Harvard Business School*, USA, Transworld International, 1990.
O'Kane, Maggie, "A public trial in Bosnia's sniper season", *Guardian Weekly*, March 19-25 1993, p. 10.
O'Rourke, P.J., "Bill Clinton", *Sunday Star Life/People*, 4 October 1992, p. 2.
Pienaar, Retha, "Freek Robinson: op die man af", *DeKat*, September 1991, pp. 38–43.
Teel, Leonard & Taylor, Ron, *Into the newsroom: an introduction to journalism*, 2nd ed, Chester, Connecticut, Globe Pequot, 1988.
The Missouri Group: Brooks, Brian S. *et al*, *News reporting and writing*, New York, St Martin's, 1980.

CHAPTER 7
WRITING WITH FLAIR

> *We should all attempt to bring quality writing, with wit and knowledge, to our work. If we succeed, newspapers will be not only informative, but also enjoyable; not only educational, but also entertaining; and not only bought, but also read.*
>
> The Missouri Group, *News reporting and writing*, p. 251.

Surveying newsrooms of reporters tapping away at their stories, many editors are asking: Where are the writers? The editor who reads this lead has reason to ask:

> Sarajevo's first war crimes tribunal began today when three Serbian men where brought to justice. The international news media flocked to witness the event.

But the *Guardian* editors who found this account of the same event know that in Maggie O'Kane they have at least one good writer on their staff:

> The state prosecutors wore their Italian wool overcoats loosely round their shoulders, Mafia style, and there were 18 butts in their ashtray before the court rose for the judge at 10:20 in the morning.
>
> The room was lit with four 1,000 watt bulbs, powered by a generator, and the sound system at the back could have served a modest rock concert. The judge at Sarajevo's first war crimes tribunal made it to the bench by crawling between the tripod legs of a TV camera and past Vioca, the stenographer, who jostled for space to type below the photographer from Reuters.
>
> (A public trial in Bosnia's sniper season, *Guardian Weekly*, 19–25 March 1993, p. 10.)

This sort of writing is not available often enough to newspaper and house journal readers. Too much of what makes it onto the news pages is flat, awkward and downright boring. The abundance of such writing may be one reason why newspaper circulation is not keeping pace with population growth and increased literacy levels. US. studies (The Missouri Group, *News reporting and writing*, p. 250) have shown that whatever else newspapers should do to attract readers, the quality of writing must be improved. In response, editors in America went to the features and life-style sections of magazines, where many good writers had fled, and brought writers back to report on hard news – and to show others how to do it.

When the *Miami Herald*'s 1986 Pulitzer Prize-winning crime reporter Edna Buchanan went off to cover a routine shooting, she filed this story:
Gary Robinson died hungry.

He wanted fried chicken, the three-piece box for $2.19. Drunk, loud and obnoxious, he pushed ahead of seven customers in line at a fast-food chicken outlet. The counter girl told him that his behaviour was impolite. She calmed him down with sweet talk, and he agreed to step to the end of the line. His turn came just before closing time, just after the fried chicken ran out.

He punched the counter girl so hard her ears rang, and a security guard shot him – three times.

(*The corpse had a familiar face*, 1987, p. 11)

Writers must possess the following three qualities: a respect for language, a vivid imagination, and the dedication to learn how to combine the two. To these qualities a journalist needs to add an instinct for news and reporting skills to get the significant details.

In this chapter, you will learn:
1. How to write with style.
2. The Wall Street Journal method.
3. Features, and some lessons, from fiction.

7.1 WRITING WITH STYLE

Good writing, according to journalism professors at the University of Missouri (The Missouri Group, *News reporting and writing*, p. 251), has five qualities:
- It is clear.
- It is precise.
- It appeals to the senses.
- It has pace, appropriate to the action.
- It is tied together with transitions.

7.1.1 Clarity

A *Cape Times* story under the headline "Judge fingers provocateurs; 'Agents' fuelling unrest – G'stone" began this way:
JOHANNESBURG – Mr Justice Richard Goldstone yesterday added two new factors to the list of the causes of violence in South Africa, saying

political uncertainty and the role of agents provocateurs exacerbated the existing climate of violence. . . . (22 July 1993, p. 1)

The writer of that lead added some linguistic uncertainty of his own. Besides, the premise is clearly false. In 1993, it is hardly original to "finger" thugs and political uncertainty as two factors that make worse the violence in South Africa.

The Missouri Group of journalism instructors suggest that before reporters type a word, they should remind themselves of three simple rules (The Missouri Group, *News reporting and writing*, p. 253):
- Rely on simple words and sentences.
- Use correct grammar.
- Think clearly.

The writer of "Quick Start: the two-minute guide to computer literacy", an article in the *Weekly Mail*'s "PC Review", followed those rules. Take this explanation of computer memory ("PC Review", *Weekly Mail*, June 1992, p. 16):

Memory: Computers actually remember nothing at all; the moment you switch them off their minds die. That's why memory comes in two kinds: active memory known as RAM, which does the thinking, and storage memory which collects those thoughts on a relatively permanent storage medium known as a disk.

RAM is measured these days in megabytes (a megabyte is roughly equivalent to a million characters). Most computers come with a megabyte RAM installed, but two or four megabytes are needed to run some heavyweight contemporary software (see later). . . .

One of the keys to clarifying complex concepts is to know how much information is enough. The writer above knew that for his purposes – the article's title is "Quick start; the two minute guide to computer literacy" – a technical definition would be inappropriate. A computer scientist may define a computer floppy disk in this way:

A disk is a flat Mylar plastic circle wated with ferrous-oxide and enclosed in a rigid plastic protective jacket. It is divided into tracks and sectors to facilitate electromagnetic storage and retrieval of data.

Our writer realized a newcomer to computers would read that and still be confused (or more confused), so he described the unfamiliar by relating it to something familiar ("PC Review", *Weekly Mail*, June 1992, p. 16):

Storage takes place in two places: a floppy disk which looks like a seven single still inside its jacket and a hard disk which looks similar, though you'd never know because it is hidden inside the computer. Both are magnetic media which record data much the same way a tape-cassette records sounds. Both kinds of disks come in different sizes, but on average a floppy disk can store two chapters of a novel and a hard disk can store a couple of novels.

The rule: use simple language to *describe* rather than *define* complex concepts.

7.1.2 Precision

Consider this lead of a short *Time* magazine story which appeared on page 17 on 3 August 1992. The quote describes how a drop in Tokyo's stock exchange had affected international stock exchanges: "The world's financial markets are so intertwined that when one itches, the others scratch."

Precision in writing means choosing exactly the right word for the job. A musician must play specific notes at a specific tempo to produce the intended melody; a writer must select the precise word and punctuation to tell an accurate tale. Reporters can make a politician say, claim, argue, announce or point out – but only one is correct.

7.1.3 Pace

Sentences, as much as words, create a mood. Short sentences convey action and tension, whereas long, drawn-out sentences tend to slow down the reader. But not always. Freelance writer Gus Silber captured the frenetic style of Radio Five's Alex Jay in a 72-word sentence which moves too fast to pause for a full-stop:

It's the Drive Show on Radio Five, and Alex Jay is back in the hot seat, jabbing digital buttons like a shuttle commander, shifting his gaze from the clock to the television to the computer screen, waving and blowing kisses at people on the other side of the looking-glass, rolling his eyes and tripping over his tongue as a minor pop singer called Prince battles to make himself heard in the background.

Alex Jay is on something. Definitely. It's called air. He lives it, he breathes it, he soars like a kite on it. Four hours a day, five days a week it's the fix that keeps him from going too sane. But when the red light fades and he floats down to earth, Alex Jay knows exactly who and what he is. . . .

(*Sunday Times Magazine*, 11 October, 1992, p. 24)

Silber finally puts the brakes on the too-busy-to-quit-now sequence by arranging softer words – "fades" and "floats" – into a plodding sentence.

89

The reader gets a chance to take a breath and learns that, occasionally, Alex Jay does too.

7.1.4 Weaving with transitions

Cutting a well-written article, like the one above, would be tough, because the reporter has been careful to weave together the action and ideas in the story by providing transitions.

Transitions are important because readers are generally curious people, but they are also pretty lazy; they certainly do not want to work too hard to get the facts. Any excuse to stop reading – a lull in the action, an ambiguous detail and they duck. Transitions keep your readers in the story, giving them no logical place to exit until the end.

Preparing a quick outline can help you organize the facts. It does not have to be formal, just jot down the topics or aspects of the topic you want to cover, then decide in what order to use them. Creating transitions is easy when the ideas follow in a logical, natural and interesting sequence.

Some techniques of creating transitions are:

7.1.4.1 Transitional words

- A peculiarity of journalism is beginning sentences with conjunctions. Something to which many language purists (like your high school English teacher) would object. Such language purists insist that conjunctions, like "but", "however", "and", should only be used to link independent clauses in compound sentences. This is not an argument. I am merely remarking that journalists do begin sentences with those little words and others: nevertheless, however, moreover and therefore. And the practice is useful.
- Also used are words of addition (like also and secondly).
- Words of movement and time, for example: when, since and while.
- Words of attribution, like: according to and he said.

7.1.4.2 Repetition

Start succeeding sentences or paragraphs with the same word:
Jon fell in the carport, a few yards from the rear corner of the house.
Jon, born in Johannesburg, has been living since 1989 with Featherstone, who is his mother's sister.

7.1.4.3 Logic

"A question precedes an answer," points out Hiley Ward (Ward, *Professional newswriting*, p. 179). Or a national problem precedes its ramifications for the local scene. Your reader can predict expected results once you have set up a logical sequence of statements or questions."

Listing items using numerals or round dots (bullets) also logically suggests a link.

7.1.4.4 Punctuation

Punctuation presents the writer with several options: using a colon will tie a group of sentences or paragraphs together; so will a semi-colon.

7.1.4.5 Balance or contrast

If, for example, you list a pro, you can use a con as contrast. Parallels can also be created by referring to the view of one side of the debate, then referring to the other side.

7.1.4.6 The camera technique

Describing a scene graphically throughout a story can hold the piece together (as Gus Silber did).

7.1.4.7 Highlighting a theme

In this section, I rely on this method; periodically, I weave in references to Gus Silber, which ties the discussion together.

7.1.5 Sensory appeal

Scanning lifeless copy, I sometimes get worked up and say to young journalists: "Do not tell me it is dry, show me the cracked mud in the park pond. Do not tell me the man is angry, show me his clenched jaw and the throbbing vein in his temple. I want to see the news, I want to choke on the acrid stench of burning tires, I want to shudder when the 11-inch hunting knife is carefully drawn across a chest until blood drips."

I owe my understanding of the importance of detail, in part, to Edna Buchanan. "What a reporter needs is detail, detail, detail," insists Buchanan (Buchanan, Edna, *The corpse had a familiar face: covering Miami, America's toughest crime beat*, New York, Random House, 1987, p. 265). "If a man is shot for playing the same song on the jukebox too many times, I've got to name that tune. Questions unimportant to police often add the colour and detail that make a story human. What movie did they see? What colour was their car? What did they have in their pockets? What were they doing at the precise moment the bomb exploded or the tornado touched down?"

Good writing has details which appeal to the senses: sight, hearing, smell, taste and touch. But a writer must know when a detail makes a story better, rather than just making it wordy. Consider this lead from *The Weekly Mail & Guardian* (Beresford, 30 July–5 Aug 1993, p. 33):

> As the dying sun filters through the rising smog of evening coal fires, the mood of bustling relaxation is reminiscent of a seaside promenade; kids playing soccer, girls and boys idling in flirtatious banter, women leaning over neighbourhood fences and their men exchanging profundities on street corners. Until 7:08 p.m.
>
> Former guerilla commander Michael Malunga says, "Look, they've all gone." And sure enough they have: wiped from view as cleanly as chalk from a blackboard.
>
> Fear is the curfew. Because this is Sebokeng and it is killing time.

The first sentence, although rich with details, provides too much useless information while the second sentence leaves the reader wondering about the significance of 7:08 p.m. In this pared-down version, unnecessary details are edited out, the scene is set in the active voice and the time reference is clarified:

> The dying highveld sun filters through the smog of evening coal fires and the mood is light: kids play soccer, boys and girls banter and flirt, women lean over neighbourhood fences and men chat on street corners. Until 7:08 p.m.
>
> Former guerilla commander Michael Malunga says, "Look, they've all gone." And sure enough they have: wiped from view as cleanly as chalk from a blackboard.
>
> Fear is the curfew. Because this is Sebokeng and after sundown is killing time.

A good writer knows when detail is appropriate. Every word must count. When space is tight, there is no place for a detail that has no job.

7.1.6 Alternative story structures

> Nearly blind, unable to walk and slowly losing her mind to Alzheimer's disease, an 80-year-old Tamarac woman begged her husband not to let her waste away in a nursing home.
>
> Sunday, Soren Korsgaard found a solution.
>
> "Two little bullets," Korsgaard wrote in a suicide note – a day before he was scheduled to put his wife of 62 years into a Plantation nursing home.
>
> Soren Korsgaard walked into his wife's room, closed the door and fired one bullet into his wife's head and another into his own.
>
> Angela Korsgaard died instantly. Doctors at Humana Hospital-Bennett tried to save Soren Korsgaard, but he died about 15 minutes later.
>
> As with everything in his life, Soren Korsgaard was meticulous in planning their deaths. This, he decided, was the only choice. . . . ("Two

little bullets; Tamarac man meticulous in planning deaths", 24 March 1992, p. 1)

Although these paragraphs open a spot news story, the traditional five W's are not strictly arranged in the inverted pyramid structure. Other story structures are being used by newspapers – and the results are usually more readable stories. The most popular is a style that has become the signature of *The Wall Street Journal*.

7.2 THE WALL STREET JOURNAL METHOD

It is not a new idea. For centuries, storytellers have used the literary device of focusing on a person as the representative of a group. The tradition continues daily in conversations: "Did you hear that the other day John's sister, the architect, was retrenched. This recession is really bad . . ."

Telling readers millions of people are starving has little impact until they see the sunken eyes and swollen belly of an infant called Peter. For some readers it is hard to relate to a statistic about 70 per cent of small businesses going under, until they hear about one woman's failed attempt at establishing her own florist.

Journalists have often used this technique, but no newspaper has embraced it like *The Wall Street Journal*. Daily, its front-page reports put a literary spotlight on the individual involved in an issue or institution. Consider this story by James Dorset entitled "Metallica Outdraws a Muezzin as Turks Flock to Arena Rock; Popularity of Western Music Boosts Promoters While Mosques Stand Empty" (*The Wall Street Journal*, 11 August 1993, p. 1):

ISTANBUL – Five times a day, the muezzin at Istanbul's waterfront Dolmabahce Mosque faces Mecca to call the faithful to prayer.

But increasingly he has had to face the music blaring from the Inonu sports stadium just a stone's throw away and drowning out his chant of "Allahu Akbar" (God is great).

Turkey has recently gained a place among the new meccas for international pop and rock concerts. With performers beating a path to Budapest, Athens and Tel Aviv, Istanbul and the Roman amphitheatre at Ephesus – where Sting has performed – are natural additions to their itineraries.

This approach works as well for local stories as it does for the national and international stories covered by *The Wall Street Journal*. Readers in South

Carolina for whom statistics released by the health department are of little interest, may read a story if it is told by using a family man affected by a disease, as in this example:

ROCK HILL – The past three weeks, 7-year-old Kevin has been sleeping on the floor beside his dad's bed.

"He's scared," said Kevin's father, Jim (not their real names). "I can't make him sleep on his own."

Kevin is scared his father will die in the night. His fears are not unfounded.

For $2^1/_2$ years, Jim has been fighting a variety of illnesses, from diarrhoea to influenza. Six months after he got sick, Jim, 39, told his son and his 12-year-old daughter that he had been diagnosed with acquired immune deficiency syndrome – AIDS. The disease is caused by the human immuno-deficiency virus, or HIV.

With a vivid image in the readers' minds, the writer moved on to the issue:

Jim is among the 12 AIDS patients reported in York County between Jan 1 1982 and Jan 31 1990, according to the South Carolina Department of Health and Environmental Control. The number of HIV cases, or people with the AIDS virus, is 78. Throughout South Carolina, 871 people have been reported to have the incurable disease. Nationwide, that figure is 121,645 and 60% of the people who have been diagnosed with AIDS have died.

All the figures – those diagnosed and those dying – double every 13 months, said Vickie Hinson, a nurse with the health department.

The face of AIDS is changing.

Jim and his scared little boy are only one family among the 871 families in South Carolina affected by AIDS, but by describing their plight in human terms, the reporter helped readers better understand the larger issue. By starting with a person, rather than an issue or institution, the journalist created empathy between the reader and the family.

7.2.1 Applying the formula in steps

The Wall Street Journal formula can be broken down into four steps:
1. Focus on the individual.
2. Transition to larger issue.
3. Report on opening focus.
4. Finish by returning to the subject of your focus or giving a summary statement.

Let us take a look at these steps.

- *The transition*
Transitions take the reader from the individualized opening to the larger story. In the AIDS article discussed above, the transition links Jim's situation to the state AIDS crisis. The writer left Jim and his family and started elaborating on the problems of identifying and treating AIDS patients.

This is the key paragraph or, in journalese, the "nut graph". Here the reporter answers the simple questions: "So what?" The nut graph usually includes most of the information given in the lead of a traditional inverted pyramid story.

- *The larger issue*
Following the transition comes the body of the story. In the story about AIDS, entitled "Face of AIDS Is Taking On New Look In S.C.", the writer analysed the statistics:

> AIDS has traditionally been considered a white male homosexual disease. But almost half of South Carolina's AIDS patients got the disease from other than homosexual sex and more than half of AIDS patients in the state are black.
>
> DHEC reports show that the top three risk factors were male-to-male sex, 54%; intravenous drug users, 21%; heterosexual sex, 7%.
>
> The DHEC statistics are likely to be much lower than the actual number of cases.
>
> A study of hospital records in South Carolina reported in the *Journal of the American Medical Association* showed that many AIDS cases go unreported.

Writing the body of a story in *The Wall Street Journal* mode is much like writing the inverted pyramid story. Until the ending you arrange the story in descending order of importance.

- *The conclusion*
Unlike the inverted pyramid, in which the importance of the material diminishes as the story concludes, *The Wall Street Journal* formula requires a strong finish.

A good technique is to return to the subject of the opening focus – in our example, Jim and his son. Because real-life stories seldom play out as neatly as fiction, it is often difficult to work the story back around to the lead. When the writer finished this story, Jim had not been cured, neither had he died. In fact, not much had changed at all. Ideally, Jim would have said something profound that would set the reader thinking.

In this case, a health department official did:
When Jim finally got approval for AZT, his T4 cell count was 143. His doctor says even with the drug, he only has six months to live.

Sandifer calls the dilemma the "God question".

"What are you going to do? You were never promised a rose garden," he said. "On the one hand, I say it is not fair. On the other hand, life is not fair."

Be careful not to confuse a kicker close with a contrived close. And definitely do not revert to the second-person and slap on the over-used line, "And what would *you* do?" – or some variation of it.

7.3 OTHER APPROACHES

The Wall Street Journal formula of leading with a focusing on an individual is the primary alternative to the inverted pyramid. Two variations of this alternative approach are stories which have scenic leads and anecdotal leads.

7.3.1 Scenic leads

Scenic leads re-create a scene, with or without the leading characters, that is significant to the point of the story. The *Chicago Tribune*'s Howard Witt used this approach when he wrote a story entitled "Radioactive river in Russia a deadly legacy of carelessness" (27 December 1992, p. 1)

MUSLIMOVO, Russia – The three overflowing cemeteries in this tiny village are situated much farther from the river than the houses of the living. That means the safest people here are the ones who are already dead.

The river – the deadly Techa River – twists like a beguiling serpent through the heart of this forsaken place, bearing an invisible poison that has touched every one of the 6,000 people who live astride its banks.

The poison is radioactivity – and there's so much of it in the Techa that ecologists consider it one of the most polluted rivers on Earth. More than 40 years ago, Soviet nuclear scientists at a secret weapons facility upstream dumped millions of curies of atomic waste straight into the river. The danger persists.

The story is not about the cemeteries, but the short opening scene slips into the transition about the cause of the radioactivity and its continued affect.

7.3.2 Anecdotal leads

Anecdotes are short narratives of incidents which attract the reader's attention. Diane Suchetka of the *Charlotte Observer* used an anecdote when she told a remarkable story of the high number of children who abuse children (28 February 1993, p. 1A):

> Zachary hated being 14.
>
> His grades were bad. Nobody liked him. His mother got on him all the time. And he never got the attention his two sisters did.
>
> But he knew how he could make himself feel better. With candy, he'd lure his sisters into his bedroom, wrestle them, take their clothes off, then fondle them and lick them.
>
> Once, he even tried to rape the older one. She was 5.
>
> "If you ever tell," he'd warn them, "I'll kill you." To make his point, he'd grab their dolls and slam them up against the wall.
>
> Then, one day while the 3-year-old and he lay naked on his bed, his other sister slipped away.
>
> "Come see what Zachary's doing," she ran and told her mother.
>
> The next thing Zachary knew, his mom was flying at him from the doorway of his bedroom, hitting him and shrieking, "I'll kill you."

Both the scenic and anecdotal approaches differ only in the leads from the basic *Journal* formula. After the opening follows the transition, the body of the story and close. Suchetka ended her story entitled "Kids abusing kids" with a return to the subject of her anecdote.

> Zachary, still in therapy two years after getting caught, is 16, charming, just a little shy.
>
> His mischievous grin and sense of humour make you like him right away.
>
> He slows his speech when he starts to talk about his past. His smile fades, his voice is lower, but he looks you in the eye.
>
> "I feel very bad about what I've done," he says, "It's destroyed the family. And it's really destroyed my two little sisters."
>
> Will he ever do it again?
>
> "I actually don't think I will," he says, "but there's a possibility. There's a possibility with anyone."
>
> His therapy, he says, has helped him deal with his own abuse. When he was 4, his mother's boyfriend beat him and fondled him. That same year, an older boy who lived nearby began forcing him to perform oral sex. Both told him the exact same thing.
>
> "If you ever tell, I'll kill you."

7.4 FEATURES AND FICTION

7.4.1 Types of feature stories

Veteran editor of the Associated Press, Rene Cappon, describes the difference between hard news stories and features this way (*The word: an Associated Press guide to good news writing*, 1982, p. 100):

The hard news story marches briskly through the whats, whens, wheres, looking neither right nor left, packing in enough details to give readers a clear picture.

In features, the immediacy of the event is secondary. The plain ladder of descending news values is replaced by human interest, mood, atmosphere, emotion, irony, humour. Features aim to give readers pleasure and entertainment along with (and, on the fluffier side, sometimes in lieu of) information.

The range of features encompasses the gourmet column and Orphaned Dog of the Week as well as news enterprise of major significance. The more compelling features supplement the straight news content in timely and topical ways: they illuminate events, offer perspective, explanation and interpretation, record trends, tell people about people.

The most common feature stories include:

7.4.1.1 Trend stories

These are the most timely. They make connections between series of actions, interests and attitudes that are moving across the city or country and affect the lives of the readers. Good trend stories not only point out the trend, but try to put it into perspective.

7.4.1.2 A profile

A profile is an in-depth look at a person, place or thing, showing all its sides so that the reader comes away from the story feeling she has an intimate and complete view of the subject.

7.4.1.3 Service pieces

Most newspapers provide an informational service to their readers. There are "What to do" and "Where to go" lists and more. Service pieces are the most obvious answer to readers who say, "We want news we can use" and cover everything from cooking to skiing.

7.4.1.4 Brighteners

Brighteners attempt to bring a smile to the reader.

7.4.1.5 Essays

Essay features give interesting and useful information, including the writer's own impressions on the topic. A good essay usually leaves the reader thinking some pro or con thoughts about the subject.

7.4.2 Learning from the short story

Because features are less bound to the moment than hard news, writers often have more time to put a story together. Unfortunately, the time is not always properly used. Some writers spend it thinking up strings of adjectives, purple passages and other decorative devices. Cappon's advice: "If you feel the decorative impulses coming on, lie down until it goes away" (*The word*, p. 100). Writing is not good if it calls attention to itself rather than the substance.

Where most hard news stories follow a set pattern, features allow the writer relative freedom. The reporter can choose any approach, be imaginative. This often leads to comparisons between features and fiction. But news reporters and fiction writers are uncomfortable cousins.

Calling a reporter's article "fiction" is likely to get him heated, at the very least. And many fiction writers balk when asked if their plots or characters are fact; many novels even carry an official disclaimer, such as: "The character and situations in this book are entirely imaginary and bear no relation to any real person or actual happening." Indeed, blurring these battle lines has landed writers from both sides in court.

This uneasy relationship goes beyond storylines to matters of style. When Pulitzer Prize winning novelist A.B. Guthrie's "The Way West" was published in 1949, he was asked whether his years as a journalist had helped him as a fiction writer. He answered with an emphatic "No!" (*Nieman Reports*, Spring 1992, p. 71)

Guthrie went further, saying journalistic experience was harmful to creative writing. News reporting stifles the imagination, Guthrie said, by its emphasis on facts and paralyses style with straight-declarative sentences.

In reply, many journalists can list reporters who have become successful fiction writers – Charles Dickens, Mark Twain and Jack London. Ernest Hemingway, for one, felt differently. Hemingway specifically credited his newspaper experience for help with his fiction.

In an interview in 1940, Hemingway recalled his time as a cub reporter for *The Kansas City Star* in 1917 and his boss, an assistant city editor named C.G. (Pete) Wellington: "Wellington was a stern disciplinarian, very just and very harsh, and I can never say properly how grateful I am to have worked under him" (*Nieman Reports*, Spring 1992; p. 71) Wellington enforced *The Star*'s 110 rules for writing vigorous journalistic English. These included short sentences, a plainness of expression and a minimum of adjectives, and avoidance of slang that had lost its freshness. "These were the best rules I ever learned for the business of writing," Hemingway said. "I've never forgotten them. No man with any talent who feels and writes truly about the thing he is trying to say can fail to write well if he abides by them."

In turn, some reporters – like Diane Suchetka – are candid about the influence of fiction on their work. Here Suchetka discusses how she put together one of her gripping features using the basic tools of fiction – scene setting, dialogue and significant detail:

I think good newspaper writing is built from the bricks and mortar of fiction and I tried to use them in this story. They are essential if you want to write an article that has impact, that makes a difference.

Ken Schell was knifed 27 times and left for dead
Why?
He's gay.

By DIANE SUCHETKA

Set up a narrative introduction. Studies show that readers by far prefer the narrative form to any other and certainly more than the inverted pyramid, now considered the worst by those studying journalistic forms. This also introduces the characters and provides a little suspense to keep the reader going. It also establishes the conflict necessary in any good work. Finally, the mention of a "faggot" provides motive and tells the reader what this story's going to be about.

1 Mark Barberree was out of work. He needed money the night he was drinking outside a Charlotte convenience store.

"I know somebody we can get," Barberree told his buddy, Larry Shrader. "This guy's a faggot. We can get away with it."

Just before 10 that night, Ken Schell heard a knock at his Chantilly bungalow.

When he opened the door, a fist hit him between the eyes. His glasses snapped and flew across the room.

Barberree, 24, and Shrader, 23, elbowed their way inside, shut the door and slid the chain across the lock.

One slammed the 42-year-old teacher into the sofa. The other drew a 7-inch hunting knife and ran the tip down Schell's forearm until blood dripped.

"What are you doing?" Schell asked. "What's going on?"

"We're going to hurt you real bad and then we're going to kill you," Shrader said.

Then he laughed.

More anti-gay acts

This lets the reader know that a cop who sees this stuff every day thought this was an unusually gruesome crime. He is the objective outsider who lends credibility. More subtle, I think, is that a police officer is willing to speak out for the victim, thus substantiating his story.

2   Today, 3½ years later, Charlotte Police Officer Bob Cooke still says it's one of the most violent crime scenes he's ever seen.

"I never will forget that house or that victim, he says."

These are the facts and figures that explain to the reader *why* we are writing this story.

3   It's one example of the violence against gay men and lesbians now surging in North Carolina and across America.

Anti-gay violence and harassment jumped 42% in 1990 in six major American cities, the National Gay and Lesbian Task Force reported last month.

In North Carolina, the number of anti-gay incidents rose 27% – from 1,204 in 1989 to 1,530 in 1990, according to the NC Coalition for Gay and Lesbian Equality.

Those statistics include two murders and 70 assaults and robberies. Not included are another 376 episodes of violence committed against gay men and lesbians by their own families.

Charlotte police don't keep statistics on anti-gay crimes. And gay leaders in South Carolina say they know of no organization gathering statistics there.

But gays aren't the only ones who say the numbers are increasing. In New York City, where police document crimes against gays and lesbians, they more than doubled last year.

> This line tells the reader that some criminals target gays. It foreshadows. It is a combination of journalistic and literary techniques.
>
> This section tells the reader where the information in this story came from, thus alleviating the need for attribution throughout and allowing the narrative form to dominate throughout the rest of the story.

4 In some cases, police say men pretend to be gay and pick up gay men to learn where they live and what they own. Then they rob or kill them.

5 Violence against gays and lesbians is like rape. Many victims don't report it. Because police reports are public record, gay men and lesbians fear that reporting crimes against them will make public their sexual orientation. Then they could lose their jobs, apartments or custody of their children.

This is the story of a hate crime. The details come from interviews and court and police records. The men who attacked Ken Schell would not be interviewed.

If Schell had been attacked because he was black or Jewish, the violence would have received much more attention when it happened, says Charlotte lawyer and gay activist Chris Werte.

"But gays and lesbians aren't thought of as human beings," he says. "They're thought of as immoral objects."

> The brief background of the main character's life gives us an idea of the sort of person he is. It gives him life, adds some depth. It also lets us know that the victim is a smart man involved in community affairs, again adding credibility.

6 Ken Schell grew up in a working-class family in Wyoming, Ohio, a wealthy Cincinnati suburb. He knew in junior high school that he was attracted to boys, but he trained himself to turn his head "like a normal guy" when girls walked by.

He didn't date, but he was bright – bright enough to win an academic scholarship to Earlham College in Indiana. In 1967, he graduated with a degree in biology.

That year, he moved to the Charlotte area for a teaching job, but he kept his sexual orientation a secret. Later, Schell, an art lover since childhood, helped start the Visual Arts Coalition and became president of the NC Print and Drawing Society.

In 1978, after a three-month relationship, he learned the man he loved did not love him. His heart was broken and he needed to talk. So at the age of 34

WRITING WITH FLAIR

Schell came out. He told his family and friends that he was gay.

No one abandoned him. He couldn't believe it. Life was easier.

Here we see he is not without faults, that he has not always used the best judgement, we see he is multi-dimensional, human. The element of surprise in the last line is designed to keep the reader reading. **7**

Then, one summer night in 1987, he picked up a hitchhiker. The man told Ken he was troubled and confused about his marriage.

They sat in the parking lot of Latta Park for two hours talking. And when Schell got ready to leave, the hitchhiker said he wanted to go home with Schell. They spent the night together.

For the next few weeks, the man kept asking Ken for money. He called – even came to his house. But Ken always said no to Mark Barberree.

He's still breathing

This entire section paints the scene and highlights the drama. Here is the blood-and-guts conflict of the story and all the detail too. **8**

"Where's your money?" Shrader yelled at Schell as he scoured each room. "Where's your jewelry? Don't you have some guns here?"

While Shrader searched for valuables, Barberree punched Schell in the face and chest again and again, pushing him into walls and from room to room.

Then he shoved Schell into a bedroom and onto the bed. He held a half bottle of red wine he'd taken from Schell's refrigerator and started splashing it on him.

"You don't have to humiliate him," Shrader said to Barberree.

"You know we're going to kill him in a minute."

The men forced Schell into the living room and demanded his car keys. I've got to do something soon, Schell told himself. If they're getting ready to leave, they're getting ready to kill me. This is it.

Schell had nothing to lose. He dived through the living room window.

Three-quarters of Schell made it past the two panes of glass and the splintered window frame, but a shard of glass foiled his escape. It sliced open Schell's leg just below his left knee.

At least the neighbours could hear him now. "Help! Murder! Help!" he screamed.

Before he could say anything else, one of the men grabbed his hair, pulled him inside and stabbed him over and over again in the back with the knife.

They pulled him to his feet and Schell instinctively blocked his face with his left arm.

Barberree jammed the knife into Schell's chest.

"You killed me," he said as he fell to the floor. But Schell could still hear voices.

"He's still breathing," Shrader said calmly. "Let's cut his throat."

"No, let's get out of here," Barberree said.

"He's still breathing. Stab him in the back of the skull."

"Let's just get out of here."

They lifted $23 from Schell's wallet and ran out the door.

Schell crawled 4 feet to the phone in the dining room, his eyes shut tight. I know I'm going to die, he thought, but before I do, I'm going to make sure they get caught. He felt for the last hole in the rotary dial, where the O would be, and dialled.

Police arrived in minutes. Officer Cooke stepped through the broken window and let another officer in through the door. They found Schell sitting on the floor like a rag doll – his legs stretched out in front of him, arms dangling and eyes shut so he wouldn't have to see the blood draining from the 27 stab wounds and cuts in his body.

During the 3-mile ambulance ride to the hospital, Schell never stopped talking to himself. With every beat of his heart, he repeated his mantra: "I will live, I will live, I will live, I will live."

This illustrates Schell's will to live and foreshadows again. **9**

WRITING WITH FLAIR

Here we use details to paint another picture, to make the reader see. This also quickly updates readers on the other two characters.

More struggle here. This was an effort to make the reader feel the pain and emphasize how much he lost.

This section explains why the main character is telling his story – motive. It is important in a story like this for several reasons. (1) The incident was dated, (2) to erase ulterior motives and assure the sceptics he was not out for gain, and (3) to enhance credibility.

In the trauma unit

10 At 1:15 that morning, Aug. 25, 1987, police found Barberree, apparently passed out, face down in a dog kennel behind his house, a German shepherd lying beside him. Barberree was spattered with blood. His white high-top tennis shoes were drenched in it.

They couldn't find Shrader.

11 In the trauma unit that night doctors pumped blood back into Schell's body. They cut him open from his breast bone to below his belly button to check the damage to his organs.

He was lucky. The knife just missed his heart, just missed his lungs, just missed his spine.

For weeks, it hurt to breathe.

The incision became infected. And four times a day, Schell endured 30 minutes of torture as a nurse used forceps to pack gauze into his stab wounds.

But he was buoyed by dozens of friends – gay and straight – who came to his hospital room, put his family up and paid for a charter plane to take him home to Ohio when he couldn't fly on a commercial flight.

About six weeks after the assault, police arrested Shrader. He had fled to Atlanta and a tipster told police he was back in town.

Three months after the attack, Schell returned to Charlotte. There were physical therapy sessions and thousands of dollars in medical bills to pay that insurance didn't cover. By Thanksgiving, he was finally able to go back to work. But not without his cane.

Going public

12 It is rare, given the strong anti-gay sentiment in the Carolinas, for a gay man to talk publicly about being assaulted. It's even rarer that he allow himself to be identified. Friends have begged Schell not to tell his story, fearing for his life.

105

But Schell, now 46, wants people to understand the horror. He says fear is constant for gay men and lesbians.

"I'm not going to live out of fear," he says. "For me to live my life publicly as who I am is an affirmation of who I am – the freedom that this country is all about.

"I hope other gay men will be less afraid to be who they are.

Schell has thick greying hair and a bushy handlebar mustache. His green eyes twinkle behind black reading glasses.

He has recovered, but his knee still throbs and his chest knots up from the stab wounds.

"I'm not vengeant," he says. "But my expectation was that these guys would be put away for 50 or 60 years."

They weren't.

13 On Nov. 13, 1987, his two assailants appeared before Judge Frank Snepp. Both, it turned out, had criminal records that included arrests for theft and assault. Shrader had been arrested for breaking a man's jaw with a baseball bat. Barberree had been convicted of assaulting a police officer.

The district attorney's office agreed to a plea bargain. Even with that, each man faced up to 60 years in prison.

In exchange for a lesser sentence, Barberree and Shrader pleaded guilty to armed robbery and assault with a deadly weapon, intent to kill.

Snepp sentenced each to the minimum prison term: 14 years. In North Carolina, inmates get one day off their sentences for every day of good behaviour. That can turn 14 years into seven.

That, says Schell, makes him feel as though he was victimized twice.

"It's appalling to me that Jim Bakker was given a longer sentence than these guys," he says. "I'm an upstanding, law-abiding citizen, except that I'm a faggot. If I wasn't, I have no doubt they would've received longer sentences."

Resolves the conflict for the other two characters.

Tells readers just how common vicious crime is.

14 Snepp, who retired in 1989, says he doesn't remember the case. "I heard hundreds of cases," he says. "I only remember sensational murder cases."

But Schell remembers every detail. And he worries about what will happen when Shrader and Barberree are released from prison.

"These guys have done this before," he says, "and they'll do it again."

Scheduled for release

This was designed to leave the reader with just a little of the fear Ken Schell feels when he thinks about those release dates. It does not wrap everything up in a neat little package. Like good fiction, it forces the reader to think about what might happen next.

15 Now Shrader leaves his Charlotte prison to work but must return at night. He is scheduled to be freed on Jan. 12, 1993.

Barberree is to be released May 18, 1994.

Both could get out earlier for working while in prison.

(Reprinted with permission)

7.4.3 Using extended dialogue

Fiction writers often let the characters tell the story. Suchetka also picked up that technique for use in her piece about Ken Schell. It worked for her, but employing extended dialogue is tricky. Consider these pointers:

- Use extended dialogue only when you meet a source who is eminently quotable or when you witness a dramatic scene – and when you have it accurately recorded.
- Few reporters are skilled enough at note-taking to get down a complete conversation by hand, so I suggest this rule: tape it, or leave it. (Suchetka relied on court records to recreate the conversations used in her piece.)
- Avoid using dialect. Not only is dialect difficult to read, but it often offends the group whose way of talking is being highlighted. If the speaker's accent is of special interest, use it only in the first quote.
- Obscenities are out – most of the time. Because newspapers are considered "family" reading, newspaper editors usually ban obscenities unless it is considered overwhelmingly significant to the story. Two reporters at *Atlanta Journal* argued just that when they put together a series on police officers and the obscenity-laden world they work in (Teel & Taylor, *Into the newsroom*, p. 150). The reporters won this quota of expletives: a couple of insults to motherhood, one slang reference to urination, and two vain calls upon God.

The rule is: do not use language that will make your grandmother blush. If your source does use expletives that are non-essential, paraphrase. And don't just substitute dashes for some of the letters. If your grandmother sees f..k, even she will try to fill in the blanks. And it is unlikely that she will come up with folk.

Assignments
1. Take a dull news report on an interesting subject and suggest ways the reporter could rewrite it with some flair.

2. Take a page from a news magazine like *Time* and underline the transitions. Which transitional devices did the writer use?

3. Using *The Wall Street Journal* formula, write three paragraphs from the following notes:

    There are 12 000 injuries in sky-diving each year – seventeen per cent of them permanently disabling the victims. Fourteen people died last year.

    Fifty-five per cent of the injuries are to the spine. Most critics blame poor enforcement of safety procedures.

    Jonathan Levy, 19, a first-year student at the Cape Technikon in Cape Town, has been wheelchair-bound since an accident earlier this year.

    On only his fourth jump, he dislocated his arm while exiting the aeroplane.

    Being unable to pull his main parachute, he opted for his reserve parachute, which had not been packed properly.

    After spiralling severely, Levy collided with powerlines and tumbled to the ground with a broken neck and lower back.

    "I guess I should have been more careful, but I just wasn't paying enough attention when we were prepping for the jump," he said from his hospital bed, two months after the accident.

    Levy studied nature conservation.

    He is an only son and his parents are very distraught.

    They are thinking of taking legal action against the Western Province Skydiving Club, to which their son belonged.

4. Write about a memorable moment in your life as an anecdotal lead to a story about how you came to be the person you are today. Include the transitional paragraph.

5. Everyone has some special interest – opera, theatre, hiking, running or volleyball. Choose one of your special interests and write a 500-word service piece about it for a specific publication.

   Interview authorities in the field, as well as participants in it. Talk to some people who don't like it at all, in order to get both pros and cons for your story. Next, think about what you like best about the subject and try to convey that to your readers. Also consider how you can point out negative aspects of the subject – and tell the reader to avoid them. Include any costs to the participant.

6. Write a 750-word profile about a historic building in your area. Besides the architecture and dimensions of the building, consider the people who made it and used it. Aim your story towards a specific publication.

7. Make a list of three trends you have noticed and discuss them with your class. Choose one on which to write a 750-word feature for a specific publication. Do not only point out the trend, but try to answer the question: "Why is this happening?"

8. The tough part about writing an essay feature is finding a suitable subject that you feel strongly about and will interest your readers. Consider the things that are on your mind and on the minds of the people you come into contact with:
   - Does your changing neighbourhood or university community engage you in some way?
   - Is there something about your career prospects that is disturbing to you?
   - Have you noticed a particular hobby or new sport becoming trendy among your peers?

   Write a 700-word essay for a specific publication.

Bibliography and recommended reading

Beresford, David, "Dusk: it's countdown to killing hour", *The Weekly Mail & Guardian*, 30 July–5 August 1993, p. 33.

Buchanan, Edna, *The corpse had a familiar face: covering Miami, America's toughest crime beat*, New York, Random House, 1987.

Cappon, Rene J., *The word: an Associated Press guide to good newswriting*, New York, Associated Press, 1982.

Dorset, James M., "Metallica outdraws a muezzin as Turks flock to arena rock; popularity of western music boosts promoters while mosques stand empty," *The Wall Street Journal*, 11 August 1993, p. 17.

"Japan's stock woes batter other markets", *Time*, 3 August 1992, p. 17.

"Journalists as fiction writers", *Nieman Reports*, Spring 1992, pp. 71–80.

"Judge fingers provocateurs; 'Agents' fuelling unrest – G'stone", *Cape Times*, 22 July 1993, p. 1.

O'Kane, Maggie, "A public trial in Bosnia's sniper season", *Guardian Weekly*, 19–25 March 1993, p. 10.

"Quick start; the two minute guide to computer literacy", *PC Review*, June 1992, p. 16.

Silber, Gus, "Hot hits and hang ups", *Sunday Times Magazine*, 11 October 1992, pp. 24–6.

Suchetka, Diane, "Kids abusing kids", *Charlotte Observer*, 28 February 1993, p. 1A.

Suchetka, Diane, "Ken Schell was knifed 27 times and left for dead; Why? He's gay", *Charlotte Observer*, 14 April 1991, pp. 1–2E.

The Missouri Group: Brooks, Brian S., *et al.*, *News reporting and writing*, New York, St Martin's, 1980.

Ward, Hiley H., *Professional newswriting*, New York, Harcourt Brace Jovanovich, 1985.

Witt, Howard, "Radioactive river in Russia a deadly legacy of carelessness", *Chicago Tribune*, 27 December 1992 p. 1, 5.

CHAPTER 8
REACHING THE MEDIA

By François Nel and Eddie Ward

> *The news release is the granddaddy of public relations writing vehicles.*
> Fraser Seitel (Director of Public Affairs, Chase Manhattan Bank), *The practice of public relations*, New York, Macmillan, 1992, p. 198.

At his desk on the fourth floor of Cape Town's historic Newspaper House, *Argus* columnist and wine critic David Biggs receives piles of mail. Many letters comment on his daily column, "Tavern of the seas". The majority of envelopes (scores each week, he says) contain press releases from organizations hoping to have their people, products and activities mentioned in Biggs' column which reaches about 105 000 readers five days a week.

About 90 per cent of those releases – the product of countless hours of work – are trashed after a mere glance. The reason? "I think it's because lots of people when they write press releases probably don't know what makes them work," Biggs says.

Many people go about writing press releases the way some primitive tribe may act if asked to build a television, he says. Using a bit of wire, rope and tree bark, they may be able to make something that closely resembles a TV, but it probably will not function as one because they do not know what makes a TV work. "It's the same with a bad press release or a bad story. It's like a TV set with no works in it," he says.

Biggs is not alone in his criticism of the waves of press releases flowing into newsrooms. A survey of newspaper editors found that the following six factors particularly goaded editors about news releases (Baxter, Bill L, "The news release: an idea whose time has gone?", *Public Relations Review*, Spring 1981, p. 30):

- Information that is not localized.
- Information that is not newsworthy.
- Releases containing too much advertising puffery.
- Releases that are too long and cumbersome.
- Releases that arrived too late to be useful.
- Releases that are poorly written.

Writing media releases remains one of the most basic tools at the disposal of public relations practitioners for reaching their target audiences. We shall look at how releases work – and how to avoid the apparent shoddiness with which they are often planned and executed.

> In this chapter, you will learn:
> 1. The format and style of releases for print and electronic media.
> 2. What goes into special media packets.
> 3. A few pointers for dealing with journalists.

8.1 HOW TO REACH THE MEDIA

Every day, every newsdesk in the country is swamped by a tidal wave of media releases, of which very few ever make it to print.

Most editors will tell you this is because PR practitioners do not know how to write. But there is more to it. The majority of PR practitioners find themselves in the crossfire between the media and their managements and they do not quite know how to balance these relationships in a way that will keep both parties happy. This is no easy task – but it can be achieved.

The key to being a successful public relations journalist lies in a thorough understanding of who expects what of you.

8.1.1 What does management want and what does the media want?

With a few exceptions, management regards newsdesks as a source of free advertising, a vehicle to tell the world just how wonderful the company and its people are – as and when management sees fit.

Management believes that it is the job of the PR practitioner to persuade newspapers, radio stations and television channels to carry glowing reports about the company in a format and language that will sell their image, products and services to their specifications. What is more, management seldom understands why this approach causes problems and often gets upset when the PR practitioner or the media (or both) suggests anything to the contrary. This kind of pressure from the top may explain why many media releases tend to resemble puffy, badly written advertising copy.

News editors, on the other hand, tend to have a completely different view of what they should publish (see chapter 1 for a complete discussion on news). Generally speaking, though, the news media consider themselves to be the watchdogs of society who have to protect the community by providing them with relevant information on which they can base the decisions that shape their lives.

In short, management wants free advertising and news editors want cold facts. In view of these apparently opposed points of view, no one can be blamed for assuming that the purposes of management and editors are mutually exclusive and that PR practitioners find themselves backed into a permanently unresolved Catch-22. They would be wrong.

Yes, bringing together the expectations of management and news editors is tough. But it can be – and is being – done. If you know what news is and you know what your company's objectives and aspirations are you can, with some effort, marry the two and write news that will satisfy both parties. The following tips will help you to achieve this.

8.1.2 Important news

You must start off with something that is newsworthy (see chapter 1 for a full discussion on news criteria). Then ask yourself: "Who cares about this information?"

If the answer is only your boss and your paying customers, the appropriate response would be to buy an advertisement. Remember, newspapers rely on advertising to pay the bills and editors are unlikely to react favourably to someone trying to con them out of money.

Of course, the opposite is true too: a manager's suspension for harassing a colleague may be generally newsworthy, but publicizing the information is unlikely to be in your company's best interest.

The recipe for a happy balance? Write a news release about newsworthy activities occurring in the area where public interest and corporate benefit overlap.

For example, if Welgemeend Wine Estate were to start exporting their product to Iceland, the information would obviously be newsworthy for the company. It is also likely that some other people – even those who never buy the estate's fine red wines – may be interested to learn that a local business is competing internationally.

News releases can be written about almost anything, but three frequent subjects are *product and institutional announcements, management changes* and *management speeches.*

8.1.3 Know your company

For a corporate journalist to be able to translate the marketing objective of her company into news she must have an intimate knowledge of the company, the image it wants to project and events taking place in the company.

She must also know the company's mission, objectives, operating philosophy and commitments. If the public relations and marketing departments are separate, she must have a clear understanding of the messages and images the marketers are projecting in order to ensure that the company's above-the-line (media advertising) and below-the-line (public contact) messages are not contradictory.

One of the easiest ways to write promotional news is to identify a number of image themes characteristic of the image the organisation wants to project and to interweave these with the news events you use to promote your company, for example:

Image theme "We are a mining house that cares for our employees and their families."
News event A mining accident.
Application In your series of news releases on the accident include quotations by a senior official on what the mine is doing for the miners and their families to support them during this trying time.

8.1.4 Know who will speak for your company

Quotes should always be attributed to an identifiable person and not just to a spokesperson. Since people identify with people it is always a good idea to identify a number of spokespersons in your organisation and, to help things run smoothly, to arrange them according to a media policy stating who says what about what, and when. For example:

Chairman/Chief Executive Officer Corporate philosophy or policy matters
Human Resources Manager Labour policy
Production managers Production-related matters.

For the sake of credibility it is important that quotes are attributed to someone who deals as closely as possible with the matter under discussion. If only the CEO issues statements the impression may be created that the company is trying to hide something. The same is true when the PR chief always acts as the company spokesperson.

8.1.5 Help your company spokesperson get to know the media

If identified spokespersons do not possess the necessary skills in media liaison, it is the PR department's responsibility to train them and to provide them with continuous back-up in media matters. The following tips may prove helpful:

- It is vitally important for spokespersons to realise that they are acting on behalf of the company and that the messages they convey must be consistent with the company image.
- Spokespersons do not have to give off-the-cuff answers to telephone enquiries. Inform them of their right to ask a journalist to get back to them after a specified period of time so that they may be able to give well-formulated answers. However, if a spokesperson has promised to get back to a journalist by a certain time, he must honour that promise.
- Spokespersons may request a draft of the article before it goes to press, but they must understand that they are only allowed to check the facts and may not interfere with the tone of the piece. Many journalists balk when a source asks to see a draft, so be very careful how you approach the journalist.
- Managers often believe they have been misquoted. However, during the interview, a journalist may summarize a lengthy answer and then ask the manager if that is what he meant. If the manager says "Yes", he can be quoted as such. This must be pointed out to spokespersons.

8.2 TARGETING THE RIGHT AUDIENCE

Your next step is to determine the potential audience and the media – or sections of the media – that target them. The only way to do this is to read, watch and listen.

Publications that list various media and news criteria are useful, but make sure you survey each media outlet yourself so that you know *precisely* what type of news each editor is looking for.

Sending out 50 news releases may impress your boss or client, but you are likely to irritate the editors whose time you are wasting – and they are likely to pay scant attention when a release with your name on it crosses their desk again.

The spray-and-pray approach – spraying out releases and praying that they will be used – yields poor results and wastes a lot of money and time. This approach also reveals much about the company: not only do they not know the media, but they often also do not know their clients and consider them to be a faceless, unidentified mass flippantly referred to as "the general public".

Companies need to know to whom they need to talk to project the image they want so that their clients will get to know and accept it. To do this they need to know who their real clients are, why they have a relationship with the company and what that relationship is. These questions will provide you with the answers:

THE BUSINESS OF WRITING NEWS

- Are the clients male or female?
- How old are they?
- What are their levels of literacy and education?
- Where do they live?
- What do they think and believe?
- What interests them?
- Which publications do they read?
- To which radio stations do they listen?
- Which television channels do they watch?

If you want to reach your target audiences, you will certainly not be successful if you use a medium that is unacceptable to them!

FIGURE 8.1 A corporate media profile pinpoints the media on which PR practitioners need to concentrate

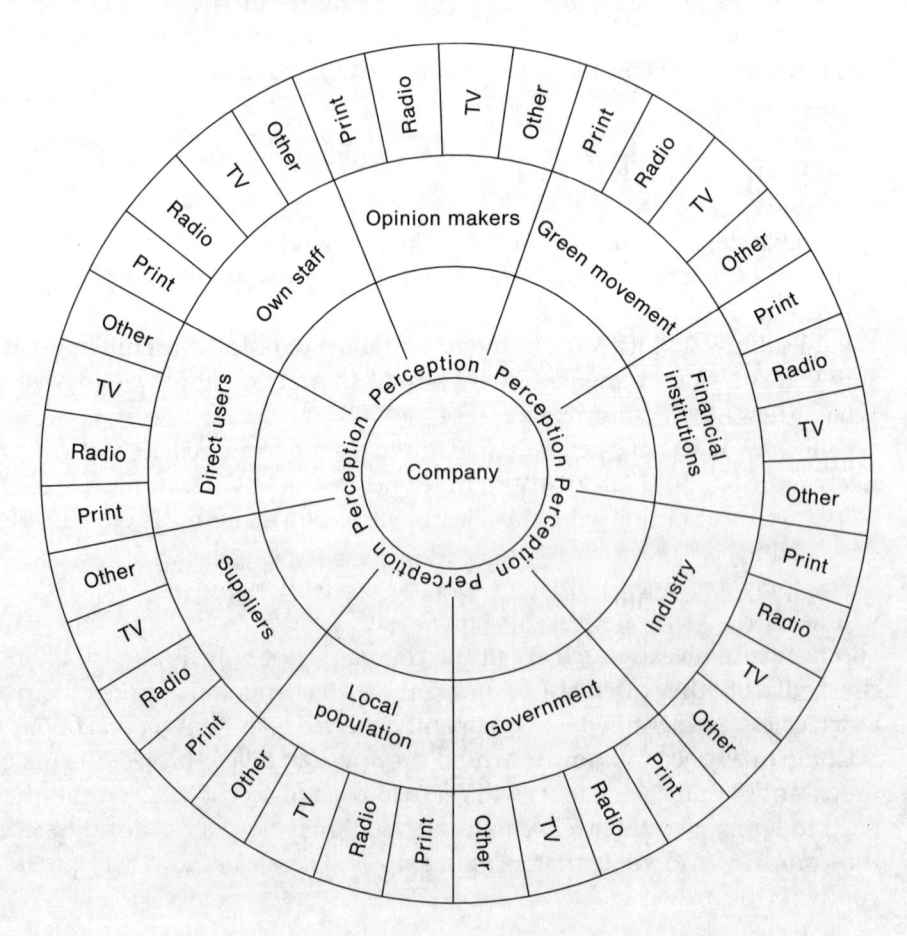

8.2.1 Creating a media profile

A corporate media profile is an essential tool in determining the media with which you need to establish good relations in order to target your message at the right audience through the right medium. This is done in two steps.

- **Step 1:** Pinpoint the interest groups your organization needs to address and get to know why they are important to your company.
- **Step 2:** Determine the media preferences of your interest groups. This will help you design your message to reach the audience directly, in a language they will understand, through the media of their choice.
- **Remember:** You are addressing *people* – not some inanimate newspaper or radio channel – and people have language quirks: bankers speak "finance", computer buffs speak "computer-ese", and teenagers use slang. Unless you speak their language via the media of their choice, they will neither understand you nor identify with you.

8.2.2 Know the media

Once you have picked the media your company needs to use, the time has come for you to get to know how those media work – and who does the work:
- Who are the people who get things done?
- Who decides what is news and what is not?
- What do they regard as newsworthy?
- Do they have any particular interests (the arts, environment, health issues) or dislikes (the arts, environment, health issues)?
- What are their style and language preferences?
- What are their deadlines?
- What can you do to make their work as easy as possible?

A key to successful media relations is to conduct yourself as a professional corporate journalist and to treat the media in the way you would like to be treated. In practical terms:
- If a reporter asks you for something, get back to him timeously so he can process the information before his deadline.
- If they use a specific style, write for that style.
- If you have to translate a release, make sure the translation is correct.

In the past, PR practitioners were often seen as a hindrance placed in the path of journalists in order to obscure what is really going on in the company. But that is changing. Companies are realizing that fair media coverage is an essential part of projecting a credible image. The better you treat the media, the better your chance of putting your side of a sticky story. And often, when a reporter needs an opinion on something related to your industry, she will ask you, the PR practitioner, because she knows you are reliable and credible. In the process you will be getting positive exposure for your organization.

8.3 THE RIGHT PRESENTATION – FOR READERS AND LISTENERS

Once you are sure you have news and you have picked your audience, as well as a publication or broadcast station that caters for them, you need to focus on presenting the information in the right way.

There is a big difference between writing for readers and writing for listeners. Readers have certain advantages over listeners. For example, a reader can scan material, focus on topics that appear interesting and reread sections that seem unclear. Listeners, on the other hand, get information in a set order and if they miss something they usually do not get a second chance. That is why we need to have a separate discussion on creating new releases for print and broadcast.

8.4 REACHING READERS

Before a release gets to your readers, it has to get past an editor who is more often than not strapped for time. For this reason the inverted pyramid style (discussed in chapter 3) remains the most effective way to organise a press release.

The first question an editor usually asks when picking up a news release is: "Is this information important?" The release writer has one paragraph – about 20 seconds – to convince the editor that it is.

Make sure, too, that you write your release in a style that suits the publication. Adding quotes from an authority in your company certainly will add some spice to your release, but be careful:
- Staid quotes filled with jargon are worse than no quotes at all.
- All quotes must be attributed. "The news release can't be used as the private soapbox of the release writer," says Fraser Seitel. "Rather, the release must appear as a fair and accurate representation of the 'news' that the organization wishes to convey." (*The practice of public relations*, p. 206.)

Target your releases carefully and try to give a local angle. The editors of the *Eastern Province Herald* in Port Elizabeth would have little use for this release:
CAPE TOWN – Patricia Jackson has been named a director of the photo lithography and printing company Graphco.

But the same release would almost certainly be used in the *Eastern Province Herald* if amended like this:

CAPE TOWN – Patricia Jackson, a graduate of the Port Elizabeth Technikon and daughter of Mr and Mrs Jason Jackson of Port Elizabeth, has been named a director of the photo lithography and printing company Graphco.

Try to get a local angle for your information, but take care not to push it – as was the case at a San Fernando Valley radio station quoted by Stephen Bates (*Anecdotes of American journalism*, p. 13). The editor had ordered that every newscast open with a local story, and so one newscast read: "Two high-speed trains collided today between Tokyo and Osaka, Japan. There were 123 people killed and several hundred have been injured. But there were no Valley residents on board."

A release must also be organized in a manner that allows the editor to use it easily. Follow these guidelines:

- *Paper*

Use plain, white paper. Expensive coloured paper with embossing and other embellishments arouse suspicion. Good editors are impressed by the news content and not the extravagant packaging.

- *Spacing*

News releases should always be typed one-and-a-half or double spaced on one side only of A4 paper.

- *Margins*

Margins should always be wide enough for editors to write in them, i.e. about 2.5 cm.

- *Type*

Use standard and upper- and lowercase type. Never use all capitals, which is very difficult to read.

- *Identification*

The name, address (if not on the letterhead), and telephone number of the release writer should appear on the release in case the journalist wants further information.

It is a good idea to list two names with office and home numbers. Give full names, not just an initial; you want the press to feel comfortable enough to call you.

Make sure you add your office hours (09:00–17:00, or whatever the case may be), because a journalist working on a deadline needs to know exactly when you can be reached where. Remember, news staff seldom work traditional banking hours.

If you are writing the release but cannot adequately field questions from the press on the subject, list the name of the person who can (see the release in figure 8.3).

- *Embargo or release date*

Indicate whether the release can be used immediately or if it should be held until a specific date. In this day of instant communication and increased competition, editors frown on embargoes. So, if you need to hold information, wait until the appropriate time to get the release to the editors.

- *Length*

"Screeds and screeds of copy helps no one," says Raymond Joseph, Cape Town Bureau Chief of the *Sunday Times*. A release should seldom be more than two pages; more than three pages can almost never be justified. Paragraphs should also be short – no more than six lines.

- *Slug lines*

Identify the story and page number at the top of each page. The terms "more" or "end" should be used at the bottom of pages.

- *Headlines*

Headlines are optional. It is better to send a release without a headline than to use a bland or misleading headline that is likely to put the editor off. Most headlines are rewritten by the sub-editors in any event. A good headline tells the story in no more than six words.

8.5 REACHING LISTENERS AND VIEWERS

Millions of South Africans get their news from radio and television: in 1993, 13 million adult listeners and 9 million viewers tuned into SABC services every day (SABC, 1993, *Radio & TV*, July/Sept., pp. 53–4).

Radio is often the primary source of news for teenagers. Many are reluctant to read newspapers and will leave the room when the TV news comes on, but they are unlikely to change stations for the few minutes during which radio news broadcasts are aired.

Getting your company's information broadcast is therefore a good idea, but you should not simply send radio stations the same release you send to the press. Consider this press release:

JOHANNESBURG – Chartered Bank today announced it was lowering its home mortgage lending rate to 16 per cent from 17 per cent, effective immediately.

Mr John E. Ashley-Brown III, President and Chief Executive Officer of Chartered Bank, said, "We are lowering mortgage rates because of increasing competitive pressures in the mortgage market and the trend of declining interest rates generally."

Mr Ashley-Brown added that this was the second reduction in the home mortgage rate in the past 12 months.

Fine for newspapers, but this rewrite would be much better for broadcast:

JOHANNESBURG – The home mortgage rate is coming down. Chartered Bank today announced it was lowering its home mortgage rate to 16 per cent from 17 per cent, effective immediately.

Bank President John Ashley-Brown said the move was taken because of competition and the general trend of declining interest rates.

This is the second reduction in Chartered Bank's home mortgage rate in 12 months.

Making the effort to tailor your release specifically for broadcasters' needs will pay off. Recently, I received the type of fax from Radio Good Hope's Programme Manager, Nico de Kock, which is a rarity for any public relations practitioner. It began like this:

It was indeed a pleasure to receive a news release in true radio style. I could not miss it and had great joy in scheduling it for broadcast.

Here are some factors I consider when preparing releases for broadcast:

8.5.1 Format

Your release is written for three audiences:
- The editor, whom you have to convince of its importance.
- The audience, whom you have to inform and, when appropriate, entertain.
- The news reader, for whom the information must be clearly set out.

To accomplish these goals you can apply the basic directives for press releases, with the following exceptions:

• *Public service announcements*

This type of announcement (e.g. a fundraising walk for the Cancer Society) is likely to be used more than once. Indicate *start* and *stop* dates.

• *Length*

Keep it *very* short. Broadcast news items seldom exceed 30 seconds; most are between 10 and 20 seconds long. At an average reading speed of 10 words per four seconds, a release should contain between 25 and 70 words.

- *Margins*
For radio releases set your margins to allow for a 75-character line, which should give you about 10 words per line (when writing in English). This will allow you to calculate the length of your release easily, without counting every word. A 20-second release, for example, will be five lines long.

- *Word breaks*
Never break a word at the end of a line or sentence at the end of a page. This is likely to make the newsreader pause at an unnatural place in the story.

- *Word count and estimated time*
Put the number of words and estimated time under the headline. Your time may be slightly off, but professional newsreaders will know how many words they read per minute.

- *Visuals*
If you are sending out a visual with your release to a television station, set your left margin to allow for a 35-character space. This will allow about five words, or two seconds per line. On the right, include a brief description of the visual (see figure 8.2).

FIGURE 8.2 The layout of a broadcast news release with visuals

```
            GARDENS PRESERVATION LEAGUE GET NATIONAL GRANT
                         (70 words; 30 seconds)

                         [EDITOR: set column to 35]

        Video                Audio

    Slide No 1           Today national recognition came to the
    (Exterior:           Gardens Preservation League's restor-
    Orange House)        ation of the Orange House. The Pretoria-
                         based National Trust for Historic
                         Preservation has awarded an R8 000 grant
                         to the volunteer group. The grant will
                         be used to fund an architect who will
    Slide No 2           prepare restoration plans for the 170-
    (Interior,           year-old Cape Town house. Following its
    Charter house;       restoration, the Orange House will be
    architect            sold to a new owner who will guarantee its
    measuring room)      future preservation.   -30-
```

- *Add print release*

A broadcast release is usually shorter than a print release. It is therefore a good idea to attach the print release to provide the editor with more complete information.

8.5.2 Style

- *Central idea*

Decide which *single idea* you want to convey to the listener in the few seconds at your disposal and discard all extraneous information. When you listen to something – a conversation, an address or a lecture – which part is likely to stick with you? If you answered "the last bit" you are right. That is why the inverted pyramid formula is not the best approach when writing for listeners.

Unlike readers who have to focus on the copy to get the information, listeners are likely to be doing something else – driving, tanning, getting dressed or fussing in the kitchen. This means that the primary job of your introduction is to draw their attention, to get them to pause and move closer to the radio.

Once you have their attention, you can move into the story. End by clearly stating the single idea you would like them to remember. Consider this example:

> If you've got a thing about creepy crawlies and the thought of stepping on a snake makes you sick, then spare a thought for John Preston from Pretoria.
>
> John's going to be surrounded by snakes ... many of them poisonous ... for up to a fortnight. He's planning to sit crosslegged in a three by four metre tank with more than 40 serpents to keep him company in a bid to break the world record for snake-sitting.

Now, cover the report with a piece of paper and answer the following questions:
- What is the person's name?
- Where does he come from?
- How many snakes will keep him company?
- How big is the tank?
- Why will he be doing it?

Quite likely you had some difficulty finding the answers to the first four questions, but I am sure you remembered straight away the guy was trying to break the world record for snake-sitting. (For a more accurate experiment, simulate a broadcast by reading the report to a friend and then ask him to answer the five questions.)

Broadcast writers often express the formula used above like this:
Tell 'em you're gonna tell 'em
Tell 'em you're telling 'em
And then tell 'em you've told 'em.

• *Immediacy*

One of the greatest strengths of broadcasting is its immediacy. Capitalize on this attribute by writing in the present or present perfect tense.

Past In Cape Town, a leading anti-apartheid activist escaped unharmed yesterday after an assassination attempt . . .

Present perfect In Cape Town today, a leading anti-apartheid activist has escaped unharmed following an assassination attempt . . .

Present In Cape Town police are searching for the gunman who fired three shots narrowly missing a leading anti-apartheid activist . . .

• *Punctuation*

Remember listeners and viewers cannot see the text. Therefore you should avoid all punctuation except for fullstops and the occasional comma. This will affect the way you structure the information.

Consider this statement:

A Zambian government official, said a South African diplomat, was pressuring foreign businessmen to relocate urban factories to rural sites.

If you were listening to it – without *seeing* the punctuation – the meaning conveyed would be quite different.

• *Use simple, declarative sentences*

The following sentence is awkward and overdramatic:

After struggling for three hours to free the mangled body from the shattered truck, firemen said the horrific crash was one of the worst they had seen in their lives.

This would be better:

Firemen with steel cutters took three hours to free the body from the wreckage. They said it was one of the worst crashes they had ever seen.

- *Numbers and statistics should be rounded off*
Nobody will remember this example of bad luck:
  A Cape Town man lost R997,983 in a three-day gambling binge at Sun City.

But stated this way, the point is certainly made:
  A Cape Town man lost nearly a million rand during a three-day gambling binge at Sun City.

- *Attribution should precede a quote*
Marketing Department director Mike du Plessis says: "The Cape Technikon is ready for the future."
  Especially in contentious statements, the attribution cannot – and should not – be held back until the second sentence:
  South African students are a shiftless, lazy bunch of spongers who should be forced to sweep the streets until they find a decent job. So said Minister Frankie Veldman at a news conference . . .

The first sentence turned a highly debatable assertion into a statement of fact, and the danger is that the audience may miss the attribution that follows (because another driver hoots, the phone is ringing or the kettle is boiling) and identify the opinion with the newsreader.
  Careful attribution is crucial where facts asserted are still to be proved.

- *Avoid direct quotes*
Direct quotes often complicate sentences unnecessarily – remember the listener cannot see punctuation marks. It is therefore better to paraphrase.

- *Pronunciation*
If your release contains names or words the newsreader may find difficult to pronounce, add the phonetic symbols in parenthesis. The *Associated Press Broadcast Stylebook* recommends a system based on the familiar principles of English usage with respect to the sounds of vowels and consonants, for example:
  Guatanama (Gwhan-tah'-nah-moh)
  Feisal (Fy'sal)

Note that the apostrophe is used to show where the accent falls. The following should cover most contingencies:

ah	pronounced like the a in arm
a	pronounced like the a in apple
eh	pronounced like the air in air
ay	pronounced like the a in ace

e	pronounced like the e in bed
ee	pronounced like the ee in feel
i	pronounced like the i in tin
y	pronounced like the i in time
oh	pronounced like the o in go
oo	pronounced like the oo in pool
uh	pronounced like the u in puff
khg	guttural
zh	pronounced like the g in rouge
j	pronounced like the second g in George
tho	pronounced like the x in Xhosa

The symbol "ow" is sometimes misunderstood, since it can be pronounced as in "how" or as in "tow". Therefore, it may be necessary to specify some pronunciations like this: "Blough (rhymes with how)".

8.5.3 Media kits

Media kits are often distributed in conjunction with an announcement or media conference. To be effective they must be easy to use and contain the right amount of information. Take care not to overwhelm the journalists.

PR practitioners should never turn media kits into some kind of lucky dip for journalists by including superfluous back editions of the company house journal and excessive corporate gifts. Stick to the basics listed below:

• *A programme of events*

If the media kit is issued to back a media conference, it is good practice to provide the journalist with a programme so that she can plan her day. Journalists are usually strapped for time and may only be able to stay for certain relevant aspects of your programme.

• *A well-written release*

Although the journalist will probably write his own report, it is a good idea to include a well-written release. If the reporter is pushed for time, he just might use it or, at the very least, it could influence him to use the news angle you prefer.

• *Copies of all speeches*

Most journalists like to follow what the speaker is saying and mark pertinent sections for later use. Copies of speeches also greatly reduce the risk of misquoting.

• *CV and biographies*

These are often referred to as a "bio" and recount pertinent facts about an individual. Most companies keep a file of bios of all top officers. When writing a straight bio use the inverted pyramid formula (chapter 4), with company information preceding personal details.

Narrative bios are written in a breezier style and will often include comments by colleagues about the person, as well as anecdotes.

A short, quarter-page curriculum vitae of each speaker is often useful, but be sure to emphasise why the speaker is pertinent to the occasion.

- *Backgrounders*

In essence, backgrounders are bios of companies. They are provided to give journalists a better understanding of the organization's structure, activities and history. Backgrounders are seldom used in their entirety, i.e. they are usually excerpted.

- *Fact sheets*

These are short – usually one page long – profiles of a person, organization or event. Fact sheets, with information listed in points under headings, are helpful to journalists who need quick access to additional material for articles.

- *Visuals*

Fraser Seitel (Director: Public Affairs, Chase Manhattan Bank) says: "Visually arresting graphics may mean the difference between finding the item in the next day's paper or in the same day's wastebasket" (*The practice of public relations*, p. 223). When appropriate, include graphics or photographs – with captions. One good visual with an extended caption is often more effective than pages of copy.

If you are operating on a limited budget – and time permits – send a page with photocopies of available photographs and phone the editors to ask which picture they would like to use.

- *Additional information*

Additional information like brochures, house jounals and annual reports should only be included when they are relevant and have a direct bearing on the content of the annoucement.

8.5.4 Working with the press

Once a release has been written and checked for errors, the task of getting it into the right person's hands remains. The following pointers may be helpful to this end.

127

- *Direct the release at the right person*
Most TV and radio stations have a news director, and all news releases should be addressed to him. Newspapers, however, are more complicated since various section editors may be interested in the news you have to offer. The following guidelines may prove helpful.

Releases aimed at a single topic (such as food or sports) should go to that section editor. If the release is of general local interest, the news editor is usually the right person for it. If one reporter covers your organization all the time, send the release directly to her.

- *When should you send a release?*
Send the release as soon as possible once the story has broken and deliver it by hand if at all feasible. Releases announcing upcoming events can be mailed one week in advance.

Keep in mind that the deadline schedules of weekly papers differ from those of dailies. You must know the deadlines in order to get the release delivered on time. The deadline of a weekly published on Thursdays may be as early as Monday.

Raymond Joseph of the *Sunday Times* office in Cape Town makes this important point: "It's not the best story and picture that makes the paper. It's the best story and picture available at the moment."

- *Exclusive stories*
The media is a competitive business environment and all journalists love scoops. If you have a good relationship with an editor in your target area, you may consider giving her an exclusive story. Never lie about giving a scoop though. You are likely to harm your relationship with an editor who expects to be running an exclusive, which she then also sees in a rival publication.

- *Press events*
Never call a press conference if a simple news release will do. News people are usually strapped for time and resent being called from their offices, getting into their cars, hunting for parking, traipsing off to a room and waiting for someone to read a statement which could just as well have been faxed or mailed.

The only reason to have a press conference is to provide an authority who will respond to journalists' questions about a complex matter or to exhibit something which cannot be satisfactorily displayed in a photograph, such as extensive restorations to a historic site.

FIGURE 8.3 A sample print news release

Cape
Kaapse
Technikon

P.O. Box 652, Cape Town 8000
Posbus 652, Kaapstad 8000

Contact: Willemien Law:
460-3257, 8:30-4:30
913-3977, evenings

Longmarket Street Cape Town 8001
Langmarkstraat Kaapstad 8001
Telegrams . TECCOM . Telegramme
Telex . 5-21666 . Teleks
Telefax (021) 461-7564
Tel.: 461-6220 Main
Tel.: 460-3911 Zonnebloem

FOR RELEASE: 14 October, or thereafter

YOUNG MARKETER OF THE YEAR - CAPE TECHNIKON

A 23-year-old Capetonian with a flair for computers, penchant for history and a seven-handicap golf record will be named the Cape Technikon's Young Marketer of the Year at a breakfast at Captain Granger's Restaurant, Granger Bay, 8:30 a.m. Thursday, 14 October.

Patrick Hall of Rosebank will receive his trophy and cash prize from Mr Louis Stander, senior manager of product marketing at Nasionale Tydskrifte, the competition's sponsor. ''This very prestigious award recognizes the Cape Technikon and career-oriented technikon education. We are doing the job industry wants,'' said Mr Mike du Plessis, associate director of the Cape Technikon's Marketing Department.

''What made Patrick Hall unique is that he ensured that his education was worthwhile by grabbing the opportunity with both hands to do his cooperative training in the marketing of information technology in the US. He deserves to win.''

On December 2, Mr Hall will compete with other third-year marketing students from technikons around the country for the national title. And Mr Du Plessis believes Hall, who matriculated from Michaelhouse in Natal, stands a good chance of bringing the award back to the Cape Technikon.

In 1989 Mr Les Herring, an entrepreneur who owns Herald Motors in Mainland, became this technikon's first national winner in the 10-year-old contest. The national competition evolved from a competition Nasionale Tydskrifte ran from 1983-85 exclusively for Cape Technikon students.

-end-

FOR: Editor, THE TATTLER
     13 October 1993

FOR MORE INFORMATION PLEASE CONTACT:

Mike du Plessis, Cape Technikon: 460-3257, 8:30-4:30, weekdays
Patrick Hall: 889-1340

FIGURE 8.4   A sample broadcast news release

**Cape
Kaapse
Technikon**

P.O. Box 652, Cape Town 8000
Posbus 652, Kaapstad 8000

Longmarket Street Cape Town 8001
Langmarkstraat Kaapstad 8001
Telegrams . TECCOM . Telegramme
Telex . 5-21666 . Teleks
Telefax (021) 461-7564
Tel.: 461-6220 Main
Tel.: 460-3911 Zonnebloem

Contact: Willemien Law:
460-3257, 8:30-4:30
913-3977, evenings

START TIME: 10 a.m. Oct. 14

<u>MARKETING AWARD FOR CAPE TECHNIKON STUDENT</u>
(80 words; 30 seconds)

A 23-year-old Capetonian with a flair for computers and a seven-handicap golf record is the Cape Technikon's Young Marketer of the Year for 1993. Patrick Hall today received his trophy from Nasionale Tydskrifte who sponsor the competition. In December Hall will compete against winners from other technikons for the national title. The technikons' marketing department head Mr Mike du Plessis said the Young Marketer of the Year award showed technikons were doing the job industry wants.

-30-

FOR MORE DETAILS CONTACT:

Mike du Plessis: 460-3257, 8:30-4:30,
                 weekdays
Patrick Hall: 887-345, evenings

Even on such occasions, be sure not to waste time. *Successful Salesmanship* editor Linda Trump notes that many PR practitioners ply the news media with invitations to social occasions and gifts "assuming that journalists simply love the distraction of breakfasts, cocktail parties, tennis matches, and the like" (*Rhodes University Journalism Review*, Dec. 1991, p. 23). Trump recounts the following anecdote:

> At a recent meeting I attended, a prominent financial editor deliberately arrived late and then interrupted lengthy introductions by stating, "Who cares who I am? Just get to the point and tell us why you dragged us out here in the first place."

Of course, the issue becomes an ethical one when showing the press common courtesies crosses the line into bribery (see chapter 11).

Fussing over minor mistakes

There is one thing that irritates journalists more than making errors and that is having someone point it out to them. Do not pester the media and make a fuss over small mistakes, but do not hesitate to request a correction when a significant error appears in print.

Please note that assignments start on p. 132.

Assignments

1. Refer to the news release in figure 8.5. If you were an editor, would you use it? Can you spot any errors?

FIGURE 8.5 A news release

MEDIA RELEASE

Witblits one

WITBLITS AND MAMPOER - A CULTURAL INHERITANCE

24 June 1992

EMBARGO: 12:00 25 June 1993

Moonshine, white smoke or white lightning, call it what you will, witblits and mampoer are as much a part of South African folklore as biltong and waatlemoenkonfyt.

Witblits is as old as South African viticulture itself and its origins can be traced back to the 17th century when Cape Brandy, as it was known in those days, was given to labourers as part of their daily ration. When the Voortrekkers packed their trunks for the trek over the Drakensberg, they took their witblits with them. They called it Cape Smoke.

Mampoer on the other hand is a truely Transvaal tradition. It owes its existence to Mampuru, a Npedi Chieftain from the Marico district who discovered that if you distilled fruit in a certain way its juice developed more than just an extra kick. Today modern distillers use a variety of fruits including peaches, apricots, cherries, apples, oranges and figs to produce their legendary liquor.

At Loopspruit, KwaNdebele, cellar master BW Myburgh distills witblits and mampoer according to time honoured tradition.

Distilling witblits and mampoer is time consuming and it takes a lot of fruit to produce only a few bottles of spirit.

First the fruit is put into stainless steel tanks to ferment for 8 to 20 days. It is then transferred to a traditional red copper still for the first of three distillation processes required to produce the final product.

Distilling witblits and mampoer is an art. To start off with, the fire under the still must be carefully regulated so as to ensure that the fruit (or mos) at the bottom of the still does not burn and ruin the brew.

Once all the alcohol has been extracted from the mos the still is cleaned thoroughly before the spirit is distilled for a second time.

more

Not all the spirit that is extracted during this second round is acceptable either. Only the so called middelloop - the spirit that is drawn off after the process has been running for about 20 minutes is deemed to be pure enough. The voorloop, distilled during the first 20 minutes and the naloop or the last third of the spirit to be distilled are then mixed and distilled once again.

Witblits was first produced at Loopspruit by ex-policeman Eric Olivier who planted the first bushveld vineyards in 1969. The original still is still used at Loopspruit today.

Loopspruit Wine Cellar, the northern most registered wine estate in Southern Africa is situated in KwaNdebele less than an hour's drive from Pretoria and is fast becoming one of the region's best known tourist attractions.

Besides witblits and mampoer Loopspruit produces an exquisite range of white wines, including sparkling wines, Blanc de Noir, Grand Vin Blanc and the Hanepoot dessert wines.

The estate offers daily wine tastings and cellar tours while traditional lunches are available if bookings are made in advance.

Cellar Master BW Myburgh, whose wine making roots lie in Stellenbosch and Oudtshoorn, has produced some exceptional wines which have received a number of top awards at major South African wine shows. In 1990 the Hanepoot Jerepico received a gold medal at the South African Championships. At the 1991 Young Wine Show Loopspruit won a gold medal for its Late Harvest, while the Grand vin Blanc and Vin de Noir won silver and bronze medals respectively.

Since 1985 the estate has been managed by the KwaNdebele Agricultural Company (KLM), a subsidiary company of the KwaNdebele National Development Corporation (KNDC).

ends

ISSUED BY: Bureau for Communication Services
KwaNdebele National Development Corporation
Moloto Rd
KwaMhlanga
KwaNdebele

CONTACT: Eddie Ward
Senior Manager: Bureau for
Communication Services: KNDC
Tel: (01215) 2331
Fax: (01215) 2231

2. Design a media campaign for a campus group (club, organisation, team). Your portfolio should include:

   2.1 Project goals
   - State what image the group would like to project, based on an interview with the leaders.
   - List the group's weaknesses and strengths.
   - Clearly state the goal(s) for this campaign.
   - Briefly explain why each target publication was chosen.

   2.2 A media kit
   - A one page fact sheet about your group (include history, goals, membership requirements, leadership, contact persons and their details).
   - A backgrounder or bio.
   - Four news releases targeting an internal publication (a house journal or student newspaper), an external publication, a radio station and a television station.

Bibliography and recommended reading

Bates, Stephen, *If no news, send rumors: anecdotes of American journalism*, New York, St Martin's, 1989.

Baxter, Bill L., "The news release: an idea whose time has gone?", *Public Relations Review*, Spring 1981, p. 30.

Bruderer, Walter, "Ensuring your press release gets published", *Business Day*, 22 July 1993, p. 4.

Hood, James, (ed), *Associated Press broadcast stylebook including the Associated Press libel manual*, New York, 1982.

SABC, *Radio & TV*, July/Sept. 1993, pp. 53–4.

Seitel, Fraser P., *The practice of public relations*, 5th ed., New York, Macmillan, 1992.

Trump, Linda, "Pr should sell, not tell", *Rhodes University Journalism Review*, Dec. 1991, pp. 23–4.

PART 2

MAKING IT LOOK RIGHT, TOO

DESIGNING FOR CHANGE

By Patti McDonald

The eighties saw a revolution happen in the world of printed media – desktop publishing. For a comparatively small amount of money, designers and journalists had the facility to write, edit and design publications in-house using personal computers and outputting fully made-up pages. These were heady days. Out went drawing boards, scalpels, reams of paper and the few remaining typewriters. Design became an exciting, flexible process as images were integrated with text and type was expanded and distorted with incredible effect – all in a matter of minutes.

But, as with all revolutions, there are many lessons to be learned. Designers and typographers, who themselves had no computer training, shuddered in horror as the "bright young things" of journalism (with no design training) churned out publications which broke all the typographic rules. Creative times countered by a lost craft and insensitive design – we have all seen it: seven different typefaces on one page, random use of point sizes, leading and, worst of all, the outlined, extra-bold, italicised, reversed out "word". There were some exceptions: Talented young artists like Nevill Brody, designer of *Face* and *Arena* magazines, flourished with tools like DTP. (When he was 31, the Victoria and Albert Museum held a single retrospective of Brody's work as a tribute to the impact of his creativity.)

The new technology not only affected the printed page, but also those who had traditionally done the printing. In Britain, where I was living at the time, the press barons took on the typographic unions – the guys who typeset and stripped-up the news pages. Who needed them when sub-editors could generate the whole page at his or her computer terminal? Craftspeople, each with a lifetime of typographic experience, joined the job queues.

As a designer with a great respect and love for typography (after all, the typographers of the past had painstakingly created every letter in the alphabet with aesthetic sensitivity, accuracy and diversity in the medium of wood and later metal), I was torn. The DTP design programmes allowed me endless creative experimentation in relatively little time. But the bitter battles fought on picket lines all around Britain over the loss of a craft tempered my glowing response to the advancement of technology.

Only when I returned to South Africa and in 1992 joined the *Sowetan* newspaper did I see how this new technology could benefit not only news pages, but also newspaper workers.

The *Sowetan*, headed by Rory Wilson, managing director, Aggrey Klaaste, editor, and Joe Thloloe, managing editor, had recently installed a DTP system. Management had made what seemed like an incredible pledge to the union, Media Workers Association of South Africa, that no jobs would be lost by the introduction of the new technology. The stripping-up department was divided into two groups: those who wanted to retrain in the DTP page make-up and those (many nearing retirement) who would continue to strip-up the classified pages, adverts and produce colour-separated film for plate-making. Within five years, the paper will be fully computerized and management has succeeded in keeping up with technology and because no member of staff has been threatened with redundancy, the new system is regarded as an exciting skills advancement challenge.

I was there to redesign the paper. Why redesign South Africa's largest selling paper? The *Sowetan* wanted to consolidate and expand its black readership of 1,6 million. Their biggest challenges: The majority of South Africans had been discouraged from reading by inadequate education policies and poverty created by political discrimination (both are finally beginning to change).

Also, many *Sowetan* readers travel far to exhausting jobs on overcrowded dangerous transport, in violent troubled times. They wanted news, but it needed to be portable and easily palatable – like the news on radio. Therefore, the redesign was also largely influenced by a need to compete with electronic media.

Following trends in newspaper design worldwide, we set out to create a faster, easier read. To present the gist of the days' news by a quick flick through the papers with a top of the page strap slugging the main elements on the page. The reader is then presented with more bites at each story – a headline and a key deck summarizing the story in two to three lines. A cleaner, modular page design broken down into a lead story, one or two second lead stories, newsbriefs columns, fact boxes, larger pictures, more colour and a page grid of four or five columns, instead of the traditional seven. We replaced the tired overused workhorse Helvetica with Franklin Gothic, a more readable sans serif typeface in a range of widths from extra-bold to light. We also introduced the serif typeface Plantin to the paper. Its open counters, readable x-height and simple serifs give the pages elegance and dignity.

Extensive market research before the redesign showed a need for a wider range of stories and information. More features, entertainment, life skills and sport was needed without losing the essential tie the paper has with the community, reporting news not found in the other papers with largely white readerships.

It was a nine-month process. I workshopped design principles for the new paper with sub-editors and a representative team of news, picture, production and advertising staff. Dummies of the paper were presented to them almost every week. By the time we were finally satisfied with the design solution every member of the *Sowetan* staff had been consulted and informed and their comments processed.

Then the technical process began. Creating templates for the specific pages with style sheets for different uses of type throughout the paper. Writing a house-style manual so that even a temporary sub-editor could follow the house style with ease. Writers were trained to write for the new design, photographers encouraged to be more creative and technically more competent because the pictures were being used in larger formats. A graphics designer was hired to produce information graphics and illustrations and to lend a creative hand to the sub-editors driven by deadline constraints and a bias towards the "word".

The remarkable spirit of the *Sowetan* made it the most exciting project I had ever participated in. There were no losers in the change which could have been traumatic. The unique management team pulled writers, photographers, sub-editors and administrative staff into a team. They were challenged by the project and honest enough to fight out objections to certain changes and they had the integrity to back-up a truly democratic consultation process. I believe we delivered a greatly improved product to the readers on July 7, 1992. An on-going process of design training and constant streamlining of the house style as well as further market research ensures that the paper remains dynamic.

At one of the final staff presentations, sixty-something "Baba" Dlamini, a father figure to most of the *Sowetan* staff, said, "When I was a young boy, I was forced to care for the cattle. I did not go to school for long. I only came to the city when I was much older. Then I began to learn again. You have designed a newspaper I can read as easily as those smart college boys in the newsroom and I want to thank you for that."

Patti McDonald has redesigned the *Sowetan* and *South* newspapers. She did post-graduate research on the desktop publishing phenomena while studying at the London College of Printing.

CHAPTER 9
EDITING

> *To entrust to an editor a story over which you have labored and to which your name and reputation are attached can be like sending your daughter off for an evening with Ted Bundy.*
> Edna Buchanan, *The corpse had a familiar face*, 1987, p. 263

Editing is the business of polishing. Awkward structure is fixed. Facts are checked. Missing information is questioned. Spelling and grammar are repaired.

It is a thankless job a lot of the time. There are no Pulitzer Prizes for editors. Like the rugby fullback who only gets attention when he misses a tackle, editors usually are in the spotlight only when there is a problem with a story, headline or caption.

This is why the best editors are experienced reporters who are well-informed, language experts and, as veteran editor Arthur Plotnik suggests, compulsive (*The elements of editing: a modern guide for editors and journalists*, London, Collier MacMillan, 1982, p. 1) But there is good compulsiveness and bad compulsiveness. Editors who are compulsive about the wrong things – like holding to favourite rules of usage, whatever the effect on communication make life unnecessarily tough on reporters. Just ask Edna Buchanan. Here is her opinion of editors (*The corpse had a familiar face*, pp. 263–4):

Over the past twenty years I have worked with some editors who did nothing to my stories but make them better. For the most part, editors mean well. But I always warn aspiring reporters to observe the three basic rules.
1. Never trust an editor.
2. Never trust an editor.
3. Never trust an editor.

They can be cavalier with your copy. They can embarrass you, lose you your sources, strip the best stuff out of your story, insert mistakes and misspellings, top it off with a misleading headline, and get you in trouble. For example, some editors – and even some reporters – do not know the difference between burglary and robbery. They consider the words interchangeable. They are not. It's the difference between finding a vacant space where your TV stood and meeting in person a masked man with a gun. That difference can mean as much as twenty years to the perpetrator and far more in trauma to the victim.

Buchanan's complaints about editors are not unfounded. Some editors, working on deadline and after reporters have left, make changes without consulting the writers – with disastrous results. Consider how the editors at *The Huntsville News* in Alabama felt when this item appeared on March 6, 1993:

Correction
In a letter from George Wolfe, published last Saturday, he wrote concerning gay sex incidents "per annum" but spelled it "anum". This typographical error led to our transcription as "per anus". The *News* regrets the error and is glad to set the record straight.

(*Columbia Journalism Review*, May/June 1993, p. 81)

Editors are the last defense against errors. They must not miss a tackle. And they must be compulsive about serving the readers.

"An editor edits above all to communicate to readers, and least of all to address the sensibilities of editorial colleagues," wrote Plotnik (*The elements of editing*, p. 2). He continued:

> Functional or reader-related compulsiveness is the neurotic drive enabling editors to do a full six weeks of work in a four-week cycle, month after month. It is the built-in alarm, the time-bomb system that glows red when there are omissions, delays and errors which, if not corrected, will devastate deadlines and subvert communications. In the editorial context, this type of compulsiveness is appropriate . . . but self-serving, retentive, fastidious, fetishist, and even some aesthetic and ethical types of compulsiveness have no place in mass communication under deadlines; they must be purged from news staff for the sake of the staff's longevity in the field.

> In this chapter, you will examine ways to guide editing compulsiveness in three areas:
> 1. Stories.
> 2. Headlines.
> 3. Captions.

9.1 COMPLETE, CLEAR, CORRECT – AND EXCITING – STORIES

9.1.1 Getting started

Begin editing by folding your hands.

Now, read – or at least scan – the *entire* story before you start fiddling. Get a sense of the piece and what the writer tried to do before you set about making any changes. Then, consider the first rule of editing:

Do not make major changes to the style and content of a story without consulting the writer.

The reasons for this are simple:
- Many a well-intentioned editor has inserted errors into the story by misinterpreting information or typographical errors (ask the guys at *The Huntsville News*).
- It demotivates writers. "I don't even read my stories in the paper any more," a Cape Town crime reporter told me. "Because it doesn't matter what I do, they change it anyway."

Fair enough, editors have to get the story into print on time – but they also have to coach writers about ways to avoid vague, incomplete and confusing stories in the future. Re-writing a reporter's story is only a short-term solution.

Sometimes, though, the writer is not available when the editor gets the story. That's when the second rule of editing comes into play:

If it doesn't check out, chuck it out. Remember, it is better not to print information than to print the wrong information.

9.1.2 Considering the content

Good grammar, perfect spelling and solid facts are useless if the story makes no sense. When editing a story's content, ask yourself the following questions:

Focus What is the point of the story?
Clarity Is that point spelled out in the lead or nut graph?
Information Is there enough information to back-up the point?
Logic Is the information arranged in a logical order?
Balance Are opinions clearly distinguished from fact? Is more than one side of the argument presented or at least acknowledged?
Originality Is the information fresh and the perspective innovative?

9.1.3 Matters of style

Having adequate information logically arranged is crucial to a good story. But it is not enough. Like spinach, stories are seldom consumed merely for their intrinsic value. It must taste good, too. That is the writer's challenge. Editors should ask the following:
- Is the information presented in a way that will involve the reader?
- Is the tone of writing appropriate for the intended medium?
- Does the lead draw you into the article?

- Is the lead clear?
- Has the writer used common, concrete words?
- Is the writing concise, free from needless words?
- Are the sentences instantly clear, free from confusing constructions?
- Are most of the sentences in the active voice?
- Are the sentences and ideas linked by transitions?
- Has a grammar and spelling check been carried out?
- Does the piece conform to the house style?

9.1.4 Line-by-line editing

The final step in editing is to proofread. Some editors suggest reading the piece once for sense, a second time for grammar and style concerns and finally reading the lines backwards. This, they claim, is the best way to concentrate on each word and not to get caught up in what is being written.

Although most editing is done electronically, final editing of publication proofs is usually done by hand. Using the marks depicted in figure 9.1 will ensure that your printer understands what you want.

FIGURE 9.1 Standard proofreading marks

Instruction	Textual mark	Marginal mark
Insert in text the matter indicated in margin	ʌ	*New matter followed by* /
Delete	Strike through characters to be deleted	♂
Delete and close up	Strike through characters to be deleted and use close-up sign	♂
Leave as printed	..... under characters to remain	stet
Change to italic	——— under characters to be altered	*ital*
Change to even small capitals	═══ under characters to be altered	s.c.
Change to capital letters	≡≡≡ under characters to be altered	caps

EDITING

Instruction	Textual mark	Marginal mark
Use capital letters for initial letters and small capitals for rest of words	≡≡≡ under initial letters and ═══ under the rest of the words	c.&s.c.
Change to bold type	∿∿∿ under characters to be altered	bold
Change to lower case	Encircle characters to be altered	l.c.
Change to roman type	Encircle characters to be altered	rom
Wrong fount. Replace by letter of correct fount	Encircle character to be altered	w.f.
Invert type	Encircle character to be altered	↺
Change damaged character(s)	Encircle character(s) to be altered	×
Substitute or insert character(s) under which this mark is placed, in "superior" position	/ through character or ∧ where required	⌐ under character (e.g. $\frac{x}{\gamma}$)
Substitute or insert character(s) over which this mark is placed, in "inferior" position	/ through character or ∧ where required	∧ over character (e.g. $\hat{x}$)
Use ligature (e.g. ffi) or diphthong (e.g. œ)	⌒ enclosing letters to be altered	⌒ enclosing ligature or diphthong required
Close up – delete space between characters	⌣ linking characters	⌣
Insert space	⋏	#
Insert space between lines or paragraphs	> between lines to be spaced	#

145

Instruction	Textual mark	Marginal mark
Reduce space between lines	(connecting lines to be closed up	less #
Make space appear equal between words	| between words	eq #
Reduce space between words	| between words	less #
Add space between letters	between tops of letters requiring space	letter #
Transpose	⎣⎤ between characters or words, numbered when necessary	trs
Place in centre of line	Indicate position with ⌐ ¬	centre
Indent one em	⌐	□
Indent two ems	⌐⌐	⊏⊐
Move matter to right	⌐ at left side of group to be moved	⌐
Move matter to left	⌐ at right side of group to be moved	⌐
Take over character(s) or line to next line, column or page	⌐	take over
Take back character(s) or line to previous line, column or page	⌐	take back
Raise lines	↑ over lines to be moved; ⌐⌐ under lines to be moved	raise

Instruction	Textual mark	Marginal mark
Lower lines	⌐___⌐ over lines to be moved ___↓___ under lines to be moved	lower
Correct the vertical alignment	||	||
Straighten lines	≡ through lines to be straightened	≡
Push down space	Encircle space affected	⊥
Begin a new paragraph	[before first word of new paragraph	n.p.
No fresh paragraph here	⌒ between paragraphs	run on
Spell out the abbreviation or figure in full	Encircle words or figures to be altered	spell out
Insert omitted portion of copy NOTE The relevant section of the copy should be returned with the proof, the omitted portion being clearly indicated.	ʌ	out see copy
Substitute or insert comma	/ through character or ʌ where required	,/
Substitute or insert semi-colon	/ through character or ʌ where required	;/
Substitute or insert full stop	/ through character or ʌ where required	⊙
Substitute or insert colon	/ through character or ʌ where required	⊙
Substitute or insert interrogation mark	/ through character or ʌ where required	?/

Instruction	Textual mark	Marginal mark
Substitute or insert exclamation mark	/ or ∧ through character where required	!/
Insert parentheses	∧ or ∧∧	(/ /)
Insert (square) brackets	∧ or ∧∧	[/ /]
Insert hyphen	∧	/-/
Insert en (half-em) rule	∧	en or N
Insert one-em rule	∧	em or M
Insert two-em rule	∧	2em or 2M
Insert apostrophe	∧	ʼ
Insert single quotation marks	∧ or ∧∧	ʻ ʼ
Insert double quotation marks	∧ or ∧∧	" "
Insert ellipsis	∧	.../
Insert oblique stroke	∧	⊘

(Source: Judith Butcher, 1976, *Copy-editing*. Melbourne: Cambridge University Press; pp. 67–70)

Before a piece is printed, the editor (and the reporter) must ask themselves: Would I take money from my pocket and time out of my day to read this article? If the answer is "no", the job is not finished.

9.2 HEADLINES

9.2.1 Choosing a style

The best stories in the world are worthless if no one reads them. The job of selling the story falls, in large part, to the headline.

Choosing the right words is difficult, and the headline writer's job is further complicated by space and design requirements. Sometimes there is only enough space for two or three words to a line, or maybe half a dozen words for headlines that are stacked several column lines deep. Editors must also decide if they want to use all capitals or caps and lowercase. These are the basic combinations:

- *All caps*
ANOTHER STUDENT VANISHES FROM WITS CAMPUS

Tests show that all-caps headlines are difficult to read (Harris, Julian *et al.*, *The complete reporter*, New York, Macmillan, 1981, p. 448). However, some newspapers still use all-caps headlines.

- *Caps and lowercase*
The standard style is to capitalize only the first letter of each word:
US Under Pressure Over Somalia Role

Another headline style requires that conjunctions, prepositions and definite and indefinite articles also be in lowercase.

- *Down style*
This is a popular contemporary option, where only the first word and proper names are capitalized:
Nothing to celebrate on this Labour Day

9.2.2 Headline designs
"Simplicity" is the buzzword in modern design. For headline writers this means shorter main heads and fewer, if any, secondary headlines. Some newspapers avoid stacked headlines entirely. Most headlines are simply one line and flushed left.

This is not just an aesthetic decision. Edmund Arnold, whose *Modern Newspaper Design* is something of a Bible in the field, says: "To the best of the knowledge that we have at this time, flush-left setting is the most effective for heads, for it is based on the instinctive pattern when the reading eye moves."

The following headline designs can be used:

- *Flush left*

Headline type is aligned with the left-hand margin of the column:

```
XXXXX
XXXXXXXX
XXXXXXXXXXXXX
```

- *Flush right*

Type is aligned with the right-hand edge of the column. The result is a ragged left edge, which can be difficult to read:

```
                                    XXXXX
                  XXXXXXXXXXXXXXXXXXXXX
                       XXXXXXXXXXXXXXX
```

- *Centred*

Each line of type is centred in the column with an equal amount of space on each side. Often, centred heads are arranged in pyramid form:

```
         XXXXXXXXXXXXXXXXXXX
             XXXXXXXXXXX
               XXXXXXX
```

- *Drop or stepped lines*

Two or three lines of approximately the same length are arranged with the first line flushed left, the last one flushed right and the centre line (if any) centred:

```
XXXXXXXXXXXXXXXXXXXX
      XXXXXXXXXXXXXXXXXXXX
            XXXXXXXXXXXXXXXXXXXX
```

• *Hanging indents*
The first line is flush left and the others, of equal length, are indented at the same space:

```
XXXXXXXXXXXXXXXXXXXXXXXXXX
   XXXXXXXXXXXXXXXXXXXXXX
   XXXXXXXXXXXXXXXXXXXXXX
   XXXXXXXXXXXXXXXXXXXXXX
```

• *Kickers*
Some headlines are written with secondary headlines or kickers above the main headline:

```
xxxxxxxxxxxxxx
XXXX XXXXXXXXX
```

• *Reverse kickers*
In these headlines the subsidiary line is run below the main headline. For a story about an 80-year old man who killed his dying wife before turning the gun on himself, *The Miami Herald* used a reverse kicker (24 March 1992, p. 1):

'Two little bullets'
Tamarac man meticulous in planning deaths

9.2.3 Principles of headline writing

A headline, advises Arthur Plotnik *(The elements of editing*, p. 6), should let the reader know how the story differs from previous stories on similar topics, and arouse the reader's interest anew.

In Cape Town, known as the Cape of Storms, the headline "Storm lashes Cape" (*Cape Times*, 8 July 1993, p. 1) arouses only a sense of *déjà vu*. And it does little to sell a story which starts this way:

> The storm-bruised Cape Peninsula continued to be lashed by gale force winds and rain that have already claimed the life of a father of two, ripped tiles off roofs, uprooted trees and kept fishing trawlers in the harbour.
>
> And the storm, with winds gusting to up 70 knots, is showing no sign of abating.
>
> A weather forecaster at D.F. Malan airport said last night that more cold fronts, accompanied by strong winds, are expected today.

Of course, the story has its own problems. Not the least of which is that the lead contains not a single item of information that would have been new to Cape Town readers, experiencing the third day of the storm for themselves; the man had died two days earlier and it is unlikely Capetonians would have needed to read the newspaper to tell them the stormy weather had continued.

The headline "Storm forecast: more ahead" zooms in on the latest information – the news – and summarizes the story.

But, there is something far worse than an unimaginative headline: a dishonest one.

"Death in the suburbs" might be a technically correct way of summarizing a story about a dog's untimely death under a car wheel. But it is an exaggeration. If a reader feels cheated by a headline, he – like any other customer – is likely to think twice before buying the publication again. Rule: do not cry wolf.

Each headline writer develops his own techniques, but there are some general principles. Some of the following are pointed out by Julian Harris *et al.* in their book, *The complete reporter* (pp. 451–2):

- Headlines should be a complete sentence with the unnecessary words omitted:
  Poor: Man sustains fatal injury
  Better: Guard killed in gun fight

- If a headline is stacked, each deck must be a full statement and stand alone:
  Poor: HUGE OIL SLICK
  100 MILES LONG
  Reported by
  Navy Ship
  Better: HUGE OIL SLICK
  THREAT TO COAST
  covers 100 miles,
  reports Navy

- Do not repeat a thought or word:
  Poor: THE MAD WORLD OF
          PETROL ECONOMICS
          Petrol pricing
          confuses consumers
  Better: THE MAD WORLD OF
          PETROL ECONOMICS
          a pricing guide for
          confused consumers

- Include a verb so that the headline does not appear merely as a label. The verb should be in the first line if possible, but a heading should not start with a verb:
  Poor: New highway
  Better: New highway opens

  Poor: Planned food scheme for city's needy
  Better: Food scheme planned for city's needy

- Use the active voice for impact:
  Poor: Strikers warned by Minister
  Better: Minister warns Strikers

- Use specific language:
  Poor: Youth injured in knife battle
  Better: Youth slashed in knife fight

- Use single quotation marks in headlines:
  Poor: "Heaven help us"
  Better: 'Heaven help us'

- Avoid using acronyms. Brevity is important, but do not compromise clarity. A headline like 'T.E.C.: IMF A.S.A.P' might save space, but few people will understand it. Only use the most common acronyms. Definitely do not use acronyms that have been in common use for less than a year.

- Words, phrases consisting of nouns and adjective modifiers, prepositional phrases and verb phrases should not be split between lines:
  Poor: Council passes sales tax despite protest
  Better: Sales tax passes despite protest

- Opinion headlines should be attributed or qualified
  Poor: Taxes too high on business
  Better: Taxes too high say businessmen

9.3 CAPTIONS

9.3.1 Caption copy

Writing captions (sometimes called cutlines) is an art. According to *The Associated Press Stylebook*, the reason so few journalists master the skill is because, for the most part, so little time is spent at it (Goldstein, Norman, *The Associated Press stylebook and libel manual*, p. 268).

But writing good captions is no mystery. Following a few basic rules (listed below), together with a touch of writing flair, can produce readable and informative captions.

- Captions aim to supplement and even explain the pictures, but they should not repeat obvious information in the photograph.

  For a photograph of a rock star on stage, *Time* magazine editors wrote (1 March 1993, p. 57):
  KNOCKOUT: Jagger mixes shin-splitting rock 'n roll with quiet surprises.

  Do not write:
  Mick Jagger plays his guitar

- While brevity is essential, captions should not be telegraphic and omit words that are important for smooth reading.

- Tense is important. Captions should be in the present tense even though the publication date may be different from the picture's action. The photograph captured a moment and froze the action.
  Write: Chief Mangosutho Buthelezi tells a crowd at . . .
  Not: Chief Mangosutho Buthelezi told a crowd at . . .

- People in the pictures should be identified by their full names and some description.

- Subjects should be identified as to their position in the picture, because many readers will probably not know them well enough to recognize them.

- When a story accompanies the photograph, the caption should not repeat lengthy facts from the article: captions are not expected to be a summary, but a supplement. However, readers should not have to read the story before they understand the significance of the photograph; people are more likely to look at a newspaper photograph than to read the copy. Photographs are usually the point of entry into the story, not the reverse.

- The caption's mood should match that of the picture. For a photo of the rocky cliffs at Chapman's Peak, *Travel & Leisure* magazine wrote (December 1992, p. 121):
  On the Indian Ocean coast, surf-sun rocks alternate with broad vanilla beaches – the beautiful face of a troubled and disturbing land.

  Do not write:
  Waves crash on the rocks at Hout Bay outside Cape Town.

  Similarly, the caption to a tragic photograph should be sober and factual; a picture of a happy scene calls for lighter lines.

- Be careful with cuteness. Magazines, especially, often use puns in their headlines. Consider these examples from the May 1993 issue of *Vanity Fair*:
  'Turns it On!' – about rock diva Tina Turner.
  'Mail Bonding' – the letters column.
  'The Heidi Chronicle' – about former stunt woman Heidi von Beltz.
  'Miami Vices' – about a new book on unethical police investigators.
  'King Kung' – about the star of a movie on the life of Kung Fu legend Bruce Lee.

  But poor puns are not funny – at best they are irritating, at worst they are insulting, both to the readers and the subject of the photograph. Take this *Sunday Times Magazine* caption (20 June 1993, p. 14), for a picture of actress Sharon Stone:
  Phew! Instinct tells me Sharon Stone enjoys showing off the kind of see-through outfits that tend to prove that, basically, she's not always as transparent as some critics would like to believe.

  Well-timed humour can be used very successfully in captions. But avoid childishness when writing for adults. The challenge is to be interesting, accurate and in good taste.

- A good rule of thumb is: if a story can be told by a photograph and a caption, it should be – and the article can be cut.

9.3.2 The format

Captions, like stories, follow a variety of formats. Let us take a look at a standard approach:

BLIND COURAGE: Sarah Johnson, 54, with her twin sons Mike, left, and Manie this week in Cape Town. Sarah, who has been blind since she was 30, reached the summit of Table Mountain during a recent expedition with her two sons. (Photo by Kim Smith.)

The various parts of the caption are as follows:

- "Blind Courage"

The overline. A few bright words to draw the reader's attention and put across the point of the picture. Use verbs in overlines, avoid labels and dull phrases.

- "Sarah Johnson, 54, with her twin sons Mike, left, and Manie . . ."

When there are more than two people in the picture, identifying one as "left" and the other as "centre" leaves the understanding that the third person is the one at the right. In the example above, Sarah is in the centre of the picture and is obviously the focus of the picture, and there is unlikely to be confusion since she is also the only woman.

If there are a number of people in a photograph and they are roughly in a line, a convenient way to identify them is "from left", followed by their names. For example:

> Registering for classes at the Cape Technikon are, from left, Daniella Arendse, Michael Truter, Salome Ries and Handri Bouwer.

When there are several rows, continue with the "from left" format, but break down the identification to front, centre and back rows. Start with the front row since readers usually focus there first.

Occasionally – thanks to inventive photographers – the subjects in a group are roughly in a circle. A helpful way to identify the people is to say "clockwise, beginning at the top with . . ." Readers, asked to examine the photograph as they would a clock, usually expect to begin at "12 o'clock".

- "(Photo by Kim Smith.)"

Photographers get credit-lines the way reporters get by-lines. Publications vary in their policy on giving credit and, at some house journals and newspapers, the sources are not credited at all, or only receive credit for exceptional work.

- Typography and layout

Many publications choose to set captions in italics, boldface or a font that is different from the body type.

Credit lines can be set with the rest of the caption; however, some publications choose to set them in very small type (4 or 6 point) and place them directly below the photograph.

> Ten tests of a good caption
> 1. Is it complete?
> 2. Does it identify, fully and clearly?
> 3. Does it tell when?
> 4. Does it tell where?
> 5. Does it tell what is in the picture?
> 6. Does it have the names spelled correctly, with the proper names on the right person?
> 7. Is it specific?
> 8. Is it easy to read?
> 9. Have as many adjectives as possible been removed?
> 10. Does it suggest another picture?

Source: N. Goldstein, *The Associated Press stylebook and libel manual*, p. 268.

Then there is a last rule, never to be violated:

> Rule no. 11: the cardinal rule
>
> Never write a caption without seeing the picture first.

Assignments

1. Edit the following news item down to 150 words using proofreading marks:

   A strike by 2,500 workers at 3 Da Gama textile plants in the eastern Cape is adding fuel to the call for a National industrial Council in the Textile Industry.

   The South African Clother and Textile Workers Union (SACTWU) this week pointed out that there are hguge wage discrepancies in the industry and thatt this is gicving some copmanies a unfair edge.

   As an example, Sactwu this week showed that worker of a grade at Da Game (spinners who are paid R125 a weak) earn half the wages thier colleagues on the same grade at the Frame clothing Company in Natal (R250 a week).

   Employees on strike are demading a R40 a weak increase back dated to January, a ten percent allowance on night shift and a service bonus of 50 cents a wekk for every uyear of service.

   Satcwu also claims that Da Gama's East London plant pays the lowest wages in the country and says the strike has won it new members.

Da Game financial director NIck pietersma acknowledged that the companies employees are 'paid less', yet he added: 'To the best of my knowledge we are thge only tectile company that is making money.'

2. Compare the stories about the same news event published in competing newspapers. Compare the headlines' content, size and style.

3. Using any newspaper or house journal, clip 10 headlines that violate the rules for headline writing. Rewrite them to correct the errors.

4. Select five faulty captions from a newspaper or house journal and rewrite them.

5. Cut three stories from a newspaper or house journal that might be improved by the use of pictures. Explain what type of picture you would use with each story. Write captions for each picture.

Bibliography and recommended reading

Buchanan, Edna, *The corpse had a familiar face: covering Miami, America's toughest crime beat*, New York, Random House, 1987.

Butcher, Judith, *Copy-editing*. Melbourne: Cambridge University Press, 1976.

Goldstein, Norman, *The Associated Press stylebook and libel manual*, New York, Addison-Wesley, 1992.

Harris, Julian *et al.*, *The complete reporter*, New York, Macmillan, 1981.

Plotnik, Arthur, *The elements of editing: a modern guide for editors and journalists*, London, Collier Macmillan, 1982.

CHAPTER 10
DESIGN

By François Nel and Eddie Ward

> *Art is wonderful. Craft is admirable. Design is teachable.*
> Edwin Taylor, former design director of
> the London *Sunday Times* and ex-managing editor
> of *U.S. News and World Report.*

To begin with: design is not just about how a newspaper or house journal looks. It's about what the publication is. It's about where it comes from, why and for whom it exists, and to what it aspires. These elements determine how the publication is presented to the world.

Design affects every aspect of a publication and every person in the newsroom – as *Sunday Star* editor David Hazelhurst explained after his publication was revamped in 1992 (*Rhodes Review*, Dec. 1993, p. 27):

> We decided on a total redesign. And by that I don't mean layout – we redesigned our approach to news, the way we wrote stories, the architecture of the stories, the layout, our typography, our use of colour – and we redefined news.
>
> Design wasn't there for designers; colour wasn't there to dazzle; headlines weren't there to be clever; pictures and graphics were there merely to be looked at; layout wasn't there to impress layout subs.
>
> *Design was there to get people to read the writers.* [his emphasis]
>
> The content was paramount – the rest, the candyfloss and pizazz that would get the stories read.

As with people, there are no set theories and rules on how to design perfect publications. But there are guidelines. And they are as important to the writers as they are to those responsible for the graphic elements in the publication, says internationally recognized design expert Jan V. White (*Ragged Right*, p. 6). "Tradition, bad guidance, and mis-education have propelled them [reporter and editors] into that boxed view that splits the team of communicators into two hostile camps: the word people and the visual people," White says.

"How to use design for editing? Start welding the two factions into one team, whose individual members understand how vital their shared efforts are to the success of the product's acceptance by the public."

Our objective, then, is primarily to help "word people" work better with the "visual people" – and get that "welding" started.

> In this chapter you will learn about:
> 1. Setting a design philosophy
> 2. Typography
> 3. Photographs
> 4. Modular and dynamic layout.

10.1 TOWARDS A DESIGN PHILOSOPHY

Louis Heyneman knows about design. He studied under some of the best as a graduate student at the University of Missouri and brought those ideas back and applied them as associate editor of *DeKat* magazine.

Heyneman, now head of the Oude Meester Foundation for the Performing Arts, also knows that there are no quick answers:

"Indien daar 'n waterdigte teorie sou bestaan oor hoe 'n koerant of tydskrif visueel daar moet uitsien, wat daarin moet staan, of selfs presies wat daarmee bereik moet word, sou mens dit bloot soos 'n koekresep kon toepas en die resultaat sou volmaakte tydskrifte of koerante wees."

[English translation: If a watertight theory existed on how a newspaper or magazine had to look, what had to appear in it, or exactly what it had to achieve, one would merely have to apply it like a cake recipe and the result would be a perfect magazine or newspaper.]

10.1.1 Basic guidelines

Although there are no fool-proof formulas, there are some good basic guidelines. Some of the best come from Jan V. White, whose many books on publication design include *Editing by design, Graphic design for the electronic age* and *Thoughts on publication design*.

- *What's in it for me?*

Potential readers are all looking to see if the publication has information they can use. Teaser boxes are the most obvious example of the what's-in-it-for-me factor. So are "blurbs" or story summaries, fact boxes and boxes that tell the reader the exact location, ticket and booking information (that means prices too!) and contact details of the play that is reviewed or bicycle race that is discussed. This factor is closely linked to the second one.

FIGURE 10.1 South Africa's fastest selling daily newspaper was redesigned by Patti McDonald in 1992. Among the changes McDonald made was to create a cleaner, modular page design broken down into a lead story, one or two second page lead stories, newsbriefs columns, fact boxes, larger pictures, more colour and a page grid of four or five columns, instead of the traditional seven

BEFORE

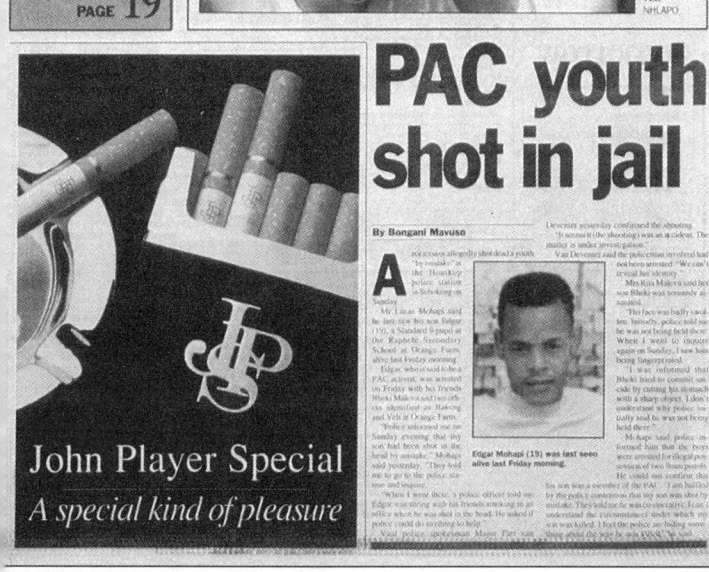

AFTER

161

- *Speed*

Many readers' attention span has been reduced to about 11 minutes – the break between television commercials. Readers want to know what's in it for them – and they want to know fast.

- *Obviousness*

This is the third crucial element. Publications must be designed and edited in a way that makes complex information simple to understand. "Information turned into visual form can be grasped faster than verbal descriptions or statistics," White says. Obviousness translates into the following elements:
— Headline typography that is bold, readable and positioned so that it shows the relative importance of the story.
— Modular page layout (see full discussion below) where stories in horizontal shapes and pictures are arranged on the page so that it is instantly clear what belongs with what, and how long an item is.
— Better cropping of pictures so that it is immediately evident what element of the picture is relevant to the story.
— Colour that is not only decorative, but helps to organize, highlight and emphasize.

- *Salesmanship*

"Readers aren't really readers," White says. "At least they don't start out as such. First they are lookers. People scan, hop and skip around, pecking here and there, searching for goodies until something catches their attention. Seldom do they start reading at the start of an article. They enter where they damn-well feel like entering. Watch how you read yourself . . . That's why we must build in as many welcoming doorways as we can. Because, once fascinated, lookers will indeed start to read."

- *Emotional involvement*

This is based on the assumption that we relate better to emotional truth than to intellectual truth. For journalists, that means more pictures and fewer long stories. Describing this factor as "news that touches your life" Hazelhurst said: "We saw no point in running long, important stories that used to feel good but weren't going to be read."

- *Guidance*

Readers want to be able to find their way around the paper easily and distinguish what is most important. Grouping stories under standard headings – for example, local news, international news and sport – and keeping them in the same place in the paper is a start.

- *Personality*

This means that the publication must have a distinctive character, in other words, you have to set design guidelines and keep to them!

- *Money*

Good design has proved to be good business. Three months after the *Weekly Mail & Guardian* was redesigned – in response to readers' suggestions – the paper posted record advertising revenues. However, beware: glitzy design alone is not enough to keep readers captivated; they also want the right stories, well written. Twenty months after the much acclaimed redesign of the *Sunday Star,* the money-losing paper was closed down. Times Media Limited managing director David Kovarsky was quoted as saying: "The regrettable closure demonstrated a lack of direction" (*Cape Times,* 20 Jan. 1994, p. 5).

10.2 DESIGN STARTS WITH PEOPLE

If the primary objective of design is to make your messages easily accessible and understandable to the target audiences that you want to reach, it is perhaps stating the obvious to say that design should start with *why* you want to say *what* to *who.*

General Sin Tju from China once said that if you want to win a battle you must know yourself and know your enemy before you fire the first shot.

The same is true of good design. To make it work you must understand what it is you want to do, why and for whom. One of the most important steps in designing an effective publication is drawing up *an editorial,* a design profile of what the publication should be, before you start visualising or writing.

10.2.1 Drawing up an editorial policy

- *Why*

Most publications fail because the editorial or design team have little or no understanding of exactly *why* they want to communicate.

Every successful publication is designed to communicate for a very specific reason.

A house journal, for example, is designed to keep employees informed about what is happening in the company; how they interface with what is happening in terms of policies and procedures; fringe benefits; and who their colleagues are and what they have achieved.

A marketing brochure is designed to inform potential clients of the benefits of a product or service in a way that will promote buying.

A magazine for SCUBA divers will be designed to keep divers abreast of the latest developments in their sport with regard to diving sites, techniques, equipment, legislation, *et cetera*.

- *What*

For a publication to be successful it is important that the editorial or design team should understand exactly what it is they need to tell their target audience. In the case of an in-house journal, for example, this will probably include corporate news, regional or divisional news, information with regard to promotions and appointments, insight into corporate philosophy and thinking, guidelines on how to derive maximum benefit from personnel regulations and procedures, feedback columns such as readers' letters and social and sport news.

- *Who*

If design is going to render the message acceptable and understandable to the audience it is essential for the editorial or design team to have a clear picture of their audience. What does your target audience look like? Are they male or female? How old are they? Where do they live? What are their interests? What are their levels of education and literacy? What language is their home language? How much do they earn?

A publication aimed at promoting better farming methods among semi-literate subsistence farmers in Transkei will not be designed in the same way as a scientific journal for academic agronomists.

- *Where*

Another factor that will influence publication design is distribution – where and how. For example, if it is to be mailed to subscribers it should have a format that can be mailed cost effectively.

- *When*

For the publication to be effective it is also important to determine at what intervals and what times during the year it should be published.

10.2.2 Publication profiles

It is only once the editorial or design team understand exactly why they are doing what for whom, that they set about deciding *how* it should be done.

A very useful first step is to draw up a design or editorial profile as a rough blueprint of how the publication will work, based on why the publication is being produced, what it is trying to achieve and who the target audience is.

FIGURE 10.2 Editorial profile and format of *Sebenza*, the civic liaison journal of the KwaNdebele National Development Corporation

---

1. **Aims**

The aims of the KNDC's civic liaison journal, *Sebenza*, are as follows:

1.1 To provide a structured medium with which to inform and educate key opinion formers and the KwaNdebele community on a formal basis.

1.2 To foster and maintain a climate of mutual understanding and respect between key role players in the KwaNdebele community and the KNDC.

1.3 To promote two-way communication between the KNDC and the KwaNdebele community.

1.4 To enhance the image of the KNDC within the KwaNdebele community.

1.5 To serve as a source of media stories and a vehicle for educating the media with regard to the activities, policies and philosophies of the KNDC.

1.6 To serve as a marketing document in providing potential new clients for KNDC's services with a track record of KNDC achievements, policies and philosophies.

2. **TARGET AUDIENCES**

2.1 **Primary audiences**

— The KwaNdebele cabinet
— Prominent opinion formers within the KwaNdebele Government Services
— Prominent opinion formers and role players within organized commerce and industry in KwaNdebele
— KNDC clients, including KAC and KUC clients
— Schools and educational institutions within KwaNdebele
— The KwaNdebele community at large

2.2 **Secondary audiences**

— KNDC's own staff and their families
— The media
— Potential new clients

3. **AUDIENCE PROFILES**

3.1 **Primary audiences**

   — Predominantly black male opinion formers and role players
   — Status and standing in the community
   — Predominantly policy makers, policy implementors, opinion formers and leaders in the community
   — Educational level: minimum matric and tertiary qualification
   — Language preference: predominantly English/Afrikaans

3.2 **Secondary audiences**

   — Predominantly white male
   — Status and standing in the community
   — Opinion formers, policy and decision makers, source of information to primary and secondary target audiences
   — Language preference: predominantly English/Afrikaans

4. **EDITORIAL CONTENT**

Corporate news
Departmental news: small business
Departmental news: training
Departmental news: housing
Departmental news: industry and tourism
Departmental news: agriculture
Departmental profile: describing services and facilities
KNDC personalia: promotions and appointments affecting the community at large
NACOC, MBA, and ACHIB news editorial reflecting policy and philosophy
Small business hints
Legal matters
KNDC calendar
List of contact people within KNDC

5. **FORMAT**

12 × A4 pages
Colour: Black and white plus one spot colour

6. **LANGUAGE**

English

7. **FREQUENCY**

Four times per annum

F/C		2	3
Corporate news		Corporate news	Departmental news (small business)

4	5	6		7
Departmental news (housing)	Departmental news (housing)	Editorial / Editorial staff	Small business hints / Legal matters	Calendar / Contact lists

8	9	10	11
Departmental news (industry & tourism)	Departmental news (agriculture)	Departmental profile	KNDC personalia (promotions, appointments)

12
NACOC/MBA ACHIB news

10.3 GRID

Very few newspapers or magazines are printed as a single mass of text across a single page. To make them more readable they are printed in a column format or *grid*.

A grid allows one to arrange text on a page in an accessible and legible format. As such choosing a grid involves a major design decision.

A grid also establishes a natural reading rhythm that helps to lead the reader through the publication. Different grid widths establish different rhythms. Large, one-column or full-page grids slow reading speed down because the reader's eye has to travel a long way across the line length. If you want your reader to ponder over what you are telling him, or make a weighty statement, a wide column grid can be a useful tool.

Narrow grids, on the other hand, make for faster reading. If you want to establish a snappy, businesslike style, narrower columns are very useful. They also work well in short, snappy news-snippet sections.

Like the human voice that becomes monotonous if the tone is not varied, a publication that uses only one column width throughout quickly becomes boring to the reader. By mixing column widths you can create a very interesting publication. However, it is essential to ensure that the widths remain compatible with regard to rhythm. If, for example, you are using a basic three-column grid you can also apply variations of it, such as 1 × col, 6 × col, and 9 × col.

FIGURE 10.3   Column formats or grids

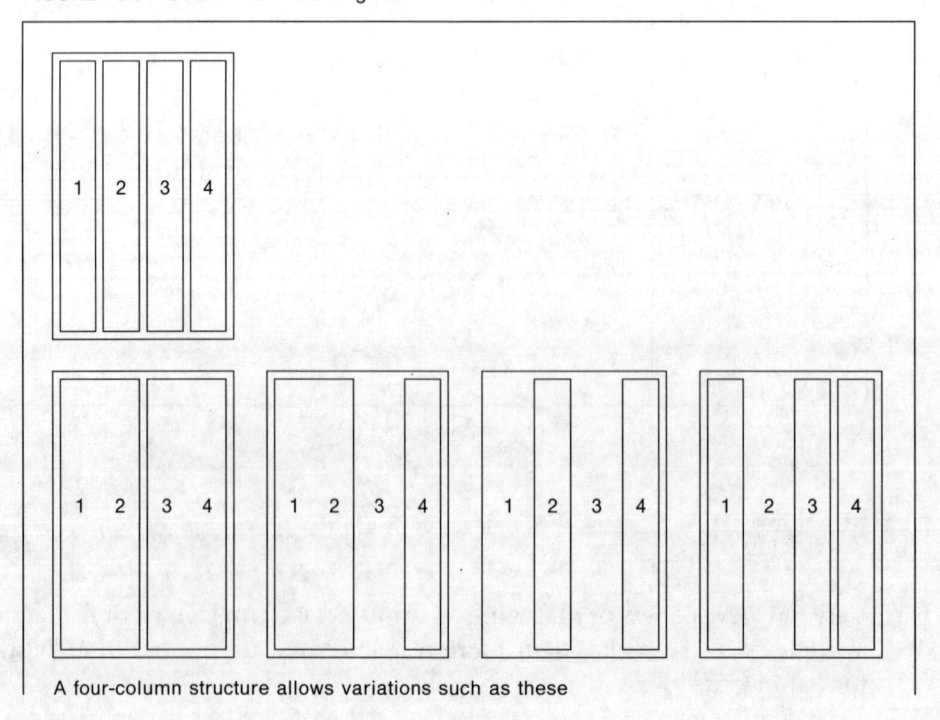

A four-column structure allows variations such as these

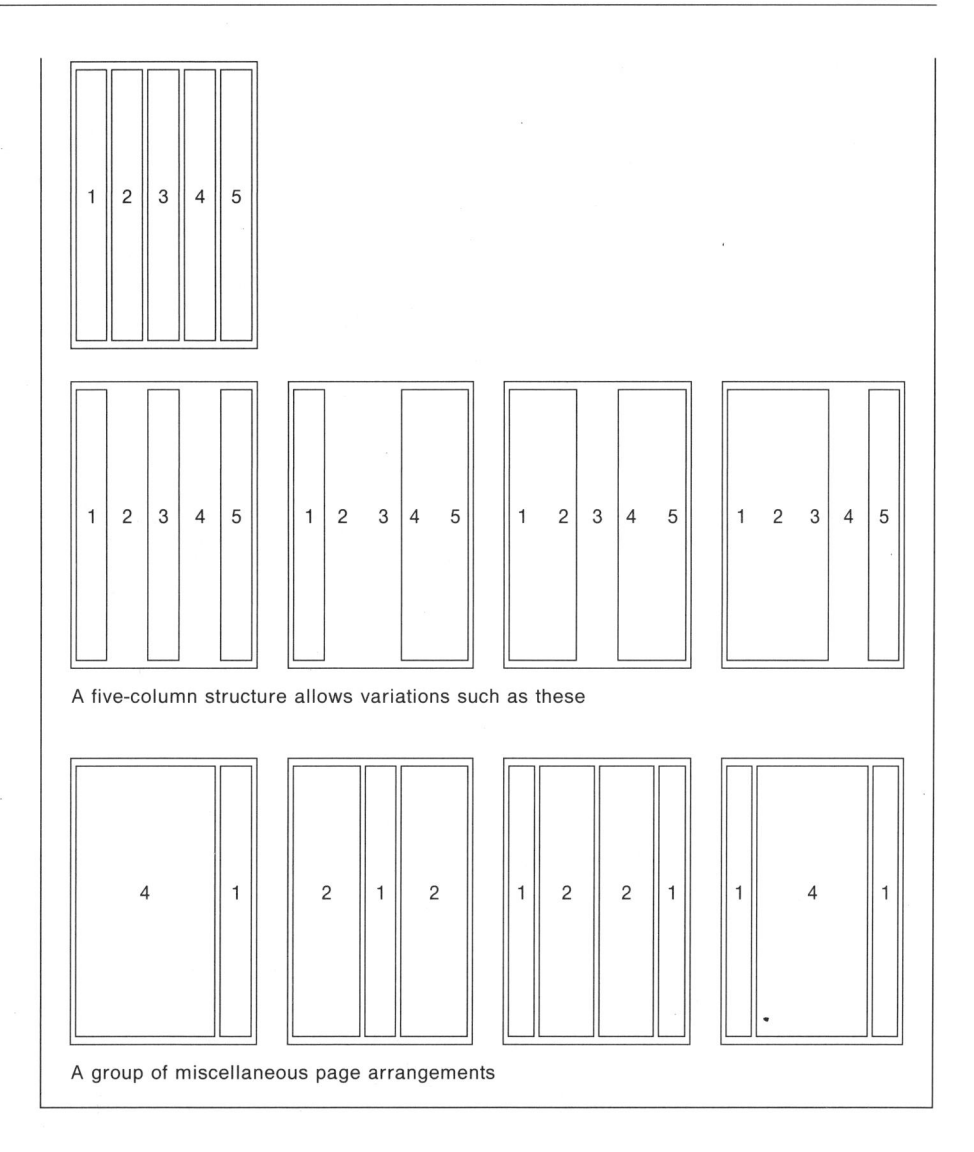

A five-column structure allows variations such as these

A group of miscellaneous page arrangements

When choosing the basic grid and column width it is important to take into account the language of the publication. Afrikaans text, for example, tends to run considerably longer than the English equivalent. If the column width used for an Afrikaans text is too narrow, it will result in numerous word breaks, thereby making the text difficult to read and to understand. Always make sure that the column width you choose will serve your purposes of design and message to the optimum.

10.4 TALKING TYPOGRAPHY

Typeface can greatly affect the appearance of a document. There are hundreds of typefaces available and choosing the right one may be quite a bewildering exercise. However, for most designers – especially those working on desk-top publishing systems – their choice is limited by what is available. This section will focus on the basic elements of typeface design that come into play when selecting a typeface.

FIGURE 10.4 Serif and sans serif typefaces

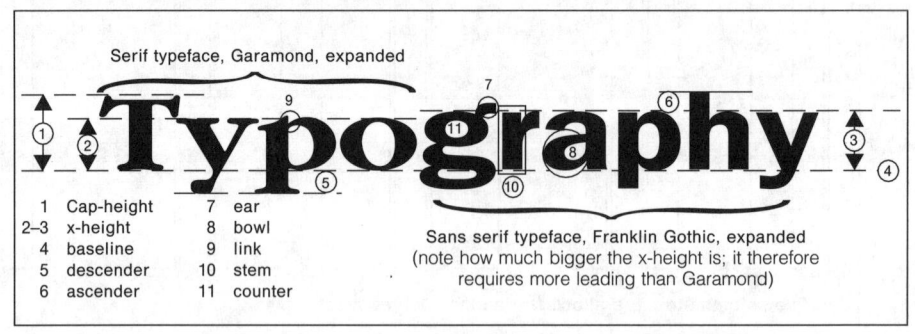

Serif typeface, Garamond, expanded

1 Cap-height
2–3 x-height
4 baseline
5 descender
6 ascender
7 ear
8 bowl
9 link
10 stem
11 counter

Sans serif typeface, Franklin Gothic, expanded
(note how much bigger the x-height is; it therefore requires more leading than Garamond)

10.4.1 The anatomy of type
The following terms are commonly used to describe typefaces.

Ascender The part of a letter that rises above the x-height, for example in b, d, f, h, k, l and t

Bowl The rounded stroke that creates an enclosed space in a character, like in the letter b

Character Individual letters, figures and punctuation marks

Counter The space enclosed – fully or partially – within a character

Descender That part of a letter that falls below the baseline

Families All the sizes and typestyles (i.e. bold, medium, light, italic, condensed, expanded, etc.) of a particular typeface

Font A complete set of characters, i.e. lower- and uppercase characters, figures and punctuation marks

Lowercase Small letters are called *lowercase* characters

Serif The lines crossing the main strokes of a character (the little feet)

Stress The direction of thickening in a curved stroke.

Uppercase Capital letters are called "caps" or *uppercase* characters

X-height The vertical height of a letter, excluding ascenders and descenders.

10.4.2 Fonts
Fonts are divided into several main categories:

• *Serif (Roman)*
These typefaces (also called *Roman*) have serifs or little finishing strokes at the end of the stems, arms and tails of characters. Serifs come in several basic varieties (full bracket, fine bracket, hairline, wedge and slab):

Full bracket serif
PLANTIN is an example of a full bracket serif face. This paragraph has been set in 10 point Plantin Roman.

Fine bracket serif
BEMBO is an example of a fine bracket serif face. This paragraph has been set in 10 point Bembo Roman.

Hairline serif
FENICE is an example of a hairline serif face. This paragraph has been set in 10 point Fenice Light Roman.

Wedge serif
LEAWOOD is an example of a wedge serif face. This paragraph has been set in 10 point Leawood Roman.

Slab serif
ROCKWELL is an example of a slab serif face. This paragraph has been set in 10 point Rockwell Medium.

Examples of Roman type include Times, Garamond, Baskerville and Cheltenham.

TIMES is an example of a Roman face. This paragraph has been set in 10 point Times Roman.

GARAMOND is an example of a Roman face. This paragraph has been set in 10 point Garamond Roman.

BASKERVILLE is an example of a Roman face. This paragraph has been set in 10 point Baskerville Roman.

CHELTENHAM is an example of a Roman face. This paragraph has been set in 10 point Cheltenham Light.

- *Square or slab serif*
These typefaces are also called Egyptian type. They were developed in Britain at the turn of the century (Sutton 1986: p. 53) not long after the discovery of King Tuthankamun's tomb. At the time the entire country was fascinated by Egyptian culture.

Examples include Rockwell, Lubalin and American Typewriter.

ROCKWELL is an example of a slab serif face. This paragraph has been set in 10 point Rockwell Medium.

LUBALIN is an example of a slab serif face. This paragraph has been set in 10 point Lubalin Graph Book.

AMERICAN TYPEWRITER is an example of a slab serif face. This paragraph has been set in 10 point American Typewriter Medium.

- *Sans serif*
Also known as Gothic, these typefaces do not have serifs ("sans" is French for "without") and have strokes that are the same thickness throughout.

Examples include Futura, Franklin Gothic, Helvetica and Univers.

FUTURA is an example of a sans serif face. This paragraph has been set in 10 point Futura Medium.

FRANKLIN GOTHIC is an example of a sans serif face. This paragraph has been set in 10 point Franklin Gothic Medium.

HELVETICA is an example of a sans serif face. This paragraph has been set in 10 point Helvetica Medium.

UNIVERS is an example of a sans serif face. This paragraph has been set in 10 point Univers Medium.

- *Text*
Also known as Blackletter, these faces are likely to remind you of the writing on old newspaper titlepieces and in Bibles. That is not surprising, since the type was introduced by Guttenberg when he printed the first Bible in 1450 and was widely in use until the 20th century. Recently this type – which is not very legible – has lost popularity.

An example is Old English.

OLD ENGLISH IS AN EXAMPLE OF A TEXT FACE. THIS PARAGRAPH HAS BEEN SET IN OLD ENGLISH.

- *Cursive*

Also known as script, these typefaces resemble formal handwriting. Most script typefaces are not easily legible and, as a rule, should be used with utmost discretion – if at all.

Examples are Palace Script and Brush Script.

Palace Script is an example of a script face. This paragraph has been set in 18 point Palace Script.

Brush Script is an example of a script face. This paragraph has been set in 12 point Brush Script.

- *Ornamental*

Also known as novelty typefaces, these come in a great variety. South African design expert Tony Sutton gives this advice (1986: p. 54); "Smart editors used [ornamental typefaces] to add impact to feature pages; wise editors don't!"

Examples include Dom Casual and Technical.

Dom Casual is an example of an ornamental face. This paragraph has been set in 14 point Dom Casual.

Technical is an example of an ornamental face. This paragraph has been set in 12 point Technical Normal.

10.4.3 Measuring type and layout

Typography and layout calculations are traditionally done in points and picas.

- *Points*

Points are small measurements, approximately the size of the mark made by a finely sharpened pencil. Small areas in a publication, like the height of type and the thickness of rules, are measured in points.

12 points equal 1 pica
72 points equal 1 inch, or 2.2 cm.

- *Picas*

Often called ems, picas are used to measure larger areas in publications, such as the width and length of columns of type and in sizing photographs.

6 picas equal 1 inch, or 2.2 cm.

- *Kerning*
This refers to the space between individual letters. Kerning is usually adjusted to make type fit better into a set space.

- *Leading*
The space between lines, usually set at 110 per cent of the type size (e.g. leading for 9 pt type will be set at 10 pt).

10.4.4 Tips on typographic communication

"Typographic clarity comes in two flavours: legibility and readability," writes Allan Haley (*Ragged Right*, No. 2: p. 9). *Legibility* is the quality that affects the ease with which one letter can be distinguished from another. *Readability* is the quality that affects the degree of ease with which typography can be read.

The following tips on legibility and readability have been compiled from advice given by design experts like Haley, Tony Sutton and Jan V. White.

- *Upper and lower case*
All caps type is more difficult to read than upper- and lowercase type. Use all caps sparingly.

- *Adequate x-height*
Remember that type measurements include ascenders and descenders. Therefore, two fonts of the same point size may appear very different.

Type with a large x-height and small ascenders and descenders will appear more substantial than a font of the same point size with a smaller x-height.

Type with a smaller x-height and longer ascenders and descenders will appear smaller than a font in which the x-height is larger.

Rule: Fonts with medium to large x-heights are more readable than fonts with small x-heights and extended ascenders and descenders.

- *Expanded or condensed*
Normal-width type is more legible than condensed or **expanded** type.

- *Too big or too small*
Type sizes of between 10 pt and 19 pt are more legible than smaller or larger sizes.

- *Italics*

Tony Sutton (1986: p. 58) says: *"Italic type can add contrast and emphasis when used – occasionally – to highlight key paragraphs of long feature items. Be careful, however, for overuse will look like a rash on your page."*

- *Too fancy*

Ordinary typefaces are more legible and readable than eccentric ones like Zapf Chancery, which has been used here.

- *Reversals and over pictures*

Black type on a white background is more legible than reverse type (white type on black background). Colour type and colour paper should be used very conservatively. Follow Edwin Taylor's advice: "Discretion is the better part of colour" (*Ragged Right*, No. 2: p. 7).

- *Line length*

Research shows that for a 9 pt typeface the most readable line length is between 11 and 14 picas (Sutton 1986: p. 56), which gives about 10 English words per line. However, newspapers have conditioned many people to scan slightly smaller columns (approx. 9.5 picas or 4 cm) with ease. Avoid using very narrow columns when designing your publication.

- *Justified left or right*

Justified and flush left/ragged right type are equally legible, provided that the justified type is properly spaced.

- *Leading*

This term refers to the space between lines of type. Body copy with one or two points of extra leading is more legible than type set solid or excessively leaded.

- *Paragraph indentation*

Some editors have decided to do away with indentations in favour of a line of white space.

Don't!

These white lines create what Tony Sutton describes as "horizontal rivers of wasted space" (1986: p. 56).

10.5 PHOTOGRAPHY

Good photographs seldom just happen. They have to be planned, as Ulli Michel knows only too well.

Chief photographer for Reuters in southern Africa, Michel was among the more than 2 000 foreign and local journalists who descended on Cape Town in the summer of 1990 to record the release from prison of African National Congress President Nelson Mandela.

Michel's snap of a smiling Mandela walking to freedom holding hands with his wife Winnie among a sea of raised fists was wired around the world and appeared on the front pages of most newspapers internationally.

"It was the most important picture of my life," Michel said (*Style*, April 1990: p. 42). "But what lengths we had to go to."

To get the shot – one of only eight frames Michel clicked before the surging crowd blocked his view – preparations began two months earlier with a task force of eight people. They planned possible routes, chartered aircraft and booked motorcycle messengers, arranged for a temporary darkroom as well as portable phones and walkie-talkies and rented a house opposite the Mandela home in Soweto. Scaffolding was ordered to ensure better vantage points.

How much did it cost to get the picture? "What, all expenses?" he asked (*Style*, April 1990: p. 43). "Oh about forty thousand rand, tops. But that's what we spent for the entire Mandela coverage, not just for the one picture. I consider it cheap in comparison to what other agencies and, in particular, the TV networks spent."

Estimates for media coverage of the first 50 steps Mandela took to freedom ranged between R2 million and R8 million – that is R40 000 to R160 000 per step.

"I've never seen anything like it before in 20 years of working for the BBC," said cameraman Francois Marais (*Style*, April 1990: p. 41). "It was the biggest single news event ever."

10.5.1 Getting the right shot

You are unlikely to cover something quite as momentous as Mandela's release, but even routine stories and photographs need to be planned. Remember the primary purpose of a photograph is not to fill a hole in your design but to *enhance your message*. To help you plan your picture to do just that, the following checklist may prove useful.

- *Why?*

Why am I taking this picture? Is it going to be used for a news story or will it be used in a marketing brochure? What am I trying to achieve with the picture? What message am I trying to put across?

- *What?*

What am I taking a picture of – a person, a product or a place?

Think about it. For example, what exactly is your product? What does it mean to your target audience and how do they "see" it? Can you find an angle that will emphasise what they see or what you are trying to say?

What is the place you are taking a picture of? A hotel, for example, is not just a building with bedrooms; it is a holiday or a home away from home. How can you convey this with a picture?

What is your organisation and how can you depict that in a photograph?

- *Who?*

Who am I taking a picture of?

The MD – sure. But, who is the MD? In a house journal you may want to depict him as a homely, approachable person. In the annual report you may want to portray him as a competent captain of industry.

Decide which aspects of a person's personality and appearance will convey the desired messages in a picture.

"Who?" will often also determine your approach to the person. If he is a difficult person, plan your approach accordingly and dress accordingly. Do not take the risk of offending your subject in an attempt to prove that you are artistic.

"Who?" will also mean having to find suitable models from time to time. As you move around your organisation make a note of who you think would work well in a photograph and keep their names on file. If you use models, however, make sure you get them to sign release forms or you could end up with an unexpected additional expense on your budget.

- *Where?*

Where can you get good photographs in your organisation? As you move around, note interesting locations.

Try looking at the world from a different angle. There is no rule that says you must stand flat on the ground. Why not climb a ladder or a flight of stairs and shoot from above, or get down on your knees – the world looks different and quite exciting from down there! (Have you ever wondered what a child sees? You can relive it!)

"Where?" is also an important point in making sure that you arrive at a shoot. Being in the right place at the right time is part of being professional. Make sure you know where you have to be to take the picture.

- *When?*

"When?" is also an important point to consider in your planning.

Make sure you know what time on what day you have to take the photographs and get there well in time.

"When?" can also refer to the time of day needed to create the right atmosphere. What do your headquarters look like at sunrise or at sunset? The best atmosphere shots do not necessarily happen during office hours. Get to know what your "wheres" look like at different times of the day.

- *How?*

Once you have gone through the 5 Ws you should be able to arrive at a pretty good "How?", which should result in a good photograph that enhances your message.

Below are a few examples of the types of picture you can take for specific situations.

10.5.2 Type of picture

In addition to layout requirements, and often more important, are editorial demands. It is usually clear from the start that certain types of pictures will be needed to illustrate a particular story. If the story is being photographed anew rather than being assembled from "stock" shots, the photographer can be given a shooting brief.

Sometimes pictures not contained in the brief may be taken during the shoot, and these may be used on their own merits. Photographs can be classified by the information they convey and the effect they have on developing a story. Not every story will require all these pictures and many photographs will fulfil a combination of several functions.

- *Point pictures*

Variously called by different magazines, point pictures are the necessary illustrations for points made in the text (hence the name). They are used even if not visually exciting and often appear small.

- *Establishing shots*

These are photographs that set the scene for certain kinds of story: an overall view of a city, for example, in which a story is set. Such pictures are generally used large and early on in a story.

- *Typical appearance/product shots*

At some point in many picture stories, whatever is being featured must be shown clearly. If the subject is an invention or a household object, the photo could simply be a routine, "no frills" still-life, but it could equally well be an exciting abstract showing the "image" of the subject rather than the subject itself. Explicitly larger subjects, such as landscapes, broaden the scope further.

- *Key personalities*

Just as a featured subject must be clearly illustrated, so must personalities who feature prominently in the story. Again, the type of picture will vary considerably according to the approach taken in the story. A formal studio portrait may be most appropriate in some instances while an "involved" reportage shot may be better in others. Typically, a portrait will be combined with several "candid" shots to give a rounded view – the portrait providing the lead picture.

- *People at work*

If the activity of a human subject is more important than the personality, it (and not the person) must feature prominently in the picture.

- *Unique images*

This category covers all surprise pictures that rely on their novelty for impact. Varieties are "first ever photograph of . . .", such as the earth seen from space for the first time, and "new views", such as the first photographs of an unborn baby in the mother's womb.

- *Sequences*

As well as fulfilling a design role, a sequence of pictures that shows the progress of action may have strong editorial value.

- *Juxtaposition*

This is an important group of image types, usually run in pairs, that work by showing relationships. These relationships often contrast – for example, the lives of the rich and the poor – or compare. Often the intention is one of deliberate surprise achieved by showing relationships of which the reader may not have been aware. The following varieties are found: unconscious mimicry (similar gestures and expressions from political opponents), scale contrast (dwarfed man/mighty works), anachronism (old-fashioned remnants in a modern city) and bizarre oddities and kitsch in context.

- *Point-of-view-shots*

Generally wide-angled, these shots show a point of view of an individual or group. The person will feature on the foreground, for instance a prison yard from a tower, with a guard right next to the camera.

- *Words and numbers*

Both of these have extra visual "weight" where they appear in the photograph and attract the viewer's eye particularly strongly. They can convey additional information, often in juxtaposition (see above).

10.5.3 Types of picture story

There are surprisingly few kinds of photographic feature run in magazines, newspapers and books, although the range of treatments can be very varied. Many magazines, in fact, plan to run a balanced selection in each issue of the kinds of feature that they favour.

- *Place stories*

Stories on particular places, from Paris to Ecuador, are popular with all kinds of magazines. They provide a good variety of shots, from small features to overall views and considerable scope for design. *National Geographic*, for example, uses this type of story regularly, with little or no news content, but taking a broad view. Treatment may vary according to the publication, from travelogue to political.

- *Periodic events*

Festivals, coronations, royal weddings have obvious – and predictable – visual interest, so the coverage can be planned and scheduled well ahead of time. In fact, some magazines are virtually obliged to provide coverage of certain events.

- *Commodity stories*

Similar in certain respects to place stories, these provide as thorough a review as possible of products used by man. The definition of a commodity tends to be quite loose, and could include rice, gold or integrated circuits.

- *"State-of-the-art" update*

A special version of the commodity story, this type of story often has a scientific, "high-tech" bias, dealing with a topic or field where there is rapid development, such as cosmology or lasers.

- *Discovery*

Sometimes related to a "state-of-the-art" update, discovery stories may deal with scientific and technical subjects, such as super-conductivity, or with discoveries in natural science, such as a newly discovered species or an archaeological discovery.

- *Social group*

Unusual or closely knit social groups are appealing subjects, provided that the coverage has sufficient depth and intimacy. A remote tribe or religious group such as the Hassidim are typical subjects.

- *Nature*

Specific nature stories tend to concentrate either on the species, such as lions in the Serengeti, or on a particular habitat, such as life on a coral atoll.

- *Biography*

This may be a fairly concise story on a personality or a longer, more evocative treatment of a historical figure. The approach can vary widely from, for example, "A day in the life of . . ." to "Following in the steps of . . ." (M. Freeman, *Encyclopedia of practical photography*, London, New Brighton Books).

10.5.4 A few pointers about working with photographers

- *Brief the photographer*

If you are not taking the picture yourself give the photographer as much information as possible about the story.

If assignment cards are used, fill in the names of the important subjects, suggestions for types of the important subjects, and suggestions for types of poses.

Consider whether you need vertical or horizontal photos to suit the page design. Also, do you need overall panoramic shots or close-ups?

Do not forget to include directions – not just an address. Also give a telephone number in case the photographer gets lost or has problems getting there at all.

- *Go with the photographer, or meet her there, if possible*

Working as a team will usually improve a story because you will be seeing the action from another point of view. Usually, the photographer will question you about the story and this, in turn, will often help you to clarify the story in your own mind.

- *Be imaginative*
If you are obliged to take yet another photograph of a cheque-giving ceremony, consider taking the photograph from a different angle or watching the recipient's face for a reaction. Avoid boring pictures of posed handshakes – grip-and-grin shots – and other clichés.

Tip: Browse through international news magazines and photography books on a regular basis, keeping your eyes open for ideas you can use to make your next photograph more exciting.

- *Do not interfere with the photographer*
If you have suggestions, be tactful. Remember photographers have professional pride and are not writer's lackeys.

- *Print them all*
Experienced house journal and newspaper editors usually choose photographs from contact sheets or proof sheets (strips of negatives laid side by side and printed on a single sheet of photographic paper). This allows them to see all the work the photographer has done. Always ask the photographer to print the full frame of the photographs and do the cropping yourself. Often photographers crop out just the extra millimetre or two you need to make the photo fit snugly into your design.

10.5.5 You as a photographer

As a corporate journalist, more often than not you will end up being your own photographer. In this regard your success will not depend only on your technical know-how and artistic flow; to a large degree it will be determined by your ability to relate to and manage people.

Bearing the following in mind will certainly be of help to you:
- The key to good subject rapport is patience and professionalism.
- Be on time every time.
- Dress properly for the occasion. If you are doing a dirty industrial shoot, jeans and a T-shirt may be fine, but they are not exactly the right attire for photographing your board of directors or a black tie gala affair.
- Always take your dress cue from the subject/s. Dress so that they will feel comfortable with you as a guest.
- When working with people *always stay in control*. If you have planned your picture in advance this is relatively easy to achieve.
- Introduce yourself politely but firmly. Explain to your subjects what you are trying to achieve and why, and then arrange them. If you are working with a difficult or moody client point out that you are trying to capture an image that will make him or her appear acceptable and professional to the

specific target audience. You can only succeed in doing him justice if he cooperates.
- Be aware of other people's personal space. If you encroach on this without asking permission and explaining why, you are likely to end up with an extremely tense subject.
- Make sure that you involve everybody present when working with a group. It takes only one bored individual to ruin an otherwise excellent shot.

10.5.6 Picture editing

You do not have to choose a great photograph. It will immediately stand out because, says Tony Sutton (1986: p. 37) "it has the impact and power which come with these factors: presence, balance, composition, surprise, subtlety, movement – or uniqueness."

To help you sift through the so-so pictures (i.e. the majority of pics that end up on your desk), Dr Mario Garcia of the Poynter Institute for Media Studies in the United States suggests you pay attention to the following factors:

- *Appropriateness*

Ask yourself if the picture is saying the right thing.

American photographer Annie Liebowitz did plenty of thinking about what would be appropriate when she was assigned to shoot a portrait of Susan Faludi, author of *Backlash: the undeclared war against American women*. Faludi had dedicated the book to her mother. That gave Liebowitz a clue. "It seemed like Susan Faludi was living the life her mother could only have dreamed of living, so I asked if they'd like to be photographed together," Liebowitz said (*Vanity Fair*, December 1992: p. 14). "She told me that no one had ever thought of taking them together before."

It is true, a single photograph can say more than a thousand words – but make sure you choose the one that is saying the right things. Do not let your urge to be creative blur your vision of what it is you want to accomplish with the photograph.

On 16 June 1976, *The World* photographer, Sam Nzima, was sent into Soweto to cover the student uprising. He saw a lot that would have made dramatic pictures: students angrily marching, burning cars, building barricades, attacking government officials. He did not click a shot. "I did not take an earlier picture of death. I saw a lone policeman trying to run from the students. He hit a pole and fell. They slaughtered him like a goat and set him alight. I couldn't take pictures then," Nzima recalled (Tyson p. 110).

When he did focus his camera, he shot six frames that included an image that, says former *Star* editor Harvey Tyson, "instantly symbolized the whole tragedy."

"It was to my mind more powerfully emotional than all the hours of harrowing TV coverage which was run and re-run around the world for days," Tyson wrote. "It was a photograph of a tall teenage boy in overalls, a shy young girl in her trim school uniform, and of her younger brother. The body of 12-year old Hector Peterson lies limply in the arms of the tall, urgently striding teenage stranger. Running to keep up, is the dead boy's sister, Antoinette Peterson. In the young faces of the two is mirrored the shock and tragedy of all that happened in Soweto that day."

The impact of Nzima's shot echoes still. Hector's funeral, which thousands attended, became the focus of the people's grief and is still recalled at annual commemorations on June 16.

Few photographs you see are likely to have the same kind of impact. But, if possible, select photographs that are able to move your audience emotionally in some way.

- *Design possibilities*

Photographs have to fit. If you are choosing a photograph, consider the design possibilities. Do you need to run a photograph down a single column? Or what about a close-up with impact? Select photographs that may be cropped to fit more than one shape.

- *Quality*

Is it technically good? Avoid photographs that are too dark, too light, out of focus or grainy. Often these flaws are magnified in print.

When it comes to printing pictures, bigger is better – usually, that is. So, if you have a particularly good picture, do not be afraid to use it big. Some newspapers, like *Liberation* in France, regularly run photographs up to half a tabloid-size page.

Editors of house journals are often required to run pictures by amateur photographers. In that case, clever cropping and down-sizing may help to disguise some of the photograph's compositional and technical flaws.

10.5.7 Cropping and sizing pictures

10.5.7.1 Cropping

Often the original print contains too much information, especially if it has to be made smaller to fit a layout. You want attention only on the important part of the image, so you must eliminate portions that do not suit your purposes, in other words, you have to crop the picture.

There are three principles to consider when you crop:
- A good photograph has only one subject or object of attention, only one area to which the eye is drawn to get the message.
- Pleasing pictures tend to be composed in thirds, not halves. It is especially important not to run a strong line, like a flag pole or horizon, through the middle of a photograph.
- Cropping should not eliminate important information. Never let the viewer suspect that something is missing.

10.5.7.2 Sizing

There are many methods to calculate how your picture will run when it is cropped and altered in size. Here are two of them:

- *The diagonal method*
  — Cover the photographs with a sheet of tracing paper and outline the area you want to use with a ruler and soft-tipped pencil.
  — Now draw a diagonal line from corner to corner of the cropped section of the photograph.
  — Decide how wide you want the photograph to run in the layout and, using a ruler, draw a line perpendicular to that width across to the diagonal line.
  — Then draw a line at right angles and extend it to the base of the photograph. Measure that line to get the new length of the photograph.

To enlarge a photograph, extend the original diagonal line and then follow the same steps.

- *The formula method*

It is best to do a layout by planning your photograph and editing your copy to fit, than to go about it the other way round. However, in practice you often have to plan to use your photograph in the space that is left over once the copy has been placed. When that happens, the formulae given below will be useful.

Note: You can begin with either the horizontal or vertical measurements. For our examples we started with horizontal measurements.

FIGURE 10.5 Sizing photographs

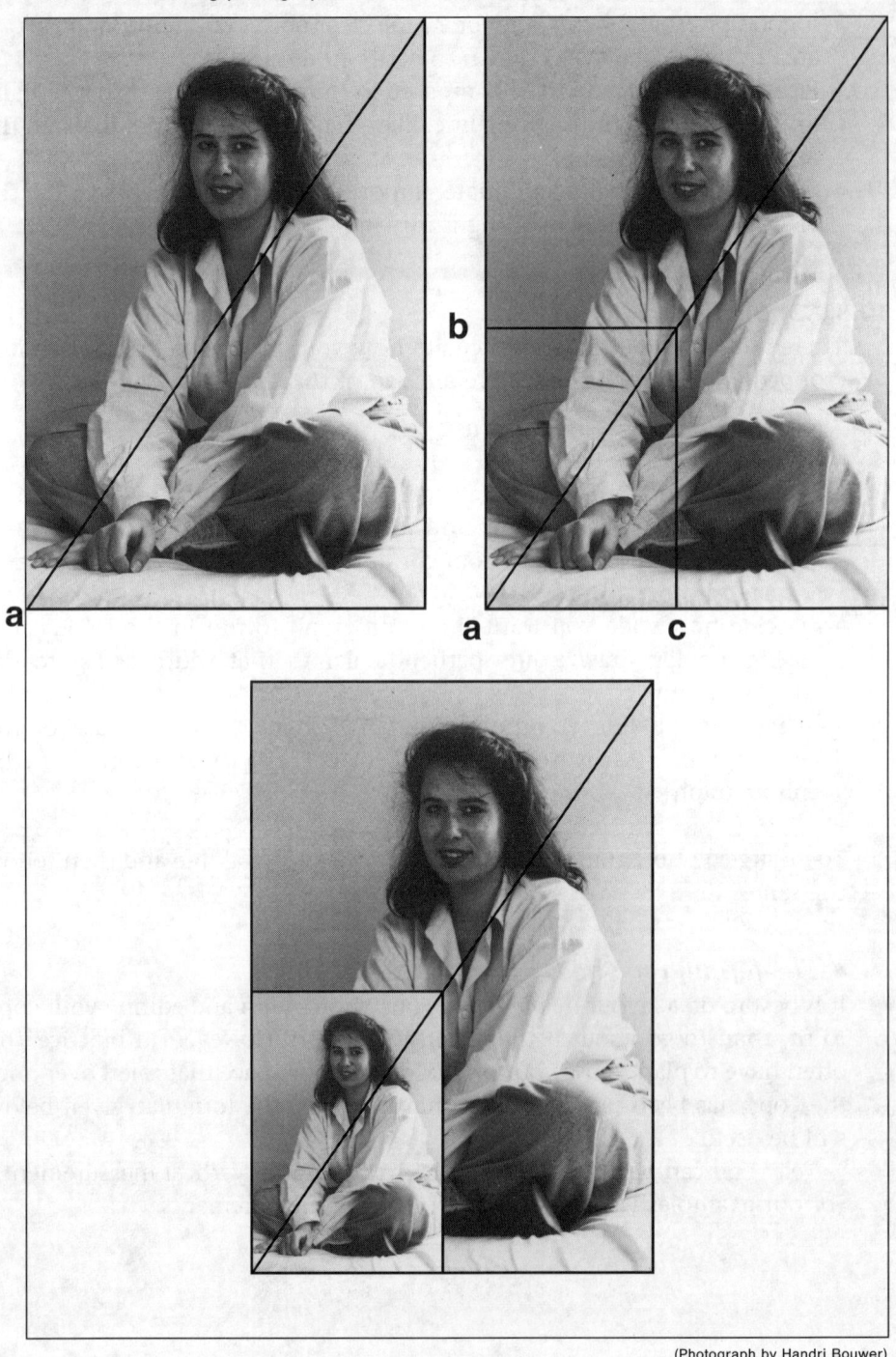

(Photograph by Handri Bouwer)

SEPARATE FILE FOR PAGE 187 WITH HALF-TONES

DESIGN

— *To reduce a photograph*

FIGURE 10.6 The formula method: reduction

To calculate the % reduction required:

Size of layout ÷ size of photograph × 100 = % reduction
= 5 ÷ 8 × 100
= 63% (rounded off to the nearest full %)

To calculate how much you have to crop the length of the picture:

Size wanted ÷ (% reduction ÷ 100)
= 7 ÷ (63 ÷ 100)
= 7 ÷ .63
= 11

Thus, you will have to crop 1 cm from the length of the photograph.

187

SEPARATE FILE FOR PAGE 188 WITH HALF-TONES

MAKING IT LOOK RIGHT, TOO

— To enlarge a photograph

FIGURE 10.7 The formula method: enlargement

To calculate the % enlargement required:

Size of layout ÷ size of photo × 100 = % enlargement
= 8 ÷ 5 × 100
= 160%

To calculate the required length of the photograph:

Size wanted ÷ (% enlargement ÷ 100) = photo length
= 12 ÷ 7 × 100
= 171%

Thus, 8 ÷ (171 ÷ 100)
   = 8 ÷ 1.71
   = 4.68 cm

You will need to crop 2 mm off the width of the photograph to make it fit the layout.

DESIGN

FIGURE 10.8 Newspaper layout: identifying the key terms in English and Afrikaans

- Teaser panel (prikkelberig)
- Titlepiece (also called the nameplate) (titelhoof)
- Overline (bostreep)
- Caption (boskrif)
- Reverse heading (omgekeerde opskrif)
- Halftone photograph (raster fotografie)
- Display type (vertoondrukletters)
- Turn line (stop reël)
- Sans serif type (skreeflose druklettertipe)
- Rule border (randomlyning)
- Splash headline (groot drukopskrif)
- Byline (outeursreël)
- Mugshot (nabyskoot)
- Initial cap, also called drop cap (begin letter)
- Serif type (skreefdruklettertipe)
- Display advertisement (vertoon advertensie)
- Lead story (hoofberig)
- Body type (hoofdeeldrukletter)

189

10.5.8 Sending photographs to the printer

Once you have decided on the dimensions you want to use, follow these steps:
- Place a sheet of tracing paper over the photograph, sticking it to the back with tape.
- Mark the area to be used with a ruler and soft-tipped pencil.
- Write the dimensions and percentage reduction or enlargement on the back of the photograph with a wax China marker or soft-tipped pencil. Never use a felt-tip marker or pen because the ink is likely to come off, smudging other pictures, when stacked together.
- Clearly mark the photograph (A, B, C or D) and the corresponding space on the layout.
- Never use staples, pins or paperclips to attach notes to photographs.

10.6 LAYOUT

10.6.1 The parts

Creating a layout is a bit like playing with Lego blocks – fitting pieces, one by one, into a single design. Doing it is not difficult, but doing it *well* requires thought and creativity.

Of course, instead of plastic blocks, the designer has to bear the following elements in mind:
- Stories of varying length
- Summary blocks or "blurbs"
- Different typefaces, particularly for headlines
- Photographs and graphics
- Number of columns per page
- Colour
- Advertisements (more often than not)
- White or "empty" space
- Layout styles, for example modular or dynamic (see below).

10.6.2 Putting it all together

Now it is time to put it all together. My approach to design is confirmed by designer Jeff Level's observation:

The news shouldn't have to be deciphered by readers – most newspapers have a crossword puzzle for that challenge (*Ragged Right*, No. 1: p. 2).

That is why I advocate simple, modular design like that followed by Cape Town's *Die Burger*, Johannesburg's *The Sowetan* and Sanlam's house journal, *Die Sanlammer*.

DESIGN

Dynamic layout, on the one hand, means that each page of a publication is approached independently with no consistency of elements like column width.

Modular layout sees every story – that means copy, headlines, photos and graphics – as a single, four-cornered module that fits into a specific page grid, with standard-sized gutters (like the lines of mortar between bricks in a wall).

FIGURE 10.9 Louis Heyneman critiques examples of modular layout configurations

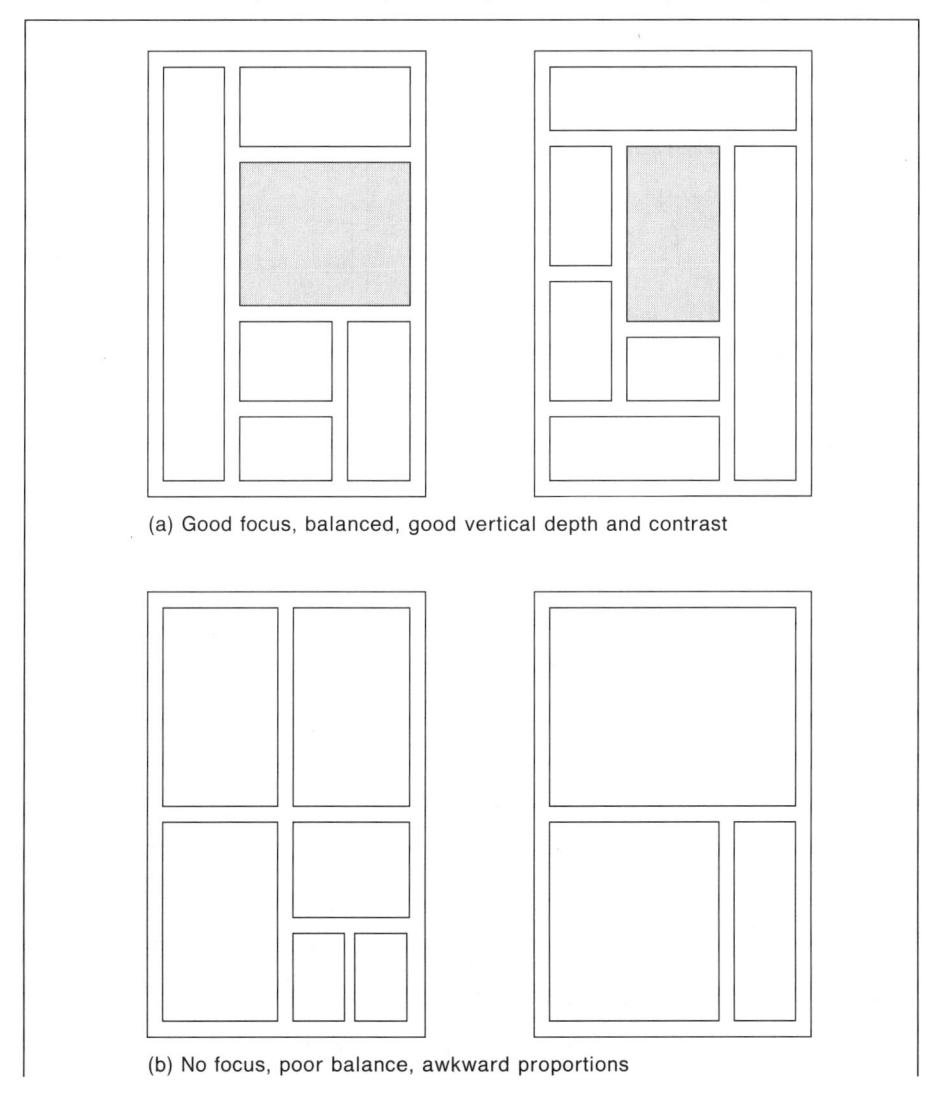

(a) Good focus, balanced, good vertical depth and contrast

(b) No focus, poor balance, awkward proportions

(c) Visually uninteresting and boring

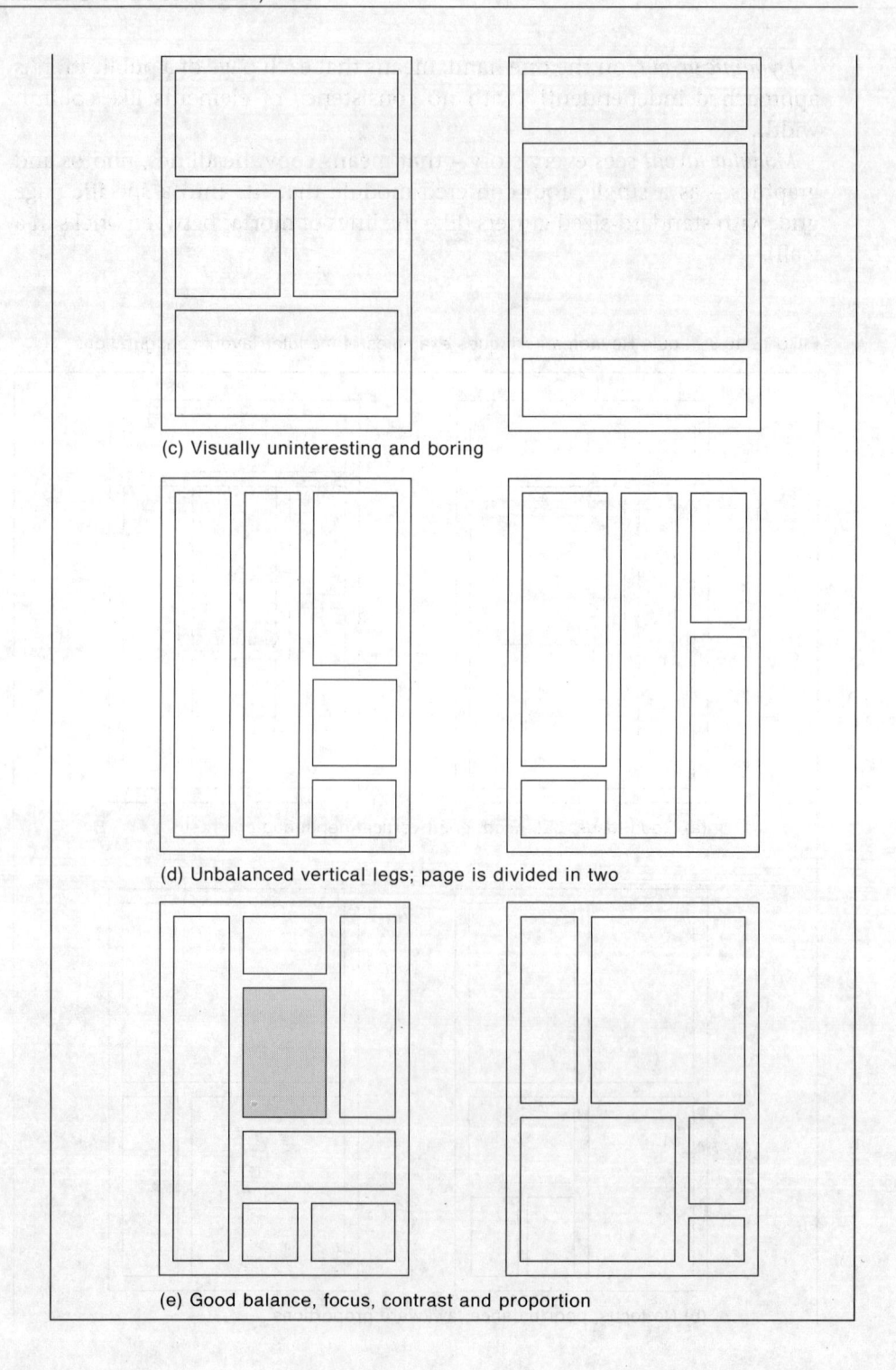

(d) Unbalanced vertical legs; page is divided in two

(e) Good balance, focus, contrast and proportion

These rectangles and squares can be used in a variety of configurations. The best combinations bear these points in mind:

- *Focus*

Each page and indeed each story must have a clear focus to direct the viewer (just like articles). Because people are more attracted to visuals than to copy, pictures and graphics usually automatically become the focal points on a page.

- *Balance*

Elements must be balanced. Take great care to ensure that headlines are appropriately sized for copy blocks. Avoid large, bold headlines on short stories and small headlines on large copy blocks.

- *Contrast*

To avoid bland layouts, you need a measure of contrast on each page to create tension.

- *Unity*

The elements must form a united whole. Using no more than four typefaces (one for copy and three for headlines), and consistent graphic elements contribute greatly to unity of page.

- *Clarity*

The information must be instantly clear – remember that a page is not a crossword puzzle.

10.7 CONCLUSION

I trust this discussion has helped "word people" to get a better understanding of both the importance and the process of design – and made them realize the challenge of competing for the attention of modern readers, products of the television age.

According to US design expert, Dr Mario Garcia, American research has shown that 77 per cent of newspaper readers do not recall life without TV and 66 per cent do not recall life without colour TV (Haffajee & Stober: p. 9).

All newspaper readers watch at least one hour of TV a day. The TV age and the pace of life have made them impatient readers, Garcia says, and today's newspapers should reflect this. "They should have the speed of television, the relaxed visuals of magazines and the directness of radio."

Assignments

1. Create a modular design for page 3 of an A4 publication using the following items clipped from magazines and newspapers:

    1 story; a headline, with a kicker; a summary or blurb; 3 photos and captions.

    Compare your effort with those of your classmates and discuss the focus, balance, contrast, unity and clarity of each design.

2. Crop and size the photograph below to fit a 3 × 3 cm space. Repeat the exercise for a horizontal space of 10 × 14 cm.

Photograph by Clifford Boobyer

Bibliography and recommended reading

Beach, Mark, *Editing your newsletter*, Portland, Oregon, Coast to Coast Books, 1982.
Ferreira, Tom & Staude, Ingrid, *Write angles – the ABC for house journals*, Johannesburg, Write Minds, 1991.
Freeman, M., *Encyclopedia of practical photography*, London, New Brighton Books.
Haffajee, Ferial & Stober, Paul, "Luring those readers from TV's glitz", *The Weekly Mail*, May 22–28 1992, p. 9.
Haley, Allen, "Why type should be readable and legible", *Ragged Right*, No, 2 Summer 1992, pp. 9–10.
Hazelhurst, Dave, "Why and how", *Rhodes University Journalism Review*, December 1992, pp. 27–30.
Heyneman, Louis, "Layout and design workshop", a two-part series presented at the Cape Technikon, Cape Town, 1993.
Sutton, Tony, *Creative newspaper design*, Johannesburg, Review Press, 1986.
Tyson, Harvey, *Editors under fire*, Sandton, Random House, 1993.
White, Jan V., "How to use design to edit newspapers", *Ragged Right*, No. 1, Spring 1992, pp. 6–8.

PART 3

DOING THE RIGHT THING

UNDERSTANDING ETHICS

By Prof. Guy Berger

Ask many journalists about ethics, and their answer is likely to be: "Huh? What's that?". But whether they acknowledge it or not, journalism is not a neutral craft nor is it a purely technical skill. Choices confront journalists constantly, and decisions have to be made one way or another. Politicians often call for "responsible journalism", demanding that those working in media pay close regard to the ethical implications of their work. Often with good reason, journalists usually reject such admonitions as suspect interference with ulterior motives.

Within their own ranks, however, there is certainly the need to exercise conscience. Yet, many media people react to daily choices with little conscious awareness of the diverse options available to them. They are motivated out of habit in some cases; in terms of their background and general outlook in others – and under instruction in many more.

Firstly, there is tradition. What would you do if you were a SABC radio programme host, and asked to announce not merely that Company X sponsored the programme, but that Company X, the best in town, was the sponsor? According to British convention, editorial and advertising should be clearly demarcated; far less so the more commercialised American style. In eclectic South Africa, different media opt for different mixes of these two traditions.

Secondly, in addition to tradition, all journalists operate in a professional context that sets parameters for them. There are news-values and modes of writing which they conform to. There are conventions, customs and policies attached to the particular medium they are working for. Often there are explicit codes of conduct to which they subscribe, voluntarily or otherwise. By their nature as journalistic employees, they are obliged to execute these as well as other reasonable instructions from their superiors – or be prepared to quit their jobs. On the other hand, some media codes are observed mainly in the breach – and by employers as much as employees. The code of conduct of the South African Press Council bans any payments by a newspaper to a person engaged in criminal activity. When the Sunday newspaper, *Rapport*, paid racist mass murderer Barend Strydom for his story during

1993, it successfully flouted the code by arguing that Strydom was no longer engaged in crime.

Besides the Press Council's codes of conduct, there are codes drawn up by the major journalism trade unions, the South African Union of Journalists and the Media Workers Association of South Africa, and each media enterprise also often has its own code.

Journalists are not free agents in full control of their production. Many of their decisions are made for them – by traditions, by the nature of their work, by formal strictures, and by order of their employers. To operate in such a situation is of course an ethical choice on its own, and one that sometimes sees journalists organizing to change things.

But usually, buttressed by their context, journalists do not see their every action as an ethical dilemma. And yet, each individual media worker – whether reporter, sub-editor, photographer, news-editor, and so on – still often does have moments of very clear, and difficult, choices.

A sub-editor operating within the constraints of news-worthiness may nevertheless still wrestle with which story to give pride of place to, which ones to cut and how to cut them. The question of whether to push home an intrusive question to a bereaved person may trouble a reporter supposed to milk the tragedy. And should a company be given "below-the-line" or free advertising within an editorial context in cases where, often with a cynical eye to corporate image, that company does a good deed or offers a journalistic merit award? Blood-and-guts photographs may bring home to readers the horror of violent death; they may also help to sell a newspaper. But does the moral imperative really rest so easily with the commercial? There are also other, sometimes more subtle, questions:

1. What gifts a journalist may accept in good conscience is determined by company policy as well as individual ethics. In an age of professional manipulation of the press by governments, politicians and companies, there are countless freebies and other goodies offered to those in the media. Accepting a free M-Net decoder and subscription may not influence a television critic's reviews of M-Net programmes. But what about being wined and dined in style by those ever-so-pleasant public relations and promotional personnel? Free tickets to the theatre may be acceptable in the case of arts critics; consider, though, a big insurance company offering financial journalists a seat in their corporate box at an international rugby tournament. The crunch choice may never come – the same

financial journalist may never be asked to suppress or to sauce-up a story about that company. But on other, less dramatic issues, there is the danger of a slow disarming of journalists. A comfortable, if not cosy, culture can grow to take the place of an erstwhile scepticism and adversarial journalism. There are plane tickets, trips and junkets, the use of a car, sponsorships, and promises of exclusive stories. Lines need to be drawn, but how and where? These ethical questions need to be posed – pre-eminently by journalistic practitioners themselves in the course of their daily work.

2. Withholding information is another difficult issue confronting journalists. In South Africa, it is not only unethical, but also illegal to identify rape victims, directly or through their families. It has been simply a convention in the USA, until the case of the 1992 William Kennedy Smith rape trial, that is, when certain television networks presented his accuser in full face to their viewers.

There are also laws against identifying children in trouble with the law, and against identifying detainees. Yet there are also cases in which these laws are defied for reasons that may be commercial sensation in some cases, or a greater ethic in other cases. *Rapport* published the photograph of Janusz Walus before he appeared in an identity parade or was charged in court with the murder of political leader Chris Hani. In another case, *South* newspaper published a photograph of a streetchild being arrested, without any of the conventional placing of disguising stripes over the eyes, under the headline: "The Face of Fear". Both cases have ethical implications.

And what about reporting information that could provoke a copy-cat effect? The difficulty is that copy-cat cases are often unintentional – a graphic report about child drug abuse on one paper saw shopkeepers calling to complain that some youngsters sought to emulate the problem. Similarly, publishing news about the horrific "necklace" form of murder in South Africa arguably helped to spread and popularize the atrocity. Should journalists publish regardless of such issues, and if not, is there not a danger of self-censorship beginning to cloud the reporting process? Withholding information also crops up in relation to the protection of sources by journalists. Many journalists refuse to give evidence voluntarily in court cases, no matter the proceedings at stake, and many South African journalists have even refused to testify when subpoenaed to do so.

The decisions involved are often personal ones, but the general working principle is that a journalist's job is to gather and disseminate information, and that actions that may hinder this mission would be avoided. The assumption is that journalistic access and credibility requires going no further than generating information; it is up to other individuals and agencies to act on it.

Collecting information can also raise tricky questions: is it ethical for a person to withhold the fact that he or she is actually a journalist? What about more extreme cases, where a journalist actually pretends to be a completely different person in order to get information. In a controversial case in 1992, South Africa's *Weekly Mail* newspaper faced a civil suit in court for allegedly having bugged the offices of former covert military operative, Staal Burger. Was the paper justified in using underhand methods to seek information about possible anti-social conspiracies?

3. Discrimination is another ethical dilemma for journalists. How relevant are characteristics like race? In road accident stories? In racially-motivated assaults or terror attacks? In crime stories? Age-ism can crop up too, as an ethical matter, in references to women as "girls", or in the general neglect of concerns of young children and the elderly. And what about gender: it seems normal to some to describe the attire of women featured in articles; to others this is a form of sexist evaluation. These are all ethical questions.

No journalist, at any level in a media enterprise, is without ethical power. Even those working under the supervision of superiors who make the decisions still have the choice to refuse to obey – even if it costs them their job. However, while it is ultimately the decision of each individual to choose what they will do, there is an accumulation of experience in the collective history of journalism. It is from tapping the wisdom of others – of colleagues, traditions, codes of conduct and so on – that a journalist is empowered not merely to make a choice, but to make an informed choice.

Prof. Guy Berger is a former editor of the left-wing alternative weekly newspaper *South*, and is Professor and Head of the Department of Journalism and Media Studies at Rhodes University, Grahamstown.

CHAPTER 11
DOING THE RIGHT THING

Everyone has the right freely to express and disseminate his opinion in words, writing and images and to inform himself. Press freedom and the freedom of reporting by broadcasting and film are guaranteed while diversity of information and opinion in the media shall be protected. Censorship shall not take place.

Resolution adopted by the South African Conference of Editors for submission to the Congress for a Democratic South Africa.

I'm not anti-censorship: I think a society at some point has a collective need and a right to say this is good or not good for society.

Paul Schrader, script writer for the film "The Last Temptation of Christ", speaking after the film was banned an hour before it was due to be screened at *The Weekly Mail* Film Festival in October 1992.

"One man, one quote," was the banner headline of the newspaper advertisement of Radio 702 in support of International Press Freedom Day in May 1993 (*Weekly Mail*, April 30–May 6, p. 19). The rest of the copy read:

A small group of men and women have dedicated their lives to protect your right to hear a point of view, formulate your own opinion, and more often than not, express it in any way you choose.

Journalists. People who dig deeper to bring you the facts and push harder to uncover the truth. And at times, put their lives in danger to do it.

We believe they deserve every bit of support we can give. Without it, we might lose the most basic of human rights.

Freedom of speech.

Freedom, though, is a big word. A typical dictionary defines freedom as the condition of being free from restraints by authority or external forces. That is only part of it – that is so-called "negative freedom". "Positive freedom", in turn, is being free to do as one wishes.

Even with a Bill of Rights, similar to the United States', which entrenches the right of free speech, citizens – and that includes journalists – cannot expect to be free from all restraints; for example, the US government bars journalists from reporting on some affairs of national security.

FIGURE 11.1 The right to write – and look: many South Africans have campaigned for press freedom

Similarly, citizens cannot expect to be entirely free to say whatever they like – to lie in court, for example.

Our concern here is specifically the freedom and independence of the media. And that, wrote British media expert David Webster (*Building free and independent media*, p. 1), depends on three factors: media regulation, the presence of able managers and the ability to be economically viable, as well as the degree to which professionalism and responsibility are exercised.

Let us briefly examine each factor:

- *Media regulation*

Webster suggests that beyond the commonly accepted laws to protect copyrights and prohibit libel and slander, no regulation is necessary. Not everyone agrees.

In South Africa, media workers have contended with government and other controls on the following:
- Topics which may be reported (for example, the judiciary, energy affairs and state security may not be scrutinized).
- Sources of information, like physicians and advocates who may not be quoted by name.
- Presentation of information, like comparative advertising.
- How information is distributed (complaints abound about government control of the airwaves, as well as the monopoly of the printed press by private conglomerates).
- To whom it may be distributed (literature as well as music and video material are subject to bannings and age restrictions).

These restrictions are upheld by the courts and the Directorate of Publications, as well as by professional bodies like the South African Media Council and the Advertising Standards Authority. But changes are being made. The most dramatic is the move to open the airwaves to private broadcasters. This and other modifications in media regulations are expected as South Africa redefines itself in a post-apartheid society.

That the controls will change is certain. That there always will be controls is as well.

- *Economic viability*

Fred M'membe, publisher and editor of a Zambian independent newspaper, summed up this point: "Financial self-sufficiency is essential for a truly independent press" (*Rhodes Review*, July 1992, p. 22). And that, he said, also goes for so-called alternative papers like *Vrye Weekblad*, *South* and *UmAfrika*, which in their early days relied heavily on funding from benevolent external financiers, especially the European Economic Community (EEC). When someone else is paying the bills, there is always the temptation to appease the financiers. "A beggar cannot be genuinely independent," he said.

- *Professionalism and responsibility*
    — A certified accountant who falsifies figures on a client's tax return could lose his licence.
    — A doctor who gives people prescriptions for drugs they do not need could lose his licence.
    — A journalist who pretends to be someone else in order to get information for a story could win a Pulitzer Prize.

Licensing journalists as a way to ensure they keep to a mandatory code of ethics – as is the case for accountants, doctors and lawyers – has long been debated. Proponents say granting licenses to journalists will ensure better qualified media workers under better control. Opponents argue that allowing only licensed journalists access to the media is a denial of free speech.

So far, no proposal to license South African journalists has been implemented. But there have been some close calls. Like in 1981.

The press should put its house in order, warned then-president P.W. Botha, nicknamed "Die Groot Krokodil" (The Big Crocodile). "If they fail to do so, the Government will take steps to do it for them" (*Equid Novi*, 1981, 22(2), p. 106). In response, the South African Media Council (since 1993 the Press Council of South Africa) was established two years later. First on their agenda: "Assist all involved in the media to maintain the highest professional standards by complying with the code of conduct" (De Beer (ed), *Mass media for the nineties*, p. 256).

The Media Council was not the first, nor is it the only group which encourages ethical behaviour (see below). But because it provides an avenue for the public to air their grievances and the industry to enforce some discipline, it is important.

Codes of conduct (like those of the Press Council, Advertising Standards Authority, Public Relations Institute of South Africa, press unions and individual media) can be helpful to journalists as they struggle to distinguish right from wrong. But such codes remain little more than lists of rules which are often thoughtlessly broken – unless they reflect the principles of individual media workers.

This chapter is not a complete discussion on the topic, and attempts only to introduce some of the basic principles on which the codes are based. We pose many questions, but only answer some. You will have to find answers to the rest from the ethical code you have built up from instruction at home, in school and church, and even in the street.

> In this chapter we shall discuss the following:
> 1. Three ethical philosophies: absolutism, antinomianism and situationism.
> 2. How some prominent editors feel about the common ethical dilemma: freebies
> 3. Codes of conduct of the South African Union of Journalists and The Public Relations Institute of Southern Africa.

11.1 THREE ETHICAL APPROACHES

First, say The Missouri Group of journalism professors (*News reporting and writing*, p. 446), is to understand that ethics is a system of principles that guides your conduct and helps you to distinguish between right and wrong or, in some cases, between two wrongs. "Conduct is based on either motives or concern about the consequences of your acts, or both. Ethics also implies an obligation – to yourself or to someone else," they wrote.

11.1.1 Absolutism

Is it ever the right to lie? "No," says the absolutist, "never – regardless of the consequences." The absolutist maintains that there is a fixed set of principles or laws from which there must be no deviation (Missouri Group 1980, p. 447). That is why absolutism is often called "legalism" or "duty ethics".

Journalists who follow an absolutist approach care only that an incident is newsworthy. They see as their duty to report all facts that are interesting, timely and significant – without fear of the consequences or favour to one group over another.

11.1.2 Antinomianism

Most thinking journalists are uncomfortable with the ethics of law, of duty and absolute obligation. So absolutism has been challenged with its opposite: antinomianism. "Antinomian" means against law. It is, therefore, a kind of "non ethics", says veteran American journalism professor John Merrill (*The dialectic in journalism*, Baton Rouge, Louisiana State University Press, 1989, p. 173).

He adds: "Opposed to standards, the antinomian needs no *a priori* guidelines, directions, or moral rules, being satisfied to 'play it by ear', making ethical judgements and decisions intuitively, spontaneously, emotionally and often irrationally."

Antinomianism, Merrill suggests, might be called "whim ethics". It is often attractive to those rebel-reporters who consider an anti-establishment stance as healthy.

11.1.3 Situationism

From the clash of these extreme ethical philosophies – absolutism and antinomianism – emerges a combined approach: situationism. Like the absolutist, the situationist makes his decisions rationally. And like the antinomianist, he believes in relativism. Situation ethics holds that there is a set of rules, but that circumstances can warrant that the rules be broken. For situationists the biggest dilemma comes from answering the question: "When is it right to break the rules?"

11.1.3.1 Solving ethical questions by invoking great thinkers

In the essay preceding this chapter, *South* editor Dr Guy Berger raises some of the ethical questions media workers encounter daily: discrimination, withholding information and accepting gifts or "freebies". These dilemmas often are similar to those great minds have tackled over the centuries. And, says US journalism professor Hiley Ward, a reporter who identifies with a great thinker or religious leader will have a lot of help in knowing what to do in difficult situations (*Professional newswriting*, pp. 531–2).

Here then are Hiley's summaries of a key idea from each of a few great thinkers:

- **Socrates** (470–399 BC) is known for this advice: know thyself.
  Journalists: Ask yourself how you feel about everything from traditions to the status quo.
- **Aristotle** (384–322 BC) held that there is a happy middle ground between the extremes of everything.
  Journalists: Avoid going too far.
- **Marcus Aurelius** (AD 121–180), who believed everyone has a conscience, argued against making judgements about others and for the spirit of forgiveness.
  Journalists: Do not condemn people for their ideas and do not hold grudges.
- **Anselm** (1033–1109) emphasized the importance of motives.
  Journalists: Examine the reasons why you want to do things.

- **Francis of Assisi** (1182–1226) wrote: ". . . where there is hatred, let me sow love; where there is injury, pardon; where there is doubt, faith; where there is despair, hope; where there is darkness, light; where there is sadness, joy . . ."
  Journalists: Be sensitive, and try to do what is good for others as well as yourself.
- **Thomas Hobbes** (1588–1679) insisted that life is a jungle.
  Journalists: Do not trust anyone.
- **Rene Descartes** (1596–1650) believed everything must be questioned, and that what is understood clearly must be true.
  Journalists: Doubt, doubt, doubt. And when something seems true, do not hesitate to act on it.
- **John Stuart Mill** (1806–1873), as the father of Utilitarianism, contended that if something is useful, it is worthwhile.
  Journalists: Follow ideas that promise practical results.
- **Jean-Paul Sartre** (1905–1980) was a leader of the Existentialist movement, which held that you are cast into the world with complete freedom and you are totally responsible for what you do with that freedom.
  Journalists: Remember you cannot pass the blame for inaccuracies on to your sources or editors.
- **Albert Camus** (1913–1960) said there are limits to everything, even if one chooses not to talk about absolutes.
  Journalists: Know your limits – professionally, personally and legally.

11.1.3.2 Conclusion

South Africa's first true newspaper, the *South African Commercial Advertiser*, hit Cape Town's streets on 7 January 1824. Publisher George Grieg and editors Thomas Pringle and John Fairbairn shared a dream which they shared with their readers on the first page:

That this, the First Attempt to establish a Medium of general Communication of the CAPE OF GOOD HOPE, should take place at the opening of a fresh season – at a time when the mind is naturally disposed to look forward with hope, that the events of the succeeding year may atone for the disappointment of the last – we cannot but think as auspicious circumstance: and, as the gradual influence of the genial Seasons rears and protects the rising blossom until the full fruit is matured – so we cannot but hope, that the Patronage of our fellow-Subjects will attend our progress, and finally crown our efforts with that reward which alone will compensate our labours – the confidence and approbation of a discerning public.

> It is the privilege of reason to view the scene of life with all its events, not merely in the light which the moment of their actual occurrence may shed upon them, but with the eye of retrospect to what has passed and of caution for what is to come; and sure, if there be a time more favourable than another, at which a reasonable being would feel disposed to look back with reflection on the past, it must at the commencement of a new season, when another year has been spared to his existence, another period added to that account which he must sooner or later be called upon to render.

The trio had battled for the freedom to bring uncensored news to the public. They knew that their battle would have been in vain if the "discerning public" dismissed their efforts with "You know you can't believe what you read in the papers". And they understood that always there are consequences to what one does.

Their perspective is echoed by John Merrill in the summary of his book, *The dialectic in journalism* (p. 243):

> The journalist who is committed to freedom is a free journalist. A journalist who is committed to ethics is an ethical journalist. A journalist who is committed to ethics and freedom is a rational, existential journalist. . . . This journalist is free because there is the will to be free, and is ethical because there is the will to be ethical. Freedom does not mean that the journalist is free to expand his or her horizons of thought and action if such an expansion is in line with the rights and freedom of others. The freedom of others impinges on the rights and freedoms of the journalists. Social rights circumscribe the journalists's freedom, but if the journalist chooses to use his or her freedom in accordance with, and for the augmentation of, the rights of others, then the journalist will have no restraint on his or her personal freedom. . . . Only when the journalist realises that both freedom and responsibility are equally necessary for authentic journalism will journalism reach a maturity that will be satisfying to everyone concerned.

The founders of South Africa's free press realized their responsibility. Follow their example.

11.2 FREEBIES

Writing for the *Rhodes University Journalism Review*, Charles Riddle asked a group of editors for their views on so-called "freebies". The article, reprinted with permission, ran under the headline: "There is no free lunch is the general feeling towards 'freebies'":

From the response to our survey (eight editors replied), it is clear that freebies in some form are generally condoned, if distrusted, by leading South African editors, and this despite the fact that everyone in (and out) of media is aware that there is no such thing as a free lunch.

At the economic level, the issue is simple: newspapers do not have the financial resources to provide as full and independent a service to their readers as they would like. Freebies, especially in the travel, entertainment and motoring areas, enable newspapers to extend editorial coverage by their own staff. As editor-in-chief of *The Star* and *Sunday Star*, Richard Steyn, notes: "If freebies were banned outright, readers would ultimately be the losers."

The danger here is well understood by all – while freebies undeniably do have beneficial spin-offs for readers, they equally undeniably also have the power to corrupt journalists. Given that donors of freebies are not after criticism – whatever their up-front person may say – the question must be: What price the South African journalist's integrity?

In answering this, the theoretical sketch of the ethical journalist – that is, the independent-minded individual who holds a brief for no-one other than the reader, who remains free of obligations other than that of fidelity to the public interest, who is sincere, truthful, accurate and impartial – can be of limited use. It is, after all, one thing to glibly reel off such qualities to a wide-eyed cub reporter, but another entirely to match them to the underpaid reality of life in the newsroom. As the editor-in-chief of *Rapport*, Izak De Villiers, notes: "Freebies should be disallowed entirely – but then again, journalists should be paid a living wage."

Generally editors seem to see themselves as the moral guardians of their journalists. Richard Steyn, Ebbe Dommisse *(Die Burger)*, Aggrey Klaaste *(Sowetan)*, Nigel Bruce *(Financial Mail)*, Ken Owen *(Sunday Times)* and Jim Jones *(Business Day)* all emphasised their discretionary powers.

The rule seems to be that freebies "of value" are always referred to the editor and, outside of free travel, nearly always refused. Ken Owen states that the rules are flexible, but for him freebies are permissible subject to his approval and only when benefit ensues to the paper.

Motoring, in the words of Derek Smith *(Eastern Province Herald)* is an area of "particular controversy" with Aggrey Klaaste stating quite openly that his journalists are "overawed by the gifts from car people". So controversial is the motoring scene that Ken Owen no longer has a motoring correspondent on the staff of the *Sunday Times* and prefers to buy in copy – thus giving his paper "a measure of protection in the editing".

This is not to say, of course, that there are no motoring journalists of integrity. There undoubtedly are, but editors nevertheless seem particularly keen to keep a close watch on motoring freebies.

Die Burger editor Ebbe Dommisse insists that motoring trips are individually approved, with the editor having final say as to which member of staff should accept.

The Star's Richard Steyn notes that mention should always be made of any free trips given by car manufacturers in any resulting story appearing in the newspaper.

For *Business Day* editor Jim Jones, the days of the "long-term trial" – which saw journalists given cars for lengthy periods – are definitely over.

Here follow some of the replies (edited in some cases for lack of space) to questions in the survey:

- *What is your attitude towards gifts to journalists on your staff?*

"*The Financial Mail* discourages gifts . . . unless they are small tokens at Christmas" (Nigel Bruce).

"No problem if the gift is small – I'd assume my staff would not or could not be bought by (say) a bottle of wine at Christmas. Anything larger should be discussed . . . (Jim Jones).

"No freebies allowed, whatsoever" (Izak de Villiers).

"Bigger 'gifts' are turned down immediately, especially if they appear to be bribery attempts" (Ebbe Dommisse).

- *What policy does your newspaper have on the issue of free movie or theatre tickets, free records or free lunches?*

"There are no free lunches" (Izak de Villiers).

"Cinema and theatre tickets are okay . . . we do not encourage free lunches for restaurant reviewers" (Jim Jones).

"Critics in entertainment can accept free records, tapes, CDs, etc; the gremlin of free lunches is debatable" (Aggrey Klaaste).

"Free lunches for restaurant critics are obviously out" (Derek Smith).

- *What is your newspaper's policy towards promotional freebies for travel writers?*

"All invitations must be to the editor to be apportioned at his discretion" (Nigel Bruce).

"Keep a wary eye on it" (Ken Owen).

"Acceptable provided no strings are attached" (Derek Smith).

"Basically we would like to finance all trips of all our journalists, but budget constraints have to be considered . . . Therefore, we accept promotional freebies" (Ebbe Dommisse).

- *What gifts are acceptable, if any?*

"A sample of a small product is okay. A car, boxes of wine, a word processor, TV set, etc. definitely not!" (Ebbe Dommisse).

"Ball pens, neckties, etc" (Jim Jones).

"A box of apples is in order. A diamond ring is not" (Izak de Villiers).

"I have once defaced and returned the title page of a special edition which I deemed an improper gift" (Ken Owen).

"No gifts are acceptable" (Aggrey Klaaste).

- *What standpoint do you hold on the issue of financial journalists dealing in shares?*

"We don't have such people on the *Sowetan*. Yet!" (Aggrey Klaaste).

"Not permitted in this company. All other journalists have to declare their holdings" (Derek Smith).

"The *Financial Mail* encourages its writers to invest in shares. They may not speculate or sell stocks forward in the hope of buying in at a lower price. All dealings and portfolios must be declared to the editor" (Nigel Bruce).

"Journalists are not permitted to accept shares or special share options. Staff members have to disclose their share portfolios to the editor and are not allowed to write about companies in which they hold shares" (Jim Jones).

"Our financial editors have to submit a complete list of their shareholdings. We regard it as highly unethical to promote shares they possess, and would take immediate action in such a case" (Ebbe Dommisse).

"All shares must be disclosed and transactions reported. My own shares, and my wife's, were put into a blind trust some years ago and are administered on our behalf – transactions are reported to us quarterly, never in advance" (Ken Owen).

- *Any other comments?*

"I generally assume staff members cannot be 'bought'. That's backed up by a requirement that any 'large' freebie be disclosed to the editor" (Jim Jones).

"The answer is to raise the qualifications, salaries, status, and self-respect of journalists" (Ken Owen).

"We do think freebies may compromise some journalists, but in the current financial climate of newspapers they appear to be a necessary evil" (Ebbe Dommisse).

"Freebies are, however, inescapable . . ." (Aggrey Klaaste).

"Provided they are modest, do not carry an obligation to provide compensatory editorial and are controlled by the editor, the *Financial Mail* has no objection in principle" (Nigel Bruce).

Used with permission.

11.3 CODES OF CONDUCT

11.3.1 The South African Union of Journalists

CODE OF CONDUCT

1. A journalist has a duty to maintain the highest professional and ethical standards.
2. A journalist shall at all times defend the principle of a freedom of the Press and other media in relation to the collection of information and the expression of comment and criticism. He/she shall strive to eliminate distortion, news suppression and censorship.
3. A journalist shall strive to ensure that the information he/she disseminates is fair and accurate, avoid the expression of comment and conjecture as established fact and falsification by distortion, selection or misrepresentation.
4. A journalist shall rectify promptly any harmful inaccuracies, ensure that corrections and apologies receive due prominence and afford the right of reply to persons criticised when the issue is of sufficient importance.
5. A journalist shall obtain information, photographs and illustrations only by straightforward means. The use of other means can be justified only by overriding considerations of the public interest. The journalist is entitled to exercise a personal conscientious objection to the use of such means.
6. Subject to justification by overriding considerations of public interest, a journalist shall do nothing which entails intrusion into private grief and distress.
7. A journalist shall protect confidential sources of information.
8. A journalist shall not accept bribes nor shall he/she allow other inducements to influence the performance of his/her professional duties.
9. A journalist shall not lend himself/herself to the distortion or suppression of the truth because of advertising or other consideration.
10. A journalist shall not originate material which encourages discrimination on the grounds of race, colour, creed, gender or sexual orientation.
11. A journalist shall not take private advantage of information gained in the course of his/her duties, before the information is public knowledge.
12. A journalist shall not engage in plagiarism and shall attribute information used in articles to the original source or individual, organisation, media channel or news agency.

11.3.2 The Public Relations Institute of Southern Africa

DECLARATION OF PRINCIPLES

Registered individuals of the Public Relations Institute of Southern Africa and Accredited Public Relations Practitioners base their professional principles on the fundamental value and dignity of the individual, holding that the free exercise of human rights, especially freedom of speech, freedom of assembly and freedom of the media, is essential to the practice of public relations.

In serving the interest of clients and employers, we dedicate ourselves to the goals of better communication, understanding and co-operation among diverse individuals, groups and institutions of society, and of equal opportunity of employment in the public relations profession.

As registered individuals of PRISA and/or Accredited Public Relations Practitioners we pledge:
- To conduct ourselves professionally, with truth, accuracy, fairness and responsibility to the public and towards our colleagues;
- To improve our individual competence and advance the knowledge and proficiency of the profession through continuing research and education;
- And to adhere to the articles of the Code of Professional Standards for the Practice of Public Relations as adopted by the National Executive of the Public Relations Institute of Southern Africa on May 3, 1993 in Cape Town.

CODE OF PROFESSIONAL STANDARDS

1. **Definition**

   Public relations practice shall be defined as the deliberate, planned and sustained effort to establish and maintain mutual understanding between an organisation and its various publics, both internal and external.

2. **Accreditation as a professional public relations practitioner**

   In recognition of the profession of Public Relations Practice the maintenance of this Code of Professional Standards signifies the following:
   2.1 That the accredited practitioner is recognised publicly as a professional exponent of the discipline of public relations;
   2.2 That accreditation provides impartial witness to the professional standing of the individual accredited;

2.3 That both the accredited practitioner and the public have the right of recourse to the Accreditation and Ethics Council of PRISA;
2.4 That the accredited practitioner may use the designation APR with his/her name;
2.5 That the accredited practitioner, in upholding his/her pledge to adhere to this Code, will continue to strive for excellence in professional conduct.

3. **Personal conduct of a registered individual and an accredited public relations practitioner**

    3.1 In the conduct of his/her professional activities, he/she shall respect the public interest and the dignity of the individual. It is his/her personal responsibility at all times to deal fairly and honestly with his/her client or employer, past or present, with his/her colleagues, with the media of communication and with the public.
    3.2 He/she shall conduct his/her professional life in accordance with the public interest. He/she shall not conduct himself/ herself in any manner detrimental to the profession of public relations.
    3.2 He/she has a positive duty to maintain integrity and accuracy, as well as generally accepted standards of good taste.
    3.4 He/she thus shall not knowingly, intentionally or recklessly communicate false or misleading information and is obligated to use proper care to avoid doing so inadvertently.
    3.5 He/she shall not guarantee the achievement of specified results beyond his/her direct control. Neither shall he/she negotiate or agree terms with a prospective employer or client on the basis of payment only contingent upon specific future public relations achievements.
    3.6 He/she shall when acting for a client or employer who belongs to a profession respect the code of ethics of that other profession and shall not knowingly be party to any breach of such a code.

4. **Conduct towards clients/employers**

    4.1 He/she shall safeguard the confidences of both present and former clients and employers, and shall not disclose or make use of information given or obtained in confidence from his/ her employer or client, past or present, for personal gain or otherwise, or to the disadvantage or prejudice of such client or employer.

4.2 He/she shall not represent conflicting or competing interests without the express consent of those involved, given after full disclosure of the facts; nor place himself/herself in a position where his/her interests are or may be in conflict with a duty to the client, without full disclosure of such interests to all involved.

4.3 He/she shall not be party to any activity which seeks to dissemble or mislead by promoting a disguised or undisclosed interest whilst appearing to further another. It is his/her duty to ensure that the actual interest of any organisation with which he/she may be professionally concerned is adequately declared.

4.4 He/she shall not in the course of his/her professional services to the employer or client accept payment either in cash or in kind in connection with these services from another source without the express consent of his/her employer or client.

5. **Conduct towards colleagues**

    5.1 He/she shall not maliciously injure the professional reputation or practice of another registered individual or accredited public relations practitioner or other professional.

    5.2 He/she shall at all times uphold this Code, shall co-operate with colleagues in doing so and in enforcing decision on any matter arising from this application.

    5.3 A registered individual or accredited public relations practitioner who knowingly causes or permits another person or organisation to act in a manner inconsistent with this Code or is party to such an action himself/herself, shall himself/herself be deemed to be in breach of it.

    5.4 If he/she has reason to believe that another colleague has been engaged in practices which may be in breach of this Code, or practices which may be unethical, unfair or illegal, it is his/her duty to promptly advise the Institute or the Council.

6. **Conduct towards the business environment**

    6.1 A registered individual or an accredited public relations practitioner having financial interest in an organisation shall not recommend the use of that organisation nor make use of its services on behalf of his/her client or employer, without declaring his/her interest.

    6.2 In performing professional services for a client or employer he/she shall not accept fees, commissions or any other consideration from anyone other than the client or employer in connection with those services, without the express consent of the client/employer, given after disclosure of the facts.

6.3 He/she shall sever relations, as soon as possible, with any organisation or individual if such a relationship requires conduct contrary to this Code.

7. **Conduct towards the channels of communication**

    7.1 He/she shall not engage in any practice which tends to corrupt the integrity of channels or media of communication.
    7.2 He/she shall identify publicly the name of the client or employer on whose behalf any public communication is made.

8. **Conduct towards the state**

    8.1 The registered individual or accredited public relations practitioner respects the principles contained in the Constitution of the country in which he/she is resident.
    8.2 He/she shall not offer or give any reward to any person holding public office, with intent to further his/her interests or those of his/her employer, if such action is inconsistent with public interest.

9. **Conduct towards PRISA and the Accreditation and Ethics Council of PRISA**

    9.1 The registered individual and accredited public relations practitioner shall at all times respect the dignity and decisions of PRISA and the Accreditation and Ethics Council of PRISA.
    9.2 Registered individuals of PRISA shall be bound to uphold the annual registration fee levied by PRISA, which fee is payable as determined by the National Executive of PRISA.
    9.3 The individual enjoying registration as an accredited public relations practitioner shall be bound to uphold the annual registration fee levied by the Council/PRISA, which fee is payable as determined by the Council/PRISA.

10. **Disciplinary rules**

    A registered individual or accredited public relations practitioner who infringes the Code of Professional Standards, in the opinion of the National Executive of PRISA or the Accreditation and Ethics Council of PRISA, shall be informed in writing and shall be given reasonable opportunity of stating his/her defence, either in writing or by personal attendance at a meeting of a Disciplinary Committee appointed by the

DOING THE RIGHT THING

> National Executive or the Council and specially convened for this purpose. If in the opinion of the Disciplinary Committee the complaint has been substantiated, the Committee will report its findings to the National Executive or the Council at its next ordinary meeting. The National Executive or the Council shall, on a majority vote, decide on the action to be taken.

Assignments

1. When the controversial religious film, "The Last Temptation of Christ" was censored an hour before it was to be screened at a Johannesburg film festival, the script writer surprised many by telling the crowd: "I am not anti-censorship." Paul Schrader explained further: "I think a society at some point has a collective need and a right to say this is good or not good for society. The starting point, for example, in America is a ruling by Oliver Wendell Holmes, a chief justice of the Supreme Court, where he says you cannot yell fire in a crowded room. That is an abridgement of speech which, everyone agrees, is improper because it creates danger.

    "The moment you accept the Holmesian dictate, you accept that censorship has a role. The question is where culture stands and how that line is drawn and how it moves."

    Compare Schrader's statement with the resolution adopted by the South African Conference of Editors for submission to CODESA, quoted at the beginning of this chapter. Write a page supporting the editors or draft an alternative resolution. Discuss your piece with your peers and try to come up with a consensus.

2. People have the right to privacy. But journalists spend a great deal of time making private affairs public. When a white, retired cabinet minister was rumoured to have an extra-marital affair with his so-called coloured secretary, journalists clamoured for the story. The couple was hounded for interviews and snapshots of the woman in scant clothing was published widely. The man's wife was also pestered until she finally closed the door with a final, "No comment". This incident raises many questions, including: Do even retired government officials relinquish the right to conduct their private lives in private? What about the woman? What about the wife?

3. Read Charles Riddle's article on freebies again. Can you pick out editors who are absolutists, antinomians and situationists from the quotes?

4. Consider Item 8 of SAUJ's code and Item C.2. of the PRISA code. Invite a public relations practitioner and a reporter to class and then discuss how these points of their codes are handled in practice.

5. Write a 10-part code of media ethics for yourself. Compare the different codes with your classmates and create a consensus version.

Bibliography and recommended reading

De Beer, A.S. (ed), *Mass media for the nineties*, Pretoria, Van Schaik, 1993.

Merril, John C., *The dialectic in journalism: toward a responsible use of press freedom*, Baton Rouge, Louisiana State University Press, 1989.

Schrader, Paul, "Who has the right to say what Christianity means?", *Weekly Mail*, 30 October–5 November, 1992 pp. 10–11.

The Missouri Group: Brooks, Brian S. *et al.*, *News reporting and writing*, New York, St Martin's Press, 1980.

Riddle, Charles, "Journalists speak; there's no free lunch is the general feeling towards 'freebies' ", *Rhodes University Journalism Review*, July 1992, pp. 20–1.

Ward, Hiley, *Professional newswriting*, New York, Harcourt Brace Jovanovich, 1985.

Webster, David, *Building free and independent media*, San Francisco Institute for Contemporary Studies. This pamphlet is available from: ICS, 243 Kearney Street, San Francisco, California 94108 USA.

For a review of tough editorial decisions in journalism ethics, consider Frank McColloch's *Drawing the line: how 31 editors solved their toughest ethical dilemmas*, published in 1984 by the American Society of Newspaper Editors Foundation, P.O. Box 17004, Washington DC, 20041 USA.

PART 4
MEDIA MILESTONES

CHAPTER 12
TIMELINE: SIGNIFICANT EVENTS IN THE HISTORY OF THE PRESS IN SOUTH AFRICA

1455 The German goldsmith John Guttenburg creates the first moveable type printing press, which eventually leads to the publication of newspapers.

1660 The first daily newspaper, *Leipziger Zeitung*, is published in Germany.

1800 South Africa's first newspaper, *The Cape Town Gazette and African Advertiser*, is published on 16 August. By order of the Governor of the Cape Colony, Sir George Young, no political news is printed.

1824 The first non-Government newspaper, the *SA Commercial Advertiser*, is published by George Grieg in the Cape Colony on January 7. John Fairbairn and Thomas Pringle are the editors.

1830 A Dutch language newspaper, *De Zuid Afrikaan*, starts in opposition to the *SA Commercial Advertiser*.

1837 *Umshumayeli Wendaba*, the first Black language (Xhosa) newspaper is published in July by Methodist missionaries. It lasts until 1841.

1844 Natal's first newspaper, *De Natalier*, appears.

1846 *The Natal Witness* is launched, the oldest daily newspaper still in existence. At first reports are printed in both Dutch and English, but eventually Dutch is dropped.

1850s The first Transvaal newspaper, *De Oude Emigrant*, printed in Dutch, appears.

1854 The Free State's first newspaper – *The Friend of the Sovereignty and Bloemfontein Gazette*, later to become *The Friend of the Free State* and then *The Friend* – is published in both Dutch and English.

1857 The *Cape Argus* is born, one of early South Africa's most influential newspapers. It is the first to use telegraph facilities.

1862 *Indaba*, the first newspaper to come out in a Black vernacular as well as English, appears.

1866 The Argus Printing and Publishing Company is formed as a public company. Among its original subscribers is Cecil John Rhodes. It remains the pre-eminent independent media owner right into the 1990s.

1874 The first important Transvaal newspaper, *Die Volkstem*, starts in Pretoria. In 1922 the newspaper switches to Afrikaans and in 1951 it closes.

1876 The *Cape Times* is launched, South Africa's first daily newspaper.

Die Afrikaanse Patriot, the first Afrikaans-language, or as it was called, Cape Dutch, newspaper appears with Rev S.J. du Toit of Paarl as the editor. It folds in 1904.

The first newspaper edited by Blacks for Blacks appears. *Isigidimi Sama Xosa* is published by Lovedale Press, a Presbyterian missionary printer.

1878 *The Natal Mercantile Advertiser*, later to become *The Daily News*, appears.

1882 The Newspaper Press Union (NPU) is established.

1884 *Imvo Zabantsundu*, the first Black-owned newspaper, appears under editor John Tengo Jabavu.

1887 *The Eastern Star*, a newspaper started in Grahamstown, is moved to Johannesburg a year after the discovery of gold and renamed *The Star*. There are already seven journals in the town.

1889 Johannesburg's *The Star* expands to a daily from three editions a week.

1891 *SA Mining and Coal, Gold and Base Minerals* first published.

1895 The first kinetoscope in South Africa is introduced in Johannesburg, six years after becoming available in New York.

1896 The Italian Guglielmo Marconi patents the wireless. He is considered the father of radio.

1902 The *Rand Daily Mail* is launched with its first editor the fiction writer Edgar Wallace.

1903 *Ilanga Lase*, the English/Zulu newspaper is started in Natal. Inkatha-controlled Mandla-Matla Publishing become its proprietors in 1987, after many years under the Argus banner.

1906 *The Sunday Times* first appears, which, together with the *Rand Daily Mail*, is considered the founder of popular journalism in South Africa. The two work in close association, although a single company is not formed until 1955 when SA Associated Newspapers (later Times Media) is formed.

Mahatma Gandhi establishes the *Indian Opinion*.

1910 *The Argus, Rand Daily Mail* and *Cape Times* create a partnership with the British news agency Reuters to establish a local agency. It is succeeded in 1938 by the South African Press Association.

1911 *Farmer's Weekly* is launched.

1915 *Die Vaderland* first appears in Pretoria. (In 1931 it is taken over by a new company, Afrikaanse Pers Beperk. Dr D.F. Malan, a Dutch Reformed Church minister, edits a new daily newspaper, *De Burger* (later *Die Burger*) and leads a new party, the Nationalists. The party has trouble raising the capital for its newspaper, and cannot find a printer to print *De Burger*. However, the company formed to publish *De Burger*, Nasionale Pers Beperk, buys second-hand equipment previously owned by the *Cape Times* which had used it to print the *Transvaal Leader*.)

1916 *Huisgenoot* is launched by Nasionale Pers.

1917 *Die Volksblad* is launched as the Orange Free State's Nationalist newspaper. It becomes a daily in 1925.

1919 Nasionale Pers launch *Landbouweekblad* in competition to *Farmer's Weekly*.

1923 The first South African radio broadcasts are made from Johannesburg by the SA Railways on December 18.

1924 Regular radio broadcasts start on 1 July with Station JB, run from a Johannesburg department store.

1926 The Scottish inventor, John Logie Baird, shows live television pictures in London.

1929 The British Association demonstrates television in Johannesburg and Cape Town.

1932 *Bantu World*, the predecessor of *The World* (1955), *Post Transvaal* and ultimately the *Sowetan*, is founded.

1934 The established press faces serious competition from outside mining via I.W. Schlesinger, who controls the African Broadcasting Company. He launches *Sunday Express* in Johannesburg and *Sunday Tribune* in Durban, and in 1937, daily editions of each. In 1939 the Rand Daily Mail, Sunday Times and Argus groups buy out all Schlesinger's interests.

1935 The first commercial radio station, LM Radio, broadcasts from Portuguese East Africa (later Mozambique).

1936 The South African Broadcasting Corporation (SABC) is established by an Act of Parliament. It takes over the African Broadcasting Company.

The British Broadcasting Corporation begins the world's first regularly scheduled television service on November 2.

1937 Dr H.F. Verwoerd, previously professor of sociology at Stellenbosch University, becomes the first editor of a Johannesburg morning newspaper, *Die Transvaler*, which was created to give the National Party a platform in the Transvaal.

1940 The SABC starts radio services for Blacks.

1943 The first public relations officer in South Africa is appointed by the South African Railways.

1947 Marius Jooste, the advertising manager of *Die Vaderland*, resigns and helps start *Dagbreek*, a Sunday newspaper. Avowed to be politically independent, the publication is financed by English business and mining capital. By 1951 many of the shares are in the hands of the Transvaal Nationalists and *Dagbreek* becomes more openly Nationalist supporting. South Africa's Audit Bureau of Circulations (ABC) is formed. The UK bureau was established in 1931 and the US bureau in 1914.

1948 The forerunner of Adindex, the Press Analysis, is started by SA Research Services, a company subsequently taken over by Franklin Research.

Reader's Digest opens up in South Africa.

1949 Capro – the organization handling the advertising for the bulk of the country's weekly newspapers starts operations. Capro is an acronym of Central Advertising and Public Relations Office.

1950 Springbok Radio, the SABC's first commercial radio station, starts on May 1. The Newspaper Press Union does not oppose commercial broadcasting because the shortage of newsprint means that they are short of space to sell to advertisers.

1951 *African Drum* is founded by Jim Bailey. West African and East African editions are later launched which have a larger circulation than the South African edition.

1956 *Bona* is launched. This magazine, together with *Drum*, gains a virtual monopoly over the Black magazine sector for the next 20 years.

1957 The Public Relations Institute of Southern Africa (PRISA) is founded.

1960 The SABC launches four Black language stations – Sesotho, Lebowa, Zulu and Xhosa – in June.

1961 The SABC makes the first FM radio broadcast. By 1965 South Africa has a national radio service broadcasting on FM in seven languages.

1962 Die Afrikaanse Pers Beperk attempts to produce a Sunday newspaper in competition to *Dagbreek*. They fail, and being in financial difficulties the company merges with *Die Vaderland* to prevent a takeover by the Argus or Nasionale. The new company, Afrikaanse Pers (1962) Beperk results.

1963 The country's first magazine gravure printing system is introduced by Nasionale.

1964 Regional radio commences with the launch of Radio Highveld on FM.

1965 *Fair Lady* is first published.

Radio Good Hope, the second regional radio station, starts broadcasting on July 1.

The Cape Nationalists launch a new Sunday newspaper, *Die Beeld*, in the Transvaal.

1967 Radio Port Natal starts broadcasting on May 1 from Durban.

Market Research Africa starts Adindex, the primary local source of advertising expenditure.

1969 The Advertising Standards Authority (ASA) and its Code of Practice is established.

1971 Afrikaans Sundays *Die Beeld* and *Dagbreek*, owned respectively by Nasionale and Perskor, merge to form *Rapport*, a 50:50 venture between the two adversaries.

1973 At the invitation of the SA Society of Marketers (now Association of Marketers), the SA Advertising Research Foundation (SAARF) is launched.

1974 Nasionale Pers launches its first morning newspaper in the Transvaal, *Beeld*, on December 16.

1975 The SABC buys LM Radio and relaunches it as Radio 5, a national "youth" station.

The first All Media and Products Study (AMPS) figures are released by SAARF.

1976 *The Citizen*, an English language tabloid daily is founded ostensibly by Louis Luyt. It is later established that the funds came from the Department of Information. *The Citizen* is then sold to its printers, Perskor.

Non-commercial television's first official broadcast goes out on January 5.

1978 SABC's TV1 goes commercial.

Bop Radio comes on air, an independent (from the SABC) station aimed at upmarket urban Blacks in the PWV area and in Bophuthatswana. It is the first of the modern homeland stations.

1979 Capital Radio commences broadcasting from the Transkei initially targeting the PWV but settles for the Eastern Cape and Natal coasts.

Radio Thohoyandou, the Northern Transvaal's Radio Bop starts broadcasting from Venda.

Finance Week comes out in independent competition to Times Media's *Financial Mail*.

Equid Novi, the first academic journal for the media, is launched.

1980 *Style* magazine's first issue appears.

Radio 702 begins beaming its MW signal to the PWV from Bophuthatswana.

MEDIA MILESTONES

1981 Maister Directories, publishers of the Yellow Pages, established.

1982 TV2 and 3 are launched by the SABC for South Africa's Black population.

Radio listeners' licences are abolished. Henceforth all SABC's radio revenues are derived from advertising and commercial ventures.

1983 Radio Ciskei is launched. Radio Lotus, an English-language station, is set up for Indian listeners in Natal and the Transvaal.

The *Beeld* (Nasionale) versus *Transvaler* and *Vaderland* (Perskor) circulation scandal comes to a head. *Beeld* gets sole control of the Johannesburg and Pretoria morning markets, *Die Transvaler* moves to Pretoria as an afternoon newspaper, *Vaderland* stays in Johannesburg as an afternoon newspaper. Perskor's Pretoria newspapers *Oggendblad* (morning) and *Hoofstad* (afternoon) are axed. Advertisers get some R1,3 million in compensation for falsified circulations.

1984 Bophuthatswana launches Bop TV.

The first South African edition of *Cosmopolitan* hits the streets mid-February.

Nasionale Pers invest in Black publishing with the takeover of Bailey Publications – *Drum*, *True Love* and the *Sunday City Press*.

The Sunday Star is launched.

The Saturday edition of *The Star* is changed from an afternoon to a morning, and pushes for property advertising, a move which precipitates the closure of the *Sunday Express* the following year.

1985 The SABC's Teledata is launched to TV viewers in the PWV area. Owners of decoder fitted TV sets can summon up to 300 pages of text 24 hours a day.

The *Rand Daily Mail* and the *Sunday Express* are closed down by SA Associated Newspapers (now Times Media).

Business Day is launched.

The Friend, the Orange Free State's only English language daily, closes down.

Durban's newspapers, the evening *Daily News* (Argus Group) and the morning *Natal Mercury* (Robinsons) are merged into one company, Natal Newspapers, which combines the printing, distribution, advertising, marketing and administrative functions of the two papers.

Ex-*Rand Daily Mail* staffers set up the independent newspaper, the *Weekly Mail*. It quickly runs into trouble with the Government, including a threat of seizure of its first issue.

The SABC introduces TV4 by using the broadcast signals of its Black TV2 and TV3 services.

1986 M-Net is pre-launched to apartment blocks, townhouses and other multi-dwellings in Johannesburg on September 28.

Breakfast TV, the SABC's TV5, first goes out on October 1.

The SABC introduces Radio Metro, a township English station targeted at Radio Bop's audience.

Cape Town's *The Argus* (Argus Group) and *Cape Times* (Times Media) rationalize operations. The *Cape Times* sells its building and moves its staff into the offices of *The Argus*, which takes over circulation and administrative functions.

The SABC restructures its radio services: Springbok is closed at the end of 1985, on January 1 the English and Afrikaans services go commercial and Radio Highveld is broken into Highveld, Jacaranda and Oranje, and Good Hope becomes Good Hope and Algoa. Radio 2000 and Orion are launched.

1987 A vintage year for magazine launches – *You* (an English version of *Huisgenoot*), *People, Inside South Africa* and *Insig*.

M-Net extends its signal to single-unit dwellings on the PWV on April 1, and to greater Durban, Cape Town and Port Elizabeth later in the year.

1988 *The Executive, Trend, Jive, Me, Talk, Career Secretary, Cover, Uptown* and *Early Times* see the light of day for the first time.

Jane Raphaely, publisher of *Cosmopolitan*, launches the new-look *Femina*.

M-Net launches its Business Broadcast facility.

After almost 75 years of newspaper publishing, *Die Vaderland* becomes a local Afrikaans/English weekly servicing the near and far East Rand. Perskor makes *Die Transvaler* its Afrikaans flagship with Johannesburg and Pretoria editions.

1989 M-Net reaches 300 000 subscribers and launches East-Net and Canal Portuguese.

Annual Media and Products Survey (AMPS) meters are relaunched.

1990 *The Daily Mail*, a daily edition of the alternative newspaper, the *Weekly Mail*, is launched and closes shortly afterwards.

Good Hope splits into Good Hope Metro and Radio Kontrei.

The SABC introduces CNN, its daytime TV news broadcast service.

M-Net reaches 500 000 subscribers and launches KTV for children.

1991 M-Net is given permission by the government to broadcast news programmes.

The Rhodes University Journalism Review is established.

Penthouse magazine is first published in South Africa.

1992 The SABC merges TV2, TV3 and TV4 into a single channel: Contemporary Community Values, or CCV.

1993 A democratically-selected board takes over the SABC.

Nasionale Pers closes down *Die Oosterlig* in East London after 56 years, while Perskor closes *Die Transvaler*, also after 56 years.

The *Weekly Mail* merges with its former international supplement, *The Guardian Weekly*, to form *The Weekly Mail & Guardian*. Parliament passes the Independent Broadcasting Commission Bill, initiated at the multi-party talks. The bill wrests control of the airwaves away from the Ministry of Home Affairs and clears the way for independent broadcasting projects.

Bibliography and recommended reading

Burns, Yvonne, *Media law*, Durban, Butterworths, 1990.

Crwys-Williams, Jennifer (ed), *South African despatches: two centuries of the best in South African journalism*, Johannesburg, Ashanti, 1989.

De Beer, A.S. (ed), *Mass media for the nineties: the South African handbook of mass communication*, Pretoria, Van Schaik, 1992.

De Kock, Wessel, *A manner of speaking: the origins of the press in South Africa*, Cape Town, Saayman & Weber, 1982.

Leahy, Mike & Voice, Paul (eds), *The media book 1991/92*, Bryanston, WTH Publications, 1992.

May, Frank A., *Joernalistiek*, Cape Town, Boeksentrum, 1963.

INDEX

Absolutism   205
Adindex   225
Advertising Standards Authority (ASA)   225
African Drum   224
Afrikaanse Patriot   222
All Media and Products Study (AMPS)   225
Analysis story   56
Anselm   206
Antinomianism   205
Argus   10, 26, 31, 111, 222, 227
Argus Printing and Publishing Company   221
Argus Newspapers   23
Aristotle   206
Arnold, Edmund   149
Ashe, Reid   7, 10
Atex Video Display Terminal   28
Aurelius, Marcus   206

Bailey, Jim   224
Baird, John Logie   223
Barnes, Clive   59
Bates, Stephen   6, 9, 57, 70, 119
Battersby, John   14
Baxter, Bill   111
Beckett, Denis   3–5, 57
Beeld   22, 224, 225, 226
Beresford, David   54, 91
Berger, Guy   197–200, 206
Biggs, David   58, 111
Boccardi, John   14
Boobyer, Clifford   194
Bop Radio   225
Boston Globe   70
Botha, P.W.   204
Breier, David   54
British Broadcasting Corporation   223

Broadcast writing style   121–6
Broder, David   12
Bruce, Nigel   30, 209–11
Buchanan, Edna   7, 87, 91, 141
Burger, Die   20, 22, 23, 28, 209, 222
Business Day   8, 209, 226
Butcher, Judith   148

Cable News Network (CNN)   227
Camus, Albert   207
Cape Argus   221
Cape Times   9, 28, 30, 31, 69, 87, 151, 163, 222, 223, 227
Cape Town Gazette and African Advertiser   8, 221
Capital Radio   225
Cappon, Rene   97, 99
Captions   154
Career Secretary   227
Carey, James   47
Carlson, Margaret   75
Central Advertising and Public Relations Office (Capro)   224
Charlotte Observer   12, 22, 52, 64, 69, 74, 96
Chicago Daily News   47
Chicago Tribune   96
Citizen, The   225
City Press   22
Clinton, Bill   72
Codes of conduct   212, 213,
Cohen, Bernard C.   15
Columbia Journalism Review   40, 142
Cooke, Janet   71
Copy-editing   148
Cosmopolitan   227

Dagbreek   224, 225
Daily News   23, 226

229

INDEX

Dana, Charles 8
De Oude Emigrant 221
De Natalier 221
De Kock, Nico 121
De Villiers, Izak 209, 210, 211
De Zuid Afrikaan 221
De Beer, A.S. 7
DeKat 79
Descartes, René 207
Design 159
Desktop publishing (DTP) 137–40
Dialogue 107
Diamond Fields Advertiser 23
Diederich, Pedro 7–8
Domisse, Ebbe 209–11
Dorset, James 93
Drum 58–9, 226
Du Toit, S.J. 222

Early Times 227
Eastern Province Herald 118, 209
Eastern Star 222
Editing 141
Editorial profile 165
Editorial writing 58
Editorial positions 23
Eksteen, Willem 20
Equid Novi 14, 15, 204, 225
Ethics 195
Executive, The 227

Fair Lady 224
Fairbairn, John 207
Farmer's Weekly 222
Feature columns 58
Feature stories 56, 97
Felder, Dov 24
Femina 227
Fiction 97, 99
Finance Week 225
Financial Mail 30, 209, 225
Flesch, Rudolph 45–6
Fonts 171
Francis of Assisi, St 207

Freebies 208
Freeman, M. 181
Friend of the Sovereignty and Bloemfontein Gazette, The 221, 226

Garcia, Mario 183, 193
Gluckman, Jonathan 69
Gold Fields Advertiser 8
Graaff-Reinet Advertiser 8
Graham, Phillip 65
Greene, Trisha 69
Grieg, George 207, 221
Grimbeek, Yvonne 10
Guardian Weekly, The 13, 16, 53, 54, 86
Guthrie, A.B. 99
Guttenberg, John 221

Haley, Allen 174
Harris, Julian 149, 152
Hazelhurst, David 24, 26, 159, 162
Headlines 148–51
Heard, Tony 30
Hefer, Stephanie 20
Hemingway, Ernest 60, 99
Heyneman, Louis 160, 191
Hobbes, Thomas 207
Holmes, Oliver Wendell 217
Hope, Bob 78
Horizon 30
Huisgenoot 223
Huntley, Dan 22
Huntsville News, The 142

Ilanga Lase 222
Imvo Zabantsundu 222
Indaba 221
Inside South Africa 227
Insig 227
Interviews 72
Inverted pyramid 52
Investigative story 57

Jabava, John Tengo 222
Jive 227

INDEX

Jones, Jim   207
Jooste, Marius   224
Joseph, Raymond   120, 128

Kansas City Star   99
Kessler, Felix   59
Kissinger, Henry   70
Klaaste, Aggrey   209, 210, 211
Kodak   28
Korybski, Alfred   16
Kovarsky, David   163
KwaNdebele National Development Corporation   165

L.M. Radio   223
Landbouweekblad   223
Layout   187
Leads   48
Legibility   174
Leipziger Zeitung   221
Level, Jeff   190
Liebowitz, Annie   165
Loeb, Richard   47
Lovedale Press   222

M'membe, Fred   203
M-Net   227, 228
Malan, D.F.   222
Mandela, Nelson   176
Marais, Francois   176
Marconi, Guglielmo   222
Marketing News   111
Matshikiza, Todd   58
McCormick, Mark H.   82
McDonald, Patti   137–40
McDowell, Frank   218
McGreal, Chris   54
Me   227
Media releases   118
Media kits   126
Merrill, John C.   15, 205, 206, 208
Meyer, Deon   26
Miami Herald   87, 92, 151
Michel, Ulli   176

Mill, John Stuart   207
Miller, Edward   12, 13

Nasionale Pers   22, 28, 222, 225
Natal Witness   221
Natal Mercury   226
Natal Mercantile Advertiser   222
New York Sun   9
New York Times   59
News   1, 6, 8, 10, 14, 17, 56
News releases   118
News writing terms   17
Newspaper Press Union   222
Newspaper style   30
Newsweek   24, 65
Note taking   82
Nzima, Sam   183

O'Kane, Maggie   86
O'Rourke, P.J.   72
Obscenities   107, 108
Oggendblad   226
Oosterlig   228
Oppel, Rich   13
Orwell, Sonia   30–6
Orwell, Angus   30–6
Orwell, George   30–6
Owen, Ken   209–11

Pendergrast, Lolo   54
Penthouse   228
People Magazine   227
Peterson, Hector   184
Photographers   24, 181
Photographs   174, 176, 181, 183
Picas   172
Plotnik, Arthur   141, 142, 151
Points   172
Post Transvaal   223
Poynter Institute for Media Studies   12
Poynter Report   12, 13
Press Council   69, 204
Pringle, Thomas   207, 221
Proofreading marks   144–8

231

INDEX

Public relations 223
Public Relations Review 111
Public Relations Institute of Southern Africa 213, 224

Radio Good Hope 121, 224
Radio Ciskei 226
Radio Highveld 224
Radio 222, 223
Radio Kontrei 227
Radio 702 225
Radio Lotus 226
Radio Thohoyandou 225
Ragged Right 159, 174, 175, 190
Rand Daily Mail 28, 69, 222, 223, 226
Rapport 225
Readability test 45, 174
Readers Digest 224
Reporter, general-assignment 64
Reporter, sports 60
Reporter, special-assignment 65
Reviews 59
Rhodes University Journalism Review 159, 203, 208
Riddle, Charles 208–11
Robinson, Freek 79
Ronge, Barry 58
Rossouw, Andre 81

Sarie 81
Sartre, Jean-Paul 207
Schlesinger, I.W. 223
Schwarz, Walter 53
Seitel, Frank 111, 127
Silber, Gus 76, 89
Smith, Derek 210
Sources 68
South African Union of Journalists 10, 69, 212
South 58, 206
South African Broadcasting Corporation (SABC) 14, 16, 223
South African Commerical Advertiser 8, 207, 221

South African Press Association (SAPA) 222
South African Mining and Coal, Gold and Base Minerals 222
Sowetan 137–40, 161, 189, 209, 223
Sparks, Allister 69
Springbok Radio 224
Star 23, 209, 222
Stevenson, Adlai 6
Steyn, Richard 209–11
Style 176
Suchetka, Diane 96, 100–7
Sunday Star 5, 11, 24, 54, 57, 72, 159, 163, 226
Sunday Express 223, 226
Sunday City Press 226
Sunday Times 7, 120, 128, 209, 222
Sunday Tribune 223
Sunday Times Magazine 76, 89, 155
Sutton, Tony 175, 183

Tafelberg 22
Talk 227
Tape recorders 84
Taylor, Edwin 159, 175
Taylor, Ron 36, 56, 57, 63, 66, 79, 107
Teel, Leonard 36, 56, 57, 63, 66, 79, 107
Television 120, 223
Thusago, Calvin 14
Time Magazine 75, 89, 154
Times Media Limited 30
Tomalin, Nicolas 6
Transitions 90
Transvaler 228
Travel & Leisure 155
Trend 227
True Love 226
Trump, Linda 131
Tuchman, Gaye 63
Typography 170, 175
Tyson, Harvey 183

Umshumayeli Wendaba 221
Uptown 227
Vaderland 222, 226